license code

IC492CA8

Username September

Password PROMOTE

Praise for
The New Entrepreneurs

"Fueled by the Internet, advances in technology give rise to a new breed of business men and women, with better tools at their disposal than ever before. *The New Entrepreneurs* forms part of the single most powerful tool of all—information chock full of statistics, demographics, success tips and how-tos from the leaders who have already 'made it.' This book is a must read for anyone looking to grow a business in the 21st Century. A masterful job."

-Ridgely Goldsborough, Publisher, *Network Marketing Lifestyles*

"In *The New Entrepreneurs*, Rene Reid Yarnell makes as compelling a case for network marketing as I've ever read. She shows us how high-tech and high-touch have come together today to enable tomorrow's entrepreneurs to go beyond making a living to making a life. Great stuff!"

-John Milton Fogg, Founder of *Upline Magazine*,
  author of *The Greatest Networker in the World*

"I strongly recommend this book for any reader—from the seriously committed network marketer to the reserved but open-minded professional who is interested in knowing more about the realities, the challenges, and the future vision of this exciting entrepreneurial opportunity."

-Dr. Charles W. King
  Professor of Marketing, The University of Illinois at Chicago

Also by the Author

The Encyclopedia of Network Marketing

Co-authored with Mark Yarnell
Your First Year in Network Marketing
Power Multi-Level Marketing
Should You Quit Before You're Fired?

For the 21st Century…

The
New Entrepreneurs

Making a Living – Making a Life through Network Marketing

Rene Reid Yarnell, M.A.

Foreword by
Dr. Charles W. King

A Quantum Leap Publication
Reno, Nevada 89509

A Quantum Leap Nonfiction Book

ISBN# 1-886039-45-3

Cover design by David Nakamoto
Page design by Michael B. Kitson, On-Call Graphics, Inc.
Indexing by Carolyn S. Dennis Indexing Services
© 1999, *Los Angeles Times,* "Cares/Zen at Work; Finding Your 'Right' Career Path—A Quiz" by Susan Vaughn, published January 11, 1999.

Library of Congress Cataloging-in-Publication Data
Yarnell, Rene Reid.
    The new entrepreneurs: making a living—making a life through network marketing / Rene Reid Yarnell.
        p. cm.
"A Quantum Leap Nonfiction Book."
Includes bibliographical references and index.
    ISBN 1-886039-45-3 (alk. paper)
    1. Multilevel marketing—United States. 2. Marketing—United States 3. Entrepreneurship—United States. I. Title.
HF5415.126.Y37 1999
658.8'4—dc21
                            99-006984

A Quantum Leap publication
95 Rancho Manor Dr.
Reno, NV 89509

Printed in the United States of America
10 9 8 7 6 5 4 3 2 1

CONTENTS

FOREWORD

Over the past two hundred years, the American and world economic models have evolved through several major eras. The basic focus of the business world has shifted from the industrial revolution...through the information age...evolving into the distribution era...maturing into the age of entrepreneurism. The Entrepreneurial Age of the coming century will potentially have an even greater and more indelible impact on the changing world order.

Rene Reid Yarnell's personal and professional profile is the epitome—a testament—to the changing cultural environment and the alternative lifestyles about which she writes in *The New Entrepreneurs* for the 21st Century. Her life's experience—from Roman Catholic nun to elected politician to professional businesswoman—makes her eminently qualified for this writing task.

Her book tracks the evolution of the process of entrepreneurism. The central theme of the book focuses on the restructuring of the work environment...from the contemporary corporate culture through the challenges of the new employment options...the traditional job market broadening to include alternative career paths.

The growing vision of the new emerging professional for self empowerment, the desire of the individual to make a broader sociological and altruistic contribution to their world, and the need for more time-freedom and less rigidity are all emphasized throughout the book. The unique opportunities of entrepreneurism, the integration of working at home and leisure life styles are clearly detailed.

The great contribution of this book is its introduction of the network marketing industry as a legitimate and realistic alternative leading the charge for entrepreneurial success! Network marketing is clearly a viable part-time supplemental or full-time income career alternative that meets the criteria of this rising new professional. *The New Entrepreneurs* presents a well organized overview of network marketing, interviews numerous corporate leaders, and details an exciting collection of personalized and compassionate success stories of network marketing achievers.

As an analyst of the literature of network marketing, I have reviewed virtually all of the major books about the industry. I strongly recommend this book for any reader—from the seriously committed network marketer to the reserved but open-minded professional who is interested in knowing more about the realities, the challenges, and the future vision of this exciting entrepreneurial opportunity.

Dr. Charles W. King
Professor of Marketing
The University of Illinois at Chicago

Founder and Seminar Leader
UIC Certificate Seminar in Network Marketing

ACKNOWLEDGMENTS

The process of publishing this book is a vivid symbol of the book's core message: holding onto our vision amidst seemingly insurmountable hurdles. Expecting a co-author, my first publisher dropped the book three weeks before completion of the first draft. Extensive complications with a second publisher led to my branching out on my own...the day before it was supposed to go to press. I kept the project moving by self-publishing until, by providence, I met the publisher of Addicus Books who contributed immensely toward raising the book to a professional standard. I now see each step of the process as an essential one that has resulted in harmony prevailing and, most importantly, that I have a book I'm proud to share with you.

I want to acknowledge those who stood by me and contributed through these various stages of growth, believing in the merit of this book.

To **Ben Dominitz** for his active and creative participation in developing the theme of this book.

To **Werner Riefling**, who reinforced his belief in this project and encouraged me; to **Bill Burkett** for his valuable copy editing genius; to **David Nakamoto** for his cover design; to **Jennifer Osborn** for her editorial and research assistance; and to **Kristen Brown** for typesetting.

To **Rod Colvin** and **Susan Adams** for their involvement in this project at a critical juncture in bringing this book to fruition.

To **Michael Kitson** for his graphic layout and design...under the pressure of awaiting the arrival of his new-born child. To **Jean Stoess** for proofreading. To **Carolyn Dennis** for indexing and final corrections.

To my long-time friend, **Robert Blair Kaiser**, author of *R.F.K. Must Die* (1970), *Melvin Belli: My Life on Trial* (1976), *The Politics of Sex and Religion* (1985), *The Autobiography of Mickey Rooney* (1991), and the stage play *Jubilee 2000* (1996)…for his research, writing, and editing contribution.

To the Direct Sales Association, and especially **Neil Offen**, for openly sharing news-breaking stories and so much valuable data from his research and surveys.

To **Father Frank Murphy** for his moral and spiritual support, his editorial contributions, and his prodding me not to give up.

To my Mom, **Helen Harrington**, who took care of everything else in my life to free me for this project.

To **Randy Sotka**, who selflessly loaned me his laptop when mine crashed in the final stages of this book.

To **Missy McQuattie**, who put up with my 4 a.m. rising and nose in my computer during our entire vacation in Maui.

To **Antonette Malloy**, for transcribing interviews and setting appointments for more interviews to keep this project moving.

To **my friends** of whom I saw very little during this project. Thanks for your understanding and for still being my friends.

To **Dr. Charles King and his wife, Sandy,** for providing an incredible working environment in our certificate course at the University of Illinois Chicago, wherein we have learned so much ourselves as we have the honor of teaching network marketing students from around the world.

To **Mark Yarnell**, for first encouraging me to write, and for our years of working so closely together to promote this industry. His newest book, *Self-Wealth*, is a motivational, inspirational book—something that Mark does like no one else I know.

To **the founders, presidents, and vice-presidents of all the network marketing companies** who so openly shared their personal visions, industry challenges, and their spirit of enthusiasm for this incredible industry.

To the many **top-level network marketers**, who disclosed their personal struggles and victories so openly with nothing held back.

Through your contributions, this book came to be published. Because of the challenges I faced in getting it to this stage, I can only believe that this book was meant to be and will serve a valuable purpose in raising the level of professionalism of the network marketing industry.

INTRODUCTION

As we turn the corner of a new millennium, a new role model is emerging for the business world. Replacing the acclaimed corporate executive of the 20th Century will be the entrepreneur of the 21st Century. In fact, it is predicted that, with the advancement of technology and the World Wide Web, entrepreneurialism will surface as "the defining trend of the business world in this next century." This conclusion is not only my own but one reached from a survey of leading Americans, commissioned by Ernst & Young.

Clearly, a new breed of professionals is emerging—professionals who are no longer satisfied with the old social mores and work ethics so prevalent at the close of the 20th Century. These new professionals are putting aside their corporate ladders and replacing them with a vision that they can create a balanced work environment that offers personal growth and fulfillment, financial rewards in keeping with how they value themselves, the chance to share their wealth, and the freedom to enjoy life. Not only employees but employers are candidates for this new form of capitalism, tired of too many sacrifices at too great a personal cost. These entrepreneurs will become the leading economic drivers, so much so that it is expected that the 21st Century could well become known as the Entrepreneurial Age.

The profession most likely to advance this Entrepreneurial Age is network marketing—an industry embodying ten million Americans, and more than three times that many worldwide. In fact, it's the fastest growing industry in the world. This is largely because it offers a viable alternative to those who've been laid off in the corporate world; or, perhaps still there, feeling trapped in jobs they despise. And success in this industry doesn't demand a degree from Harvard or MIT. It's for people who like people and enjoy serving and supporting others, for people who want to own their own life but still be given the chance to "shoot the moon" financially.

Not a Ponzi Scheme

Maybe you are among those who consider network marketing to be a Ponzi scheme. Charles Ponzi was a slick, very well-dressed Bostonian who, about 1920, promised investors extremely high returns on their money. Ponzi paid out high interest to the early investors with the money derived from later investors, and that encouraged lots of their friends to join in, until, one day, they all realized that Charles's plan could only work as long as new investors kept coming on board.

Ever since then, a good many fast talkers have tried their own Ponzis. Relying on the propensity of some to look for a fast, easy buck, they do pretty well, for a time, until their Ponzi plan collapses and they're hauled into court. There, a district attorney-type tells a jury how it all works. The DA shows them a chart that looks very much like a pyramid, with the Ponzi schemer on top and a bunch of very disenchanted people at the bottom.

Our Country Founded on the Framework of a Pyramid

Network marketing is not a Ponzi scheme. In fact, it is not a scheme at all. It bears one strong resemblance to a pyramid, and that is its compensation plan. It's a legitimate way of selling all kinds of products and services, from shampoo to vitamins to telephone and Internet services. Most of us do this all the time, without thinking much about what we're doing—and never dreaming we might get paid for it. For example, we see a good movie, and we tell our friends not to miss it. They go see it and tell their friends. And so on. But no one gets paid for doing that. In network marketing, we tell our friends. And we get paid. And so do they. And so do their friends. If someone were to draw up a chart, it would look very much like a pyramid.

But then, a lot of things look like pyramids. The truth is, we all live in a pyramid of one sort or another. A family tree is a pyramid. The US government is a pyramid. General Motors is a pyramid. So is the Roman Catholic Church.

Take a look at the Great Seal of the United States. Where can you find one? It's on the back of every US dollar bill ever printed. We probably touch the Great Seal every day without ever thinking about it. If we take time to look at it, we see an unfinished pyramid, with an eye in a triangle, surrounded by rays of glory. Over the eye, we see the words, "Annuit Coeptis." At the base of the pyramid, we read, "Novus Ordo Seclorum." As those on the dollar bill's design committee explained back in 1782, that pyramid signifies strength and duration. The eye over it and the mottoes above and below it allude to the many signal interventions of Providence that favor the American cause. In other words, our nation's Great Seal expresses the belief that "Providence favors our undertakings in a New World Order."

This new world was built on a principle of democracy. While structured within the framework of a pyramid, Thomas Jefferson and our Founding Fathers envisioned it as a world where all men were created equal.

The American Dream Has Become a Nightmare

Fast forward now to modern times. And what do we see? The American Dream of our forefathers has become a nightmare for all too many workers.

More and more people are realizing that Monday is an awful way to spend one seventh of their life. They hate the very thought of going to work. And those who keep track of such things tell us more suicides are committed on Monday morning before nine o'clock than at any other time of the week. Today's workers can hardly wait for Friday to roll around, and have even developed their own special cheer (and a chain of bar-restaurants) to mark it: TGIF! Thank God It's Friday!

Emerging to offer an alternative way to make a living—and live—is network marketing. The difference between a corporate and a network marketing pyramid is simple and straightforward. In a multi-level marketing pyramid, individuals start out at the top as the president and CEO of their own businesses. They then proceed to build their organization, in pyramidal fashion from the top down, looking first for their vice-presidents who make up the "front line" of their corporation. The twist to this approach is that, for those who are so inclined, although they may be in frontline position to their sponsor, they can, in turn, set themselves up as the CEO of their own business. And that process can be duplicated again and again.

In network marketing, we once again bring democracy to the workplace. We are in charge of our own lives. No one tells us what to do. We don't have a job in the traditional sense of the word. We don't commute to work. We don't race out of the house to catch the 7:15 to Grand Central Station, or fight the freeways in a carpool. We conduct our business from home.

Working from Home

It's ironic. Americans spent most of the 20th Century moving from the farm to the city. Now, as we enter the 21st Century, more and more men and women are moving back to the farm...in a metaphorical sense. Some Americans, indeed, are moving from the city to more rural locations where they can have chickens and ducks. But many more of us have figured out a way to earn a living by staying home, whether in the city, suburbs, or the country.

The point is that we're leaving the rat race, and doing our work at home. No more commutes of an hour or more. Now we're getting our work done in the hours from eight to two or three p.m. And we're home when our kids get out of school. Or, if we've reached that time in our lives when the kids have moved out, we're off to the golf course, the tennis courts, the local fishing hole, or to contribute time and money to serve those less fortunate than ourselves.

We can do this, of course, because we've joined the communications revolution. We have phones, fax machines, fax-on-demand; we've signed up for e-mail or web TV; we conduct meetings by video conferencing or teleconferencing and virtual office systems. Working from home has become a viable option for some corporate employees as well as new entrepreneurs like us. By the year 2000, experts predict that 40 to 50 percent of all businesses will operate from home.

With the convenience of technology, traditional businesses are having employees work from home at certain times. The federal government supports and encourages "telecommuting."

Of the estimated 60 million home-based businesses in the United States alone, general contracting, construction, computer services, business consulting, cleaning services, real estate, painting, crafts, trucking, and marketing head the list, in that order. But clearly, network distribution is the rising new home-based profession for the coming millennium.

Home Businesses Attract Professionals

Why are so many professionals drawn to work at home? It offers a low-risk venture with the potential of an exceptionally high return. And with network marketing you have no overhead, no accounts receivable, no payroll, and no geographical restrictions. Network marketing is a business that can be conducted from anyplace in the world. Anyone can become a network distribution success, independent of gender, race, cultural heritage, education, or other social or economic background. The key determinant of success is the individual's personal connections and genuine commitment to hard work sustained over time.

As more professionally-educated and financially-successful attorneys, physicians, dentists, teachers, chiropractors, professors, corporate CEOs, and entrepreneurs join our industry, we can expect more and more socially-conscious men and women to enter the network marketing industry. These folks will attract other men and women like themselves, people who will continue to raise the bar of professionalism in our industry. The kind of experience and credibility they bring can only *enhance* network marketing, making the industry even more effective in creating a legitimate, efficient, and rapidly growing channel of distribution for moving an ever broadening array of products and services to customers around the globe.

Freedom from Professional Slavery

As we move into a new millennium, it is natural to want to create new paradigms. Gerry Spence, in his book *Give Me Liberty*, proposes: "The new paradigm for success in America must be person-based, not money-based. A successful person is one who has acquired not great wealth, but great personhood. The wealthy man who has not become a person is only an empty machine powered by churning greed. The individual who has achieved personhood is a lily in perpetual bloom. The paradigm of wealth as virtue, of money as success, of profit as the ultimate human goal, is the most enslaving value of all."

Network marketers, as a body of people, are on a campaign to set people free from modern-day wage slavery.

"By slavery, the old or the new, I mean that state in which the person has no effective control over the course of his or her life," says Spence in his book. "Despite his freedom to jump from job to job or junket by jet from beach to beach, if no matter how he schemes or toils he cannot explore his boundless uniqueness, if he has lost his only power, the power of the self, he is enslaved."

Our modern-day enslavement is an accident. No one ever intended it to happen.

"Man is born free," asserted Jean Jacques Rousseau, the French creator of the Social Contract, "yet he is everywhere in chains."

For us to liberate ourselves as a nation, there must be some visionaries who rise to lead us from our contemporary captivity.

Dare to Be Open to Change

"Great spirits have always encountered violent opposition from mediocre minds," Albert Einstein reminded us. Such minds are always on the sidelines watching the parade go by. Companies such as IBM and AT&T were nearly lost by clinging to their closed systems and conventional definitions of progress. Don't make the same mistake. If what you are doing now will not create the results you want for a quality life, be willing to explore new options. There are others who have gone before you who have been where you are.

Some of the most valuable information in this book comes through a collection of accounts from network marketing representatives all the way from Boston to Brisbane and from Texas to Taiwan, providing human roadmaps by professionals who have led the way. I have dedicated more than a decade of my professional life to this industry and have chosen to put my reputation on the line for it. While others contribute their academic expertise and research to this industry, I bring hands-on experience, having worked with my business partner to build a large network distribution organization that was eventually comprised of more than 200,000 distributors in 27 countries.

I offer this as a resource and reference book for those who want truthful and accurate facts, statistics, and data on the evolution of the network marketing industry. I offer it as a self-revelation of its memoirs by those who have "walked the walk" of the industry. In addition to contracting with a professional indexer, I have personally dedicated hours to constructing the index, making it easy to access pertinent information. As one friend said who has helped read and edit this book, "*The New Entrepreneurs* recounts the history of where the network marketing industry has been, where we are, and where we most assuredly will be."

Often, writers are able to produce their best work during painful periods. I acknowledge that I wrote this book at a time when I was undergoing one of the most difficult transitions in my own life. This book was cathartic for me. Needing isolation, I used this time constructively. It is my hope that the result, namely, the publication of this book, is as rewarding for you as it was healing for me.

Changing Trends Lead to New Entrepreneurial Age

I believe that this remarkable industry will be responsible for changing social trends over the next few decades. Entrepreneurs who spend more time working from home will be better mothers and fathers, there when their families need them rather than stuck in gridlock on a freeway. They will reestablish priorities and create lives with a more elevated sense of purpose and fulfillment. With more capital in the hands of responsible entrepreneurs, I expect to see countless people make more money than they ever dreamed possible. And many of them will use their newfound wealth for altruistic causes.

These entrepreneurs are carrying us across the threshold of a new age—the Entrepreneurial Age—with legions of network marketers leading the way. Through this new rising profession, these spirited networkers have the opportunity to change the business world as we know it. For those of you who choose to become part of this profession, we welcome you and congratulate you for a thoughtful decision.

Together, through this industry, we have the opportunity to reestablish a "Novus Ordo Seclorum," a New World Order for the 21st Century. And as we participate in the groundswell of the driving force behind the evolution of this global, pyramidal industry, we may, for the second time in history, again be able to say, "Annuit Coeptis," Providence favors our undertakings.

As we face the dawning of a new millennium, let us welcome in a new breed of entrepreneurs...who will give rise to a new Entrepreneurial Age!

Rene Reid Yarnell
Reno, Nevada
September 4, 1999

To the many professionals coming into the Network Marketing arena,
    You are to be acknowledged for your values and your openness
        —and the confidence you've shown in your own judgment.

To the millions of network marketers who are proud to call yourself so,
    You are to be respected for your belief and trust
    —belief in your product
        and trust in that special person who invited you to join.

To the pioneers who have been in the industry for a time,
    You are to be honored for your vision and determination
        —and seeing what others could not yet see.

To those whose lives have intertwined with my own,
    I am honored to walk among you
        —and call you my friend.

Together we are changing society and prioritizing its values.
    We are creating a new era for the 21st Century
        Where work and leisure and growth and altruism are all interwoven
            —and history will call it the Entrepreneurial Age!

PART I

Network Marketing:
An Alternative to
Today's Work Environment

"Your work is to discover your work and then, with all your heart, give yourself to it."

—*Buddha*

CHAPTER 1

Corporate Stress Drives Professionals Out

I hadn't seen Rich for a while. He and his wife, Betsy, were having dinner at one of our local hangouts. They were talking quietly when I walked up to their table and joined them for a few minutes. I couldn't help but notice that he looked stressed. I asked him what was happening.

He was forthright.

"I've been fired," he said.

I thought back to the last time that we had talked. He had been debating with himself—whether to stay in a secure job as a vice-president of a local hotel-resort, or take a higher-risk position as president of another company. He took the riskier job. It hadn't worked out.

He and Betsy told me a little about how it all came crashing down. I shared a recent experience with them of how both my marriage and my business relationship had ended. In a way, I had been fired, too. Talking about our respective crises helped us both, and, for that moment, brought us closer. Success had kept us apart. Our mutual firing brought us together.

"So," I probed, "what's ahead for you?"

He shrugged. "I don't know. I'm not sure anyone in corporate America knows. Nothing's for sure, except that nothing's for sure. Everyone's scared. And, if they aren't, they should be."

Rich summed up precisely the predicament facing an aging workforce in a downsizing corporate world.

If we expect the world to meet us on the terms of yesteryear we are kidding ourselves. Job security is a thing of the past. All the more so if you are over 40. Computers and technology have made the United States more globally competitive.

If you are among the 78 million boomers in the workforce, you are especially vulnerable. You may find yourself looking over your shoulders while also worried about bumping into someone in front of you. You can't move ahead; there's no room. And right behind you, there's another generation coming up fast.

Network Marketing Welcomes Corporate Refugees

Tom Alkazin considers himself blessed to have personally experienced the trauma caused by corporate downsizing as early as the mid-70s, long before it became a prevailing trend. Within 18 months of joining his computer science company as a new college grad, the guillotine chopped off numerous positions.

"Seeing massive layoffs firsthand showed me just how devastating they can be. I'll never forget the trauma of those good people," he said. "It was the point of no return for me."

Fortunately for Tom, he had also joined the oldest and largest networking company during this period of his life. Faced with a strong dose of reality, Tom turned what he had intended to be a part-time MLM endeavor into a full-time, had-no-choice career. With no safety net, he was driven to succeed. Each level in an MLM compensation plan is given a name. Tom quickly earned his first milestone of achievement, a diamond pin, and found an even more valuable jewel in his future wife, Bethany. Theirs is one of countless marriages that have emerged from this industry. Finding a life partner with like values and goals is one of the innumerable potential benefits.

"The premise that I gradually came to discover was that there are several essential virtues in making this kind of a home business go: company and products, system and compensation," Tom explains.

"Examine the stability of the opportunity and vision of the company principles. (1) Do you personally love the results you experience from the products? (2) Make sure the compensation plan is financially beneficial for the serious network marketer as well as the casually active person. (3) You want to know that the company has a far-reaching corporate vision but can also focus closely on the needs of new members. If the company is aware of your personal needs, then you can start building your confidence about the industry. (4) Make certain you are comfortable with the system the company uses. Bethany and I have found great success with a system of marketing that is non-confrontational, meaning that we teach people how to advertise their business in such a fashion that others will call them. It's much easier to present a product or an opportunity when there's already interest coming your way.

"You will want to define your objectives. Based on your circle of influence, resources, and desire, how fast would you like to move? You will want to set specific goals with specific time periods. The most important thing you can do to achieve these ends is to utilize your line of sponsorship. Let them be your coach. Then be prepared to move quickly and take massive action."

Today the happily married couple resides in Carlsbad, California, with their two teenage boys and a younger daughter, all at a Christian school in which both parents are deeply immersed. Bethany is a volunteer and Tom is a school board member and basketball coach. They are deeply rooted in their faith and committed to their family.

"We feel the success we've experienced in this business is reflective of our values. 'As we sow' our support to others in the relationships we form through the building of our organization, 'so shall we reap' the personal and financial rewards."

The pain and devastation of early corporate downsizing has never left him, and is undoubtedly part of the reason that he and Bethany have a committed philosophy about treating their business associates with dignity and support. After a professional lifetime in MLM, Tom is a strong proponent that network marketing extends a real home, in every sense of the word, to corporate refugees and those people whose lives have all too often been torn apart by corporate America.

Women Execs Find Haven in Network Marketing

The finished-at-40 syndrome is not biased. It discriminates against men as well as women. For ten years, Carol Waugh was a major account salesperson with Xerox Corporation. But in her 40s, she knew the company could hire three people right out of college for her base salary alone. After ten assignments in ten years, she was exhausted, and knew that she had to find a way out.

5

"You know you are about to crack when you leave your keys in the car, lock it," she laughs, "and discover the motor is still running."

When Carol decided to leave Xerox, her interviews with other companies brought her to the realization that the corporate finished-at-40 culture was the same everywhere. She heard about network marketing, but couldn't envision herself being a part of what she perceived to be a pyramid scheme. In April 1991, she received a company magazine from Rita Davenport, a friend since 13, about the new network marketing company of which Rita was president. Rita was pictured sitting with the company founder at a black baby grand with the title "In Perfect Harmony." Carol thought "Why not give my friend the opportunity to help me learn something new?"

Carol confessed her resistance to the network marketing industry. "The biggest challenge was my ego. Coming out of a corporate background, could I make money selling cleansing cream and lipstick after working with a major corporation doing half-million-dollar office equipment deals? The worst part was feeling I wasn't being taken seriously...as if my family and acquaintances were thinking, 'Oh, bless her heart, it didn't work out at that big corporation. Now she's going to go sell lipstick.' I didn't want people to think I was moving backward rather than forward when I joined the industry. I dreaded telling anyone what I did for a living because I didn't know what to say I was doing. I really had to humble myself to learn new things as a beginner in this business."

But as it turned out, Carol didn't really have to start over. She came to understand that she had been training a lifetime to be a leader in this industry. She brought many years of organizational skills, teaching capabilities, professionalism, credibility, work ethic, and enthusiasm.

Now when Carol is at social events and people ask her what she does, she tells them, "I work from home much like President Clinton...only I make more money." Or sometimes she'll say, "I hunt elephants.... I look for big people who want big results and have big dreams but don't want to work for peanuts."

With success comes respect. Ironically, what begins for most professionals as fear of losing credibility if they join a network marketing company results in enhanced admiration once certain milestones have been achieved. Says Carol: "One of the greatest things about this business is the dignity and respect that comes once you have created and built an organization."

> # There are numerous couples today who are choosing to create a marriage and a merger by working together in business.

The belief factor needs time to develop. Professionals need to make a commitment and not look back. Carol characterizes what happened to her as "a spiritual awakening, a kind of anointing."

Carol does not portray the business as a means of getting rich quick, but it has been about getting richer and richer the more she kept focused, disciplined, and consistent in her business. After five years, Carol and her husband were debt free, living in Brentwood, Tennessee, taking six-week vacations annually, contributing to charities with gratitude, investing in stocks, bonds, and mutual funds, and driving her white Mercedes Benz paid for by her company. Carol Waugh never intended to end up in network marketing. Today, she has a business that is equivalent to about six McDonald's franchises. Carol's daughter, Leslie Huskins, recently became one of the company's youngest regional vice-presidents, and they are the first mother-daughter vice-president team in their company.

Couples Create a Marriage and Merger

There are numerous couples today who are choosing to create a marriage and a merger by working together in business. They want to have it all: a deeply loving relationship and a successful business partnership. Leaving their respective professions behind, they want the luxury of working jointly from their home. Kerry Brown and Richard Larkin are two such people.

"Richard, you're crazy! What on earth are you thinking?" Richard Larkin had heard this so often that when he didn't, he held back. But when he heard those magic words "You're crazy!" he knew it must be right.

Kerry Brown and Richard Larkin were born in Saskatchewan, Canada. Both of their parents were successful small business owners. Kerry's entrepreneurial parents left Saskatchewan when she was ten to move to the West Coast. There, they started their own jewelry business where she worked after school, weekends, and Christmas holidays. Richard's father owned two gas stations where Richard honed his entrepreneurial skills. Richard headed west with all his personal belongings in his new Honda

7

Civic at the age of 18 for his first sales job in the car business. He rose quickly to the top salesperson position. He then entered the fast-growing franchise industry in 1978 and worked as a broker.

In the meantime, after graduating from the University of Victoria with an Honors B.A. in Anthropology, Kerry realized that even though she enjoyed her subject, it was not going to provide her with the kind of income that matched her talents. Like most college grads, she entered a field totally devoid of her education: real estate. It proved to be a very successful career choice for her; she was in the top one percent of the income earners in her market. She was the owner of her own Century 21 franchise for two years, and elected as director of her local and provincial real estate boards. She loved the income, but had no time to enjoy her life.

In 1980, Richard introduced jet skis to Vancouver Island by setting up a rental operation at a resort on a local lake. The banks, friends, and just about everyone said it would never work. "You're crazy! Don't do it." It not only was extraordinarily successful, but has grown into one of the hottest sports ever to hit the water.

Richard's next move was to enter the indoor sun-tanning field, which at that time was virtually unknown. "Richard, you're crazy!" Ah, yes! That heartening affirmation! Soon he found himself involved in one of the fastest growing industries in the early 1980s.

In 1991, he was approached by a potential franchise client to analyze a network marketing company. Not terribly enthusiastic, Richard took a look at the industry and the particular company. He became convinced that network marketing was the "people's Franchise," allowing distributors to be in business for themselves, with a proven track to run on, and without significant financial risk. Once again he heard those stimulating words, "Richard, you're crazy!" and he knew it was the right move.

After working 60 to 70 hours per week for 12 years in residential and commercial real estate, Kerry assessed her options and realized she had the same two choices many successful people face. "I could either work myself to death or 'buy' some of my time back by giving up a substantial amount of income." That's when Richard introduced her to network marketing.

Although initially resistant, what attracted her was the opportunity to create her own work hours, use her creativity, work out of her home, and most importantly, have the opportunity to work with Richard.

In January 1992, Kerry and Richard began their career in network marketing and found that their part-time income quickly surpassed their previous incomes, and soon went full-time. After seven years and three companies, they feel very thankful that they were introduced to the industry. Yet they allowed many people to slip away by thinking they were too successful to even be interested. Their breakthrough came when they shifted from finding mid-range successful people to approaching those who were dissatisfied and willing to make the changes necessary to take control of their lives.

"No longer 'ships passing in the night,' we have the freedom to spend our time the way we want to," Richard reflects. "There are millions of people out there who would love to do what we do. It's natural now to get up when we want to, have breakfast with our son, and begin making phone calls mid-morning. This is the part that's really hard to describe to people who are still in traditional business."

The relationships that have resulted from our business have been immensely rewarding and fulfilling," Kerry reflects. "We love spending time with our people, so there's no longer a separation between work and pleasure. When we're giving a private presentation in a lovely home, sharing a glass of wine with good people, I have to pinch myself to believe I'm actually working. Developing a partnership with people, helping them realize their dreams, and in turn creating long-lasting relationships is what network marketing is all about."

It's been a while since Richard has heard "you're crazy." He has some simple advice for anyone else who is fortunate enough to have these words spoken: "Pay twice as much attention. Follow your heart and trust your own instincts."

Women Stepping Off the Corporate Ladder

"Many women have given up climbing the corporate ladder to succeed. The focus now is female entrepreneurs," says Lillian Vernon Katz, chairman of the National Women's Business Council.

"When I went into business, nobody knew what a woman entrepreneur was, " Katz says. "Today, we are a force to be reckoned with."[1]

Women-owned companies employed 15.5 million people and cranked out some $1.4 trillion in sales in 1994, the last full year for which data was available.

What has begun in the 90s will accelerate at the turn of the century as we see more female entrepreneurs emerging in the business world.

We see a similar trend in network marketing in the number of professional women who are choosing to get involved—not just to sell products—but for the purpose of building a business.

Network marketing presents women with a unique opportunity in business. Free from the confines of glass ceilings, as well as the many political games and the often-biased advancement and pay policies of traditionally male-dominated work environments, women have found that a home business allows them to be at home with their families.

Liz Walcher, a stockbroker with Merrill Lynch for several years, was ready to make a change. She had paid a high price for her success.

"If you want to continue to climb that corporate ladder, you have to sacrifice all the things you really value," she says. "Your relationships are sacrificed, your family is sacrificed, and ultimately you end up being the sacrifice. That was clearly happening to me.

"I was always being made enticing offers by headhunters but I had reached the point that I was ready to accept an offer with another financial services firm. I never saw my family because of my long hours and my international travel and (if you can believe this) the big enticement was that this new firm was promising me two secretaries to make my work load less.

"I believe I got involved with network marketing through sheer divine intervention. The owner's daughter of the daycare center where I dropped off my youngest daughter for 12 hours a day (it makes me sick to admit this) began talking to me. She looked me straight in the eye, and said, 'I know you're successful. I know you make a lot of money. I know you have a title and work for an important firm. But are you happy?' No one had ever asked me that question before. It really made me stop and think, and I realized that no, I wasn't happy."

Liz was introduced to network marketing as a means of spending more time with her family.

> **Developing a partnership with people, helping them realize their dreams, and in turn creating long-lasting relationships is what network marketing is all about.**

Free from the confines of...traditionally male-dominated work environments, women have found that a home business allows them to be at home with their families.

"But I couldn't see myself working in her company as a cosmetic lady," she recalls. "A financial manager, yes—a cosmetic lady, no! She gave me information to read when I got home. I threw it away when I cleaned out the car that evening. She called me the next day to follow up. I lied and told her I had lost the literature."

Her friend's daughter "overnighted" another set of brochures, audio and video tapes, and called back two days later.

"She reminded me of myself when I really, really, really wanted an important account," Liz admits now. "I respected her tenacity and follow-up."

On a sleepless night occasioned by job-related stress, Liz got up and watched the video.

"I was mesmerized...completely transfixed. Call it totally taken and touched by the looks of genuinely happy women collecting diamond rings, trips around the world, cars, and huge paychecks, even bigger than my own. And they didn't have the financial compliance division, the SEC or FTC breathing down their necks!

"When I was with the brokerage firm, many times my women clients would ask me what it took to find a job like mine. They wanted a position where they could call the shots, a job where they could become financially independent. There was no way I could help them back then. But now, by developing this networking business, I could help other women build a business where they could call the shots, have the paycheck, and have the lifestyle, with it all built into one."

Liz likens a network marketing business to a financial portfolio. "First you start with safe, sound investments, your inventory and product sales, which bring you a consistent return," she says. "Then you diversify your portfolio with investments that are going to bring you higher returns over time. The principles of building the portfolio, building the customer base, and building a sales team all seemed like one and the same to me.

"To be successful in corporate America, you have to be productive...even if that means making compromises on the things you care about," Liz

11

says. "The priority is not how you feel about yourself, or your happiness, or your well-being. The focus is all about being productive for the bottom line at any cost. But in our industry, it's different. You have to build people up from the inside out. When you can build self-esteem in someone and help them focus on their dreams, then they are fulfilled and the productivity will follow."

Physician Saves Her Own Health with MLM

Dr. Daria Davidson began her career in healthcare in 1974, first as a registered nurse, and since 1984 as a board certified emergency medicine physician. Most of her medical career was spent at a large trauma center in Wichita, Kansas.

Although she had a vibrant career, it came at great cost. Years of sleep deprivation, relentless stress, poor eating habits, and a dose of bad genes led to a diagnosis of breast cancer at the age of 41. Both Daria's mother and grandmother had breast cancer. One of her greatest concerns was the health of her twin daughters. Having raised them as a single parent since medical school (the divorce rate of first-year medical students is quite high), the three of them are very close. Yet, they had little time together as Daria was constantly at the hospital. Worn out by her so-called life, she began to search for an alternative to her medical practice.

When a physician colleague came to her with information about a new division of an established health company, the product that offered a natural solution to high cholesterol got her attention, not from a business standpoint but from a healthcare perspective. If this product actually worked, was safe, and available without a prescription, it would substantially decrease the risk of coronary artery disease.

Then her mind began working overtime: "If this product is so good, why don't they just sell it in stores?" After more study, she found her answer. From a corporate business standpoint, network marketing allowed the parent company to replace the fixed expenses of retailing (multiple levels of mark-up and advertising) with the variable expense of commission-based sales. The company needed to pay only after the product was sold. No more products needed to be manufactured than what the market would bear; the company needed only ship the product once, directly to the customer.

As Daria puts it, "A light went on and I realized that network marketing really was a legitimate and reasonable option for bringing products to the end-line user. It is so much simpler and more straightforward than conventional means of product distribution."

She made the decision to get involved on a part-time basis, in spite of her busy practice. She already had no time for herself or her family. Unless she did something different, that wasn't going to change.

Dr. Davidson made a move to Seattle and was able to gradually back out of her medical practice in exactly 32 months. She now earns a solid six-figure income with her network marketing business and practices medicine ten hours per week for the personal and professional satisfaction.

When asked for advice by other medical professionals, she has a simple response: "Make your decisions based on fact, not perception, so that what you choose is right for you. If you want to build your work around your life and not the other way around, take action. Don't let outdated or erroneous information determine your future. We all must live with the rewards and the consequences of our decisions. I am happy that I put my fear aside and took action. More importantly, ask my children: they're happy too!"

Company President Enjoys Freedom as Distributor

After receiving her MBA in Marketing and Finance, Janice DeLong began her career as a commodities trader. From there she moved into venture capital and spent the next seven years working for a firm that placed $100 million under her management.

"I enjoyed working with all the start-up companies. My job was to get them to a place where we'd either sell them or take them public," she says. "But they were never my baby, so I began looking for something where there would be a lasting relationship."

One day in 1990 she saw an ad in the New Canaan, Connecticut, *Advertiser* that said, "Entrepreneur looking for another entrepreneur to

---

I realized that network marketing really was a legitimate and reasonable option for bringing products to the end-line user. It is so much simpler and more straightforward than conventional means of product distribution.

13

start a business. Only requirement: sense of humor." That was all it took for Janice to step out of the employment world of high finance into the entrepreneurial business world.

"We set out to develop a line of naturally-based skin care, nutrition, and household cleaning products," she says. "After a year of preparation, we then began exploring our best avenue for marketing them. Someone suggested network marketing. Since neither of us had any preconceived opinions about that form of product distribution, we stayed open and attended a gathering of about 500 networkers in Stanford. We were impressed. It made economic sense from both the distributor and corporate perspective. Why not redirect the conventional advertising budget toward compensating distributors who spread the word to their friends and associates?"

She joined the Direct Selling Association (DSA) so she could learn from the experts, and became deeply involved with the organization, sitting on their Board of Directors, joining their International Council, and chairing the Interactive Marketing Council.

The company was successful, but there was a downside. "As president of the company, I felt responsible 24 hours a day for the welfare of thousands and thousands of distributors. You are responsible for getting them the right products, the right compensation plan, shipping problems, all the taxes being paid. And that is a lot of pressure. After having my eyes opened to how much freedom there is in being a distributor, in 1998 my partner and I made the decision to merge with a stable, expanding network marketing company. Why? After working on the corporate side for so many years, and never having control of my own life, I could continue to build a thriving business but have my life back."

So she surrendered the reins, became a distributor, and found time to "smell the roses along the way."

There are very few executives—even of the network marketing type—who won't, in a moment of honesty, admit at least a tad bit of envy, if not full-blown preference, for the lifestyle of a distributor. More and more corporate founders are stepping "down" to the good life, building a global network while working from home, and enjoying the balance of family, good friends, and business all wrapped into one.

African American Woman Lawyer Finds MLM

Often it is those who have the most to overcome who excel. Jonell Clark has conquered what others might consider inspiring but challenging obstacles to achieve her dreams. As an African American woman and lawyer, Jonell was enjoying a rewarding career in full-time practice in Stone Mountain, Georgia, but something was missing. She had money to spend but her time wasn't her own. She lacked a sense of passion and of genuinely effecting change in people's lives.

As a result of some physical problems she experienced in 1985, a friend, Shirley Carmike, told her about some nutritional products and encouraged her to try them. Jonell was so impressed with the results that she inquired about the marketing opportunity. Her friend was in shock because no one at that time had ever asked about joining her in business. And, besides, who would have expected Jonell Clark, an attorney, to be interested in selling?

"She was a close personal friend and someone I trusted," Jonell says. "That was important because previously I had never allowed anyone to come near me talking about selling anything. But the more I listened, the more I believed in the impact this could have on my life and the lives of others. As I look back, I can see that I went through a three-step process. First, I put my faith in God, believing that what I was doing was right and good. Secondly, I was totally and completely committed to the industry. Third, I went to work armed with the impassioned belief that I would have the success I envisioned. Prosperity didn't come easily or immediately, but it did finally present itself overwhelmingly.

"Through this industry, I have been able to help so many people expand their consciousness and enhance their standard of living. Whether they're joining me in business or just using our products, I make sure that people know how much I care about them. This is an industry in which anyone who is able to dream and willing to work hard can be successful. I come from a very, very impoverished background. Where else but in America could this have happened to me? Network marketing is truly an opportunity for all people everywhere to realize their dreams."

Business Owners Lured into Network Marketing

So much of life is spent searching for our niche (our chair, our tree, our piece of land), both in business and in our personal lives. Bob Hydeman was no exception. In 1972, he began a commercial real estate business in Dallas, Texas. Sixteen years later, in 1988, a major real estate depression in Texas destroyed his company. He managed to repay $15 million in debt and narrowly avoided bankruptcy. He even sold his homestead of 19 years

> **Bob had absolutely no interest in the industry and said so in no uncertain terms. His friend's reply was "What do you have that is better, Bob?"**

and conveyed the proceeds to his lenders in order to protect his integrity and personal self-image. It was a rags-to-riches story in reverse.

No longer even a home owner, Bob went from being a multi-millionaire to worse than bankrupt. With his life in shambles, at 52, he felt his future looked extremely bleak. It was during this time that a friend, formerly the head of a $4 billion division of a financial institution, invited him to join a network marketing company. Bob had absolutely no interest in the industry and said so in no uncertain terms.

His friend's reply was, "What do you have that is better, Bob?"

After a moment's pause, Bob responded, "When can we get started?"

Based on his own experience, Bob feels that the industry offers numerous benefits, particularly for those like himself who have crossed the half-century mark of their lives:

- *Low risk versus high rewards:* The ability to begin a networking business for a few hundred dollars with the potential to earn millions. How many people risk their life savings in traditional business, only to see their venture go down?
- *Leverage:* An opportunity to build through people. As John Paul Getty said so well, "I'd rather have one percent of a hundred peoples' efforts than a hundred percent of my own."
- *No restrictions:* On the size of your group or the territory where you can sell. This is unlike conventional businesses where the sales force undergoes annual reviews, often with commissions adjusted down as territories are reduced.
- *In control of your own life:* No boss, no quotas, no time constraints, and no dress code. Unlike corporate life, you choose your own hours, full or part-time, and set your own goals.
- *No liabilities:* No bank loan, no office lease, no overhead, no employees. Unlike owning a conventional business, your sales force

consists of all independent contractors and you enjoy the autonomy of working out of your home.

- *Residual income:* Your income continues as long as your organization is productive. In conventional business, your income stops when you leave the company.

As Bob thinks back on his real estate career, it doesn't begin to compare to the advantages of network marketing.

"At the height of my real estate business over a sixteen-year period, I had ten associates for whom I was liable and three staff. I had a long-term office lease and a gross overhead of $30,000 per *month* before I received an income, which fluctuated dramatically from year to year depending upon the economy. In comparison, I currently have a Network Marketing organization that totals in the hundreds of thousands of independent distributors and growing. Although many of them are beyond my pay level, I have stability and therefore security unlike anything I ever experienced in real estate. Unlike real estate, the stability of my networking business is not tied to the economy. I work out of my home and my annual expenses are approximately $30,000 per *year*. I've accomplished this in five years and my income has shown steady growth—much more consistent than my years in real estate. Presently, my business is on automatic pilot and I own my own life. But at any time I choose, I can retake the controls."

More and more professionals, like Bob Hydeman, are finding their niche in network marketing, leaving behind the stress of owning their own business. In short, they are tired of the chase.

Every morning in Africa, a gazelle wakes up. It knows it must run faster than the fastest lion or it will be killed. Every morning a lion wakes up. It knows it must run faster than the slowest gazelle or it will starve to death. It doesn't matter whether you are a lion or a gazelle. When the sun comes up…in traditional business, you'd better be running.

In contrast, so much of our industry is about working cooperatively with those in our organization. Our success is intertwined with their success. It exhibits neither the competitiveness of traditional self-employment nor the dictatorial nature so prevalent in corporate America. Network marketing calls upon us to lead by example, celebrate the victories together, and offer support to each other when those times of discouragement set in.

So often this support is like the child who saw his next door neighbor sad after the death of his wife. Upon seeing the man cry, the little boy went into the old gentleman's yard, climbed onto his lap, and just sat there. When his mother asked him what he had said to the neighbor, the little boy said, "Nothing, I just helped him cry." It is such shared moments that create the essence of which network marketing is made.

CHAPTER 2

The Changing Work Culture

Career change is a normal part of corporate life today. It would be naïve to go to work for a company and think you would be there forever. Some industries are clearly part of the future. Others are like switching seats on the Titanic. As we are shifting from a managerial society to an entrepreneurial one, it is important to your personal planning that you are fully aware of this transformation.

Baby Boomers and Lost Expectations

As baby boomers, we can remember a time when our grandparents and parents worked their whole lives for one company. In my case, I grew up in a matriarchy. I remember my grandmother working as a bookkeeper for more than forty years for the *Dallas Morning News*. For the sake of their families, our precursory generations gave of themselves on an implied promise that they'd get a small degree of prosperity in exchange for a lifetime of loyalty to their employers.

After college graduation, our generation moved toward having both spouses in paying jobs. We moved around a bit, searching for better pay or better hours or more rewarding opportunities. We thought we'd surely find our niche, a place we could call home, with the kind of company that would underpay us at the beginning of our careers, pay us well in our 30s, and overpay us as we hit our 50s. We thought we would get more perks with age, even after we'd reached our peak, and that the company would stand by us in our later years (like companies stood behind our parents and grandparents). We believed that we would receive good health coverage and a reasonable pension program to carry us into our retirement years.

Baby Boomers Attitudes Change

If you are 40 or over—a baby boomer—you are caught on the cusp of the job revolution. You started your career thinking much like your dads: land a good job with a good company and work hard. Now you have been "downsized," or wonder when your turn will come. Either way, you may not be financially or psychologically ready for this. You may believe there is something shameful in it.

The job market today does nothing to assuage that feeling of shame. Many older job seekers with flawless résumés, solid experience, and Ivy League educations simply can't find work.

"Companies are laying off middle managers, and there's a reluctance to let them back in," says Larry Merris at Lancaster Employment and Training Agency in Pennsylvania.[1]

According to Exec-U-Net, a Norwalk, Connecticut, job information organization, the length of your job search increases with your age. Compared to a 35 to 40-year-old executive, Exec-U-Net found it takes 18 percent longer for a 41 to 45-year-old to find a job. For someone 46 to 50, it takes 24 percent longer. That number jumps to 44 percent for someone age 51 to 55 years old and 60 percent for those aged 56 to 60. The problem is not that there are not enough jobs for older workers, but that those over the age of 40 have to overcome certain prejudices, including the perception that your skills are outdated or salary demands are too high.

> **The problem is not that there are not enough jobs for older workers, but that those over the age of 40 have to overcome certain prejudices, including the perception that your skills are outdated or salary demands are too high.**

"It's just a mentality that exists in American business, especially with companies that downsize, that that particular age group is marked, that they're past their most fruitful years," says Bob Ward, manager of Denver's Forty Plus, a nonprofit networking and job services group for executives over the age of 40.

There are exceptions. Bill Wells, vice president of business development with Lee Hecht Harrison recruiters, says start-up companies in the technology field value experienced managers. Entrepreneurs may have the technological expertise, but lack the managerial skills to bring the technology to market.

"They need someone who can come in and do it, who doesn't have to be taught," says Wells.

There's only one catch. This is a buyer's market. The number of men and women aged 45 to 54 in the labor force stood at nearly 17 million in 1980. In the year 2005, according to the Bureau of Labor Statistics, that number will more than double. It's the old law of supply and demand.

According to a 1998 Retirement Confidence Survey released by the Employee Benefit Research Institute, 75 percent of those interviewed believe they will have to work beyond the age of 65. That means there will be more and more senior job seekers out there. You will almost surely have to settle for smaller salaries.

Little Security Past Forty

A funny thing happened on our way to retirement. The men and women who are my peers in their 50s and 40s have come to learn that companies with a tradition of standing by them are now just as likely to replace them with someone younger. This someone will earn half as much as they do, get less vacation time, need fewer dollars put into their pension plans, and require far less expensive medical benefits and insurance. We should have seen it coming back in 1989, when the American workforce first began to shrink. Since then, U.S. companies have laid off some three million employees, under the new rubric called "downsizing."

As Pat Buchanan told the story in 1996 (he was then running for his party's presidential nomination), this was nothing less than the abandonment of the American worker by heartless corporate executives. *The New York Times* ran similar editorial laments about greedy capitalists. But, the big American corporations—and, inevitably, many small ones, too—believed they must either throw some people overboard...or sink.

General Motors cut its workforce after years of losing market share to Japanese auto manufacturers. GM-Hughes Electronics (and all the other aerospace giants) cut thousands of jobs when the Cold War ended. Sears shed 50,000 people during the 1990s as more and more of its customers migrated to new competitors like Wal-Mart. In January 1996, AT&T announced that it would lay off 40,000 white-collar employees. Said its CEO Robert Allen: "We make the necessary, even painful changes today, or forfeit the future."

And the beat goes on. According to Challenger, Gray and Christmas, U.S. companies announced the elimination of some 600,000 jobs in 1998, and promised more cuts to come. In December 1998, Boeing announced it would cut 53,000 jobs over the next two years, well beyond a previous forecast of 28,000.

In January 1999, BankAmerica Corporation officials announced they would pare 18,000 positions worldwide, which is 10,000 more than they predicted eight months before when BankAmerica Corp. merged with NationsBank Corp. In the same month, January 1999, the *Los Angeles Times* said Compaq would cut 17,000 jobs, as opposed to an earlier estimate in April that the computer firm would trim only 1,000 positions.

Though statistics on this are harder to pin down, corporate insiders claim the first people to go were often the oldest. The reasons were purely pragmatic. "For my salary," says one 51-year-old man who was laid off in 1998, "the company could hire two 28-year-olds."

Over 40 Now a Minority

What happens if you're fired? You go and get another job, right? Well, yes, but only if you're young enough. According to Henry Conn and Joseph Boyett, authors of *Workplace 2000: The Revolution Reshaping American Business,* people beginning their careers in the 1990s will probably work in ten or more jobs for five or more employers before they retire.

Older workers will have a much harder time. David Opton, executive director of Exec-U-Net, says he tells people between 40 and 45 who are considering a new job to hurry "because the door closes at 45." It can get worse. When you're filling out forms at a Westech Career Expo, the nation's largest job fair, you now qualify for "professional minority status" if you are over 40. At 40, you're now a minority! At 40, you don't even bother looking in some fields.

Since the advent of the two-paycheck household, this country has had a large, underpaid minority. We are called women.

"I've had people in their late thirties tell me they've had someone look at them and say, 'Wow, you're kind of old for a programming job, aren't you?," says Paul Kostek, president of the Institute of Electrical and Electronic Engineers, USA.

Executives once spoke of reaching a plateau. In the February 1999 issue of *Fortune,* Nina Munk summed up the situation: "If their path no longer led upward, at least they were in a stable, safe place. Now the plateau is a narrow ledge. Suddenly...growing numbers of 40-somethings are slipping backward."

Women Struggle in the Workplace

Since the advent of the two-paycheck household, this country has had a large, underpaid minority. We are called women. According to a White House task force, women earn just 76 cents for every dollar that men earn. This is an improvement over the 63 cents per dollar women "enjoyed" in 1979, according the U.S. Bureau of Labor Statistics.

Rather than wait for the government to enforce equality, more and more women are deciding to leave their j.o.b.s (journey of the broke) to become entrepreneurs. Many of us gave up on corporate jobs after finding wages stagnant and feminist rhetoric about self-fulfillment empty. Juliet Schor, author of *The Overworked American,* reported that 28 percent of the respondents in a recent survey had made a voluntary change in lifestyle that involved a significant reduction in earnings as they moved to a less stressful job, turned down a promotion, or refused relocation.

More and more mothers are working part-time and they routinely make less an hour than full-time workers doing the same job. I see another new trend: If women can work at home making a significant fraction of the money they made in the secretarial pool, they'd still prefer to be with their kids. Some creative entrepreneurial women are learning they can stay at home with their kids *without* sacrificing their income.

Even so, the number of women 45 and older employed or looking for work swelled from 14.8 million in 1988 to 20.3 million last year, according

23

to the U.S. Department of Labor. With this increase, it is clear that women as well as men are looking for the solution to financial stability in their lives. This seems to be so whether they are married or single.

"Age plays differently for women than it does for men," says Deborah Chalfie of the American Association of Retired Persons (AARP). "Baby boomers have a much stronger attachment to the workplace than…their grandmothers, so it's likely to become an increasing issue."[2]

The challenge is even greater for women executives who aspire to the top. The typical Chief Executive Officer this year is 56 years old, male, white, and Protestant. In the past, it has proven nearly impossible for a woman to break through the bias in favor of men.

Age Bias

Companies are encouraging older workers to retire early as part of their downsizing efforts, but the good news is that many are hiring them back on a temporary basis. Of 460 large corporations surveyed, 75 percent reported that they retain retirees as consultants or seasonal workers, according to the Commonwealth Fund, a philanthropic organization. All kinds of companies—not just fast-food chains—are seeking older workers to occupy part-time jobs with flexible hours.

"Age discrimination is rampant and illegal, but it probably affects lesser-skilled workers more than it does professionals," suggests Patrick Burns, spokesperson for the National Council of Senior Citizens.

"Opportunities abound in consulting and teaching for former executives, as long as you keep current by joining professional organizations, attending conferences, and speaking and writing on topics related to your field," he says.[3]

Age bias is exactly that—a bias that has little or no foundation in fact. At the same moment 77-year-old John Glenn was undergoing endurance tests in July 1998 to prepare for his chance to go back into space, Jim Tatum was pedaling across Texas in the over-70 division of a cross-country bicycle race.

By some measures, Glenn is old. Of the 3.05 million Americans born in 1921, less than half (1.34 million) are still alive. But the meaning of "old" has evolved. People are living longer, healthier lives. Life expectancy rates have risen dramatically over the last 50 years. Seniors are undertaking new endeavors that would have seemed inconceivable to the youth-obsessed American culture back in 1962, when Glenn became the first American to orbit the Earth.

"Remaining active helps you to remain active," said the former astronaut with a smile.

Glenn recounted a recent airport encounter with a fellow senior citizen, who told him, "You're really making it possible for me to do something."

"And I said, 'What's that?'" Glenn recalled.

"If you can go back into space," the man said, "then I can climb Mt. Kilimanjaro after all."[4]

Everyone has a subconscious, if not conscious, awareness of role models. After Roger Bannister ran the first four-minute mile, 11 other long distance runners broke his record in the next two years. The more we see vibrant, active 70 and 80-year-olds leading full and productive lives, the more likely we will be to get out there and live our lives outside the box of stereotypes when we reach their age.

Mary Lou Wilson is a septuagenarian enjoying her "golden years" with a lifestyle that includes work. Although she has been involved in her field for more than 20 years, it wasn't until January 1991, already past the "normal" retirement age, that Mary Lou first heard about the network marketing company with which she is now affiliated. More and more so-called "retirees" (a word that should itself be retired) are going to find ways to blend usefulness with the joys of their "golden years."

Workers Not Paid Their Worth

At the end of the millennium, workers across corporate America hoping for generous pay raises in 1999 should prepare themselves for some bad news: employers in general are holding the line. Instead companies will use non-traditional pay programs to attract talented hires and reward top performers. Stock options, signing bonuses, gain sharing, and performance-based pay are now being used by companies facing a tight labor market and mounting profit pressures.[5]

Little or Nothing Toward Retirement

According to the National Commission on Retirement Planning, approximately 50 million workers have no pensions, and 14 percent of people age 51 through 61 have nothing saved for retirement. Only 29 percent of those in that age range have $100,000 or more in retirement savings, and 18 percent have less than $10,000.[6]

Between 33 to 40 percent of Americans are not saving for retirement. Most of them believe they have too many pressing financial responsibilities today to save for tomorrow, according to a 1998 Retirement Confidence Survey. About 40 million people work in businesses with 100 or fewer employees. And 25 million of them aren't covered by a retirement plan at work. For most of them, this is not a concern. Retirement is not on the mind of average workers. They've been dealing with a divorce, $19,000 in credit card bills, and trying to make their monthly mortgage, car, and child support payments. Their only concern is getting through the week.[7]

Baby boomers are notorious for not thinking about retirement. After all, we have always conquered the economic world and somehow we'll do it again when that time comes in our life. But the reality is that the future of Social Security is looking precarious, company pension plans are meeting only minimal needs due to the frequency of job switching, and IRAs are predicted to become obsolete if retirees are forced into higher tax brackets.

Our future income rests squarely on our own shoulders. A 45-year-old earning $60,000 a year today will need to save an average of $3,679 each month for a total of $2,167,320 by age 65 to produce the equivalent annual income, assuming a 3-percent inflation. A 45-year-old earning $35,000 a year today will need to save an average of $2,146 each month for a total of $1,264,260 by age 65 to produce the equivalent. A 35-year-old earning $60,000 a year today will need to save an average of $1,954 each month for a total of $2,912,700 by age 65 to produce the equivalent income power. A 35-year-old earning $35,000 a year today will need to save an average of $1,140 each month for a total of $1,699,080 by age 65 to produce the equivalent income power. A 25-year-old earning $35,000 a year today

> **Retirement is not on the mind of average workers. They've been dealing with a divorce, $19,000 in credit card bills, and trying to make their monthly mortgage, car, and child support payments. Their only concern is getting through the week.**

will need to save an average of $654 each month for a total of $2,283,420 by age 65 to produce the equivalent income power.[8]

"People are living too far beyond their means," says David Wyss, an economist at Standard & Poor's. "They can't keep it up forever."

An estimated $12 billion over and above what was earned was taken out of American savings accounts. This is important because it is indicative of how much U.S. workers will have when they retire.[9]

If you are 40 years old and making $40,000 annually, to retire comfortably at the level at which you've become accustomed, you will need $1 million in savings. That will require faithfully setting aside over $800 a month for the next 25 years. That kind of commitment just doesn't seem to be happening among today's spend-crazy boomers.

Low-Rung Workers Shortchanged

It is often lower-rung workers who are unable to profit from the benefits and perks offered by employers. They may not be able to afford a computer needed to work from home or they may be factory workers whose job demands that they be on site. A study by The Conference Board found 66 percent of employers say telecommuting is hard for lower-earning employees to use.

"If a company doesn't think it through, they may set up programs that don't take into account lower-wage workers," says Ann Vincola, senior partner at Corporate Work/Life Consulting in Boston.[10]

There's a clear message here: employees can no longer depend on companies to assume responsibility for them. They must begin taking steps to take care of themselves, especially in the area of benefits and long-term pension programs.

New Technology Brings Global Competition

Computers. One word tells us much of what has happened. Two other words tell us the rest of the story—global competition.

For most of us, technology means computers and all the tools we attach to them—the satellite dishes and cables and modems and telephones that we use to collect, store, and disseminate information. The first computers were giant machines that would fill entire rooms, which had to be air-conditioned to keep the radio tubes that ran them from overheating. Then came the transistor. And then the integrated circuit. No more tubes. No

> **If you are 40 years old and making $40,000 annually, to retire comfortably at the level at which you've become accustomed, you will need $1 million in savings.**

more huge rooms. By 1980, one $2,000 personal computer had the power of an old IBM mainframe that had once cost several hundred thousand dollars.

Along came Apple. Along came Microsoft. Along came Intel. By the mid-1980s, computers were transforming our shops and offices and banks and phone companies, and the pace of change only accelerated in the 1990s. In 1997, 36 percent of the companies in the *Inc.* magazine list of the 500 fastest growing companies were in some facet of the computer industry. And if companies weren't making computers, or selling them, they were using them. Suddenly, computers were like noses. Everybody had one. And with them companies attained unprecedented new productivity...and profit.

It happened just in time, because now U.S. companies were challenged by global competition. In the 1990s, some three billion new workers, producers, and consumers joined the international marketplace. Many U.S. companies went abroad themselves, to save labor costs, and they triggered like moves by their competitors, forcing everyone to become leaner and meaner.

One executive, Albert Dunlap, then CEO of Scott Paper and later of Sunbeam, found fame simply for his ruthlessness in terminating workers. The business press called him Chainsaw Al. He was so proud of that nickname he wrote a book celebrating himself, *Mean Business.* Other managers loved the book. They made it a best seller. They followed Chainsaw Al's example, and the rest was history. Managers figuratively fired up their own chainsaws, and, again, generally used them to lop off graying, long-term, committed heads.

American business was making its internal adjustments to the challenges of global competition and technological change.

Employees Leaving Giant Corporations
Many employees now go to work for big companies to get their on-the-job training and then switch to the small-to-midsize companies

responsible for driving job growth today. Many of the smaller companies have been expanding progressively while such corporate giants as IBM, Philip Morris, and RJR Nabisco brutally slash their payrolls.

It is these smaller entrepreneurial businesses that help explain why the U.S. is adding more than 200,000 new jobs and more than two million workers are joining the nation's payrolls each year.

Smaller employers are unquestionably feeding on the restructuring of corporate America, many of them hiring experienced workers laid off by bigger companies.[11]

Employee Agitation Growing

Almost everyone starts out working for someone else. If you are like most employees, you embraced your first job and all subsequent ones with all the excitement that goes hand in hand with experiencing something new. Before long, you find yourself stifled and your talents circumscribed by protocol. "We've never done that here before," you are told.

You contend with office jealousies and are irritated by obstructive chains of command. You learn the art of covering your behind with endless memos. You try not to anger supervisors who fear that you may soon surpass them. At some point, you may even reflect on the difference between present "wage-slave" work and actual bondage on an antebellum plantation.

The rise in retaliation claims with the Equal Employment Opportunity Commission (EEOC) reflects the growing unrest among employees across the nation. Total charges for race, sex, age, religion, and other forms of discrimination have swelled from 63,898 in 1991 to more than 80,000 in 1998.[12] Attacks on corporate management are increasing.

"It used to be you expected to be a lifer at a company. Now, jobs are more like way-stations," remarked Ronna Lichtenberg, co-author of *Work Would Be Great If It Weren't for the People,* "so there's less time to get to know someone. And there isn't the incentive to work things out."

"Work has become a predominant feature in everybody's lives," says Lee Bolman, a leadership professor at the University of Missouri in Kansas City. "People want work to mean something. They're looking for shared beliefs."

Employers are seeing the spirituality emphasis as a way to ease alienation among workers buffeted by business changes. "There's a lot of cynicism in the workplace," says Craig Neal, co-founder of the Heartland Institute, an Edina, Minnesota, group that fosters social and spiritual change. "People want to be fulfilled in their life."[13]

Downsizing Aftermath

Business and industry are thriving, but a lot of people aren't. Workers who didn't get downsized were left wondering who was better off, the ones who were fired, or the ones who weren't. They had increased work loads. They were suffering from stress, anxiety and lassitude. Worst of all, they were so afraid of being fired that they stopped telling the boss the truth as they saw it, falling back to simply agreeing with him, even when he was wrong.

In such workplaces the satire of Scott Adams, creator of the cartoon Dilbert and the bard of downsizing, is timely. The Dilbert Principle supplanted the outmoded Peter Principle.

And here is a disturbing result of people trying to deal with their frustration over the job situation: more than 1,000 Americans are murdered on the job every year, 32 percent more than the annual average in the 1980s. According to Joseph Kinney, executive director of the National Safe Work Institute in Chicago, "Violence directed against employers or former employers is the fastest-growing category of workplace violence."

If you don't die on the job, there is a good chance you will be maimed. A 1993 survey by Northwestern National Life Insurance reports that more than two million employees suffer physical attacks on the job each year. And more than six million are threatened in some way.

All in all, there is neither safety nor security in the workplace today. Loyalty is no longer a value in corporate America, so workers and managers are forced to always be on the lookout for something better. The upside is that workers are developing keen survival skills due to their understandably circumspect attitudes.

Corporate Execs Find New Start in MLM

Forty-something middle managers have become a dime a dozen. By 2003, more than half the nation's workers will be age 40 and over.

On January 6, 1998, Fed Ex delivered letters to the homes of 389 Gerber Products sales people telling them they were out of work. Of those 389 employees, nearly 70 percent were over 40. One of them was Tom Johnson. He had been selling Gerber baby food for 27 years, starting when he was

21. Shouldn't he have known he was vulnerable? "Right up until D-Day, I was convinced I wouldn't be hit, what with me calling on national accounts and all," Johnson says. It's human nature that causes us to be blind-sided. No matter how often we hear stories of corporate ruthlessness, of 45-year-olds being replaced by 28-year-olds, we believe it won't happen to us.

"I sat in my chair and read the letter eight times. I just couldn't believe it," Tom remembers. "It was like someone grabbed me and hit me as hard as they could right in the stomach. I thought, 'God, all I've done and all I've worked, and it doesn't mean a thing.'"

His unemployment checks, at $476 every two weeks, ran out months ago. He had sent out about 400 résumés, and still hadn't found a job. If truth be told, his chance of finding anything that comes close to paying what he earned at Gerber is probably zero.

The Tom Johnsons of the world are the most likely candidates for MLM as they are being replaced by the Gen Xers.

Why Work for Someone Else?

There are countless options available to you both within and without the confines of corporate America. What you choose is entirely within your control. Make a list of your priorities with the most important at the top. Then ask yourself this all-important question: Can I attain my dreams and achieve my priorities by working for someone else? If the answer is not a resounding *yes*, it may be time for you to weigh other career options.

How often have we heard that if you always do what you've always done, you'll always get where you've always gotten? Every one of us is in charge of our own personal and professional excellence. If this can be reached in the environment in which we presently find ourselves, it is up to us to make it happen.

> **Loyalty is no longer a value in corporate America, so workers and managers are forced to always be on the lookout for something better.**

Mel Zeigler, founder of Banana Republic clothing stores, once said: "A leader discovers the hidden chasm between where things are and where things would better be, and strings up a makeshift bridge to attempt the crossing. From the other side, they guide those who dare to cross this rickety traverse until the engineers can build a sturdier span for all."

If you are happy where you are, but just need to step forward and improve the current situation, just focus, and do it. If it is beyond your control, then get out and create a better way for yourself.

You have options and it really is that simple.

New Options and New Hope

Working for someone else no longer seems to be the answer. Why not work for yourself?

"You mean, create my own job?" you ask. "Isn't that a bit impractical?"

No. It has never been more realistic. Almost 19 million Americans work for themselves, the vast majority of them running single-person businesses out of their homes. Many of them are people who were downsized in the 1980s and early 1990s.

These corporate refugees found they could sell their services back to the very companies that fired them in the first place, often for more money. By some estimates, one-third of all corporate refugees go out the back door, turn around and walk in the front door. They have the inside track on the company's needs, and sell their expertise to their old employers and new customers as well as independent contractors.

The same forces that create the pool of refugees also create a demand for their services.

"As corporations diminish," says Charles Handy, visiting professor at the University of London School of Business, and author of a book about the changing workplace, "huge markets are opening up for precisely the people who are being displaced."

Those with vision and belief in themselves are not crying "poor me" for long. These professional emigrants understand today's business climate and do not miss an opportunity. They are making history. They start up new franchises and small business ventures everywhere, and enjoy life as perhaps never before. Slim chance that you could entice these new entrepreneurs to return to corporate America. They've realized that they can shape their own culture, free at last from the entrapments of big business protocols, even if they must sacrifice secure salaries and big expense accounts.

Can I attain my dreams and achieve my priorities by working for someone else?

"As they find their footing," continues Charles Handy, "these corporate refugees are beginning to have a broad impact on the world around them. With their knowledge, insights, and expertise, they are transforming some long neglected nooks of the U.S. economy. They're revitalizing old-fashioned 'metal-bending' companies with new technologies and marketing savvy. They're introducing a new level of professionalism to family businesses across the nation. And they're bringing new financial and operating sophistication to the world of franchising."

If you wait around for corporate America to return to the so-called days of security, you might also hope for Tinkerbell to land on your windowsill. Corporate America hasn't been able or willing to soften the hard reality for the men and women over 50 who are out of work. If we are talking about security here, then maybe we all have to ask ourselves where true security lies. Psychologically speaking, security lies within. Maybe we have to grow up and look to ourselves instead of others.

"This is all fine," you say, "if I don't fail." Right. Many small businesses and franchises do fail. Many consultants will wait in frustration for accounts to walk in out of cyberspace. And some of those who do get the business will find themselves working grueling hours for a fraction of their old company pay and benefits. One human resources manager offered this piece of advice for those who confront this challenge. "Make your own opportunities, whether it is inside the company you are working for, or outside it. Keep developing your skills, rid yourselves of the notion that you can move ahead by staying put, and keep repeating the mantra that security cannot come from your bosses or anyone outside of you."

CHAPTER 3

Consider Starting Your Own Business

There may have been a time not so very long ago when many of us—average Americans—felt stuck in our jobs. We were frightened by the threat of being downsized and scared to strike out on our own—damned if we did, damned if we didn't. You may recall that we had double-digit inflation in the 1970s and 1980s, and factories, particularly in the East and Midwest, were closing by the scores. So many of us hunkered down in our boring jobs, doing what we had always done.

Then, in the early 1990s, the economy began to take an upswing. One Saturday morning early in 1999, we woke up to read these headlines on page one of *The New York Times*: "Economic Growth In Last Part Of '98 Was Robust 6.1 Percent; Tied Top Rate Of The 90's....With Pace of Inflation at 0.7 Percent, Expansion; Now at 8 Years Gives No Sign of Ending."

Amazing. This was a decade that began in doom and gloom. But now, here, in the last year of the decade, it is all boom! With unemployment at an all-time low in many states, it began to dawn on even the dullest of us that the U.S. economy was going great and getting better. So much so, *The Times* could report on Feb. 27, 1999, "The economic expansion that began in early 1991 is completing its eighth year, with no end in sight."

What happened? Let's look at the statistics.

"Since 1980, the U.S. economy lost some 43 million jobs through downsizing and other structural changes. Economists call them 'sunset jobs.' "In their place," analyst Horace Brock points out, "71 million new jobs have been created. That's a net gain of 28 million jobs, or nearly seven times as many as the economies of continental Europe, which together are larger than America's, gained in the same time." These are "sunrise jobs" in industries that have a brighter future and in most cases pay better than the median wages.[1]

Entrepreneurs on the Rise

Entrepreneurs are creating many of these "sunrise" jobs. Who are they? They're people who choose to be in business for themselves, intent on gaining personal independence and, for many, prosperity beyond their dreams. You remember that character in Shakespeare who said that "...Some are born great, some achieve greatness, and some have greatness thrust upon them?"

In the 1990s, a lot of people who may never have otherwise thought of themselves as entrepreneurs suddenly had "greatness thrust upon them." They were fired from their jobs, or they could see the handwriting on the wall—that they'd probably be fired soon. Or perhaps they were just fed up with their bosses from hell, so they decided that they had to do something else. Some ended up starting their own companies. Some ended up working solo.

By some estimates, 25 million Americans are now doing exactly that. "Not long ago people would disguise that they were working from home; now they're celebrating it," says Daniel Pink, a former White House speechwriter. "This is a legitimate way to work. It isn't some poor laid-off slob struggling to find his way back to the corporate bosom."

It isn't just those being laid off who are interested in going into business for themselves. According to *U.S. News & World Report*, there is an increasing interest in entrepreneurship among college students and those

---

Entrepreneurs are...people who choose to be in business for themselves, intent on gaining personal independence and, for many, prosperity beyond their dreams.

---

pursuing a business degree. In fact, more than 400 programs now offer courses in entrepreneurship, up from 16 in 1970, and funding for entrepreneurial programs is nine times what it was in 1980.[2]

Why did so many men and women become entrepreneurs in the 1990s? Simply because they could, and the momentum was moving in that direction. Times had changed, and the world was full of new opportunities, triggered by these trends:

Outsourcing

All those companies that had downsized or, as their corporate public relations people preferred, "rightsized," still had work to be done, more than the employees that were left in place could handle. So they farmed the work out, often to some of those very people who had been invited to leave a few months before. The companies called it "outsourcing."

Fewer Capital Demands

Those whom the companies called back to work tended not to need heavy equipment, or even an office or a lab outside their homes. Armed with a computer and modem, a phone and a fax, they were in business. So, new entrepreneurs who worked as consultants often didn't have to raise huge sums of money to start their own businesses.

Abundant Credit

Getting money to start a business has always been the biggest obstacle for many entrepreneurs. But a thriving economy and a swarm of investors made rich by entrepreneurs have made the necessary money available.

Joseph Sansone, CEO of Pediatric Services of America, operates a business that makes it possible to take premature babies home sooner than in the past. His business would have gone nowhere in the 1970s. Ventilators and other life-support systems were too unreliable, and even if they weren't, he wouldn't have been able to raise capital to buy the equipment.

"Now," Sansone says, "I could raise 50 times what I raised the first time."

Seed money is always more available during times of economic growth. Venture capitalists say there's more financing available today than at any time in the past 50 years. Says one of them: "This transcends the wild, crazy times of the '80s."

Proven entrepreneurs are courted by venture capitalists. Most start-ups, however, must begin like Narenda Popat, a native of India and co-founder of NetScout Systems, who won an Entrepreneur of the Year Award in 1998. When he started out, Popat had $750 and some credit cards, no money in the bank, a second mortgage on his house, a lot of rejection, and a difficult time speaking English.

"I didn't know if I'd have a next day," he says.

By the time he received his award, Popat had 150 employees, and some $12 million in the bank, and he was moving into a new plant that very week.

Technology

Communications has become easy. We can link our telephones to computers and facsimile machines and, with cellular technology, we can fax and e-mail on the road, in our cars, on trains, on flights across the world, or (yikes!) even from poolside (or courtside) at our local country club. Computer technology isn't only a tool. It's a product, too.

In the past, someone who wanted to go into business usually figured out how much it would cost to make and distribute a product, then determined if it could be sold at a reasonable profit. Maybe you did this when you were a kid. In school, maybe, you learned how to build a birdhouse. Then you went to the lumberyard, bought some wood and some nails and some glue for $15 and then, in your dad's workshop or the garage, you built six birdhouses, which you sold for $5 apiece...and made a profit of $15. But today, a young person learns Java and HTML, figures out how to make web pages, and sells them for thousands of dollars each. What's he selling? Knowledge and skills that others are willing to pay for, and handsomely at that. There is real value here or people wouldn't pay.

Public Acceptance

William Bartmann, CEO of Commercial Financial Services in Tulsa, was a 1997 Ernst & Young Entrepreneur of the Year. Bartmann remembers when people such as he used to be called "swashbucklers and hip-shooters." Now, he says, "society thinks it's cool to be an entrepreneur." Bartmann is 49, and he's not new to the entrepreneurial world. He has been self-employed since he was 22. But in 1987, he was $3 million in debt, and about to default on a $1 million bank loan. Did he give up? No way. He convinced the bank that it had little to lose by lending him an additional $13,000 to start a company that collects bad debts by being understanding

Today's heroes have a vision that they make happen, instead of waiting to get lucky.

rather than pushy. We don't have to wonder how Bartmann, saddled with debt, got that idea. It was an idea that worked so well he paid back the loan in two years. He now employs 1,800 people who are most happy to be understanding.

Bartmann says the U.S. business world is filled with people who have followed the same entrepreneurial path, like Herb Kelleher, who built Southwest Airlines from scratch; and Bill Gates, who founded Microsoft in 1975 and became unimaginably rich in less than a decade. Today's heroes have a vision that *they* make happen, instead of waiting to get lucky. Suddenly, getting rich seems within reach.

A New Zeitgeist

There's something else going on in American society: time has moved up on the priority list. Somewhere in the past couple of decades, many of us have figured out ways to stop working hard and start working smart. We have a reason—we're learning how to enjoy life. Working smart, we take more time with the kids, smell the flowers, or take art classes so we can paint them. We do volunteer work in our churches or pitch in at the local homeless center. We need to do less getting and spending (as the poet Wordsworth said, "laying waste our powers") and start doing more for others, which makes us feel better about ourselves.

Key to Any Entrepreneurial Venture

Back in 1994, Peter Lowe, a man who has been taking "Success Seminars" on the road to big arenas around the country for several years, tried to explain the success of his philosophy to a journalist named Richard Reeves. Lowe had filled the Cow Palace in San Francisco with more than 20,000 folks who paid $225 for a day's worth of inspiring talk by men and women who had not only made it big, but were sure they could help others do the same. Pitchman Zig Ziglar is one of Lowe's regular stars, but Lowe also persuaded winning coaches like Lute Olson of the University of Arizona and Lou Holtz of Notre Dame to share their winning formulas.

His audience included hundreds of Bay Area telephone company employees, sent by AT&T executives the same day they announced that over the next two years they would be eliminating 15,000 jobs in their long-distance-services unit. In essence AT&T was telling its own people, "Look, there are changes going on in the telephone business. You may have to get off our gravy train and actually build one of your own." Indeed, many of the AT&T people attending that Success Seminar at the Cow Palace were motivated to go out and become entrepreneurs.

"It's not money or power," Peter Lowe told Reeves. "People want love, happiness, and peace. What we're doing is not 'get rich quick.' It's moral and spiritual; this lays a foundation for a new way of life."

Lowe had to be right, if only because it's a lot easier to be moral and spiritual if you know where your next meal or mortgage payment is coming from. That's the way it is with economic necessity; if you can't see the end of the road, you do what you have to do to keep moving in that direction.

This even happens in China, according to a February 1999 editorial in the *Far Eastern Economic Review* called "Smarter: Thank Goodness for Entrepreneurs." The editorial reported a survey by the Chinese Academy of Social Science and the National Industrial and Commercial Association showed that about 73 percent of heads of Chinese private companies got no further than middle school—6.4 percent only had a primary education. The editor of the *Review* concluded, "Those least likely to slot themselves into the system are creating their own space. Let's just call it enterprise."

"When times get tough," said this editor, "Asians don't gripe, they get to work. Often for themselves."

He reported that during a recent downturn in the Hong Kong economy he wandered into a local neighborhood and found two new vegetable

---

It's not money or power.... People want love, happiness, and peace. What we're doing is not "get rich quick." It's moral and spiritual; this lays a foundation for a new way of life.

---

stalls and two new discount candy shops—the most favored start-up businesses in recession-stricken Hong Kong. Why vegetables and candy?

"Because, however bad the times, people still have to eat and parents still buy treats for kids, only now they look for value. And you don't need a Harvard MBA to figure out that fresh produce and cheap sweets are low-cost inventory that turn over quickly. The upshot is that capital isn't tied up with slow-moving stock, so cash flow is steady. How's that for smart business planning?"

Smart is the right word. Entrepreneurs who have to live by their wits tend to be—no surprise—witty people. According to Sumaria Monhan-Neill, who is a professor of entrepreneurship at Roosevelt University in Chicago, "To succeed, a person has to be innovative. Some would call it bizarre." Take Mike Turk, for example. Somehow he came into possession of 1,000 teak trophy bases. Probably saw them at an auction, found no one bidding on them and got them for pennies a copy.

Turk had an idea for a way to move his trophy stands that was bizarre enough. He bolted deactivated Army surplus hand grenades to the teakwood bases and sold them for $15 apiece as desk ornaments. So what made these curios move off the shelf in explosive fashion? Turk attached a plaque to the teak-grenade keepsake. It read: "Complaint Department. Take a number." The number was attached to the detonating pin.

Attitude Is Everything in Business

Okay, so not everyone is a Mike Turk. But then, you may not have to be. I like to think that the main thing you need is attitude. It is more important than ability.

What kind of attitude? It helps if you're a positive thinker. Uh huh. Everybody says that. Hey, you may already have enough of this positive attitude to make it as an entrepreneur. (The very fact that you are reading this book might give you a clue. You've got an open mind. That's definitely a start.)

More? You need more? Okay. Here's a little way to test yourself. A quiz, adapted from a 1999 piece in *The Los Angeles Times* by Susan Vaughn. Go ahead. Take it now. Be honest with yourself. Then we'll take a look at your answers and see whether you have the kind of attitude that makes for a successful entrepreneur.

1. You win a $350,000 MacArthur Genius Award. You:
   a) Quit your job and move to a ranch in Montana to contemplate nature.
   b) Quit your job, but remain in the same vocation.
   c) Stay at your job. It is extremely fulfilling.
   d) Quit your job, buy a Mercedes, do serious shopping in Beverly Hills and have that surgery you've been coveting.

2. In your present job, you make:
   a) Very little contribution to society, but you are trying to change that.
   b) A modest contribution to society.
   c) A formidable contribution to society. You take delight in helping others.
   d) No contribution to society, which is fine.

3. When did you last perform an unsolicited act of kindness at work?
   a) Last week.
   b) Yesterday.
   c) Today.
   d) There is no one at your job you want to assist unless you have to.

4. You perform your job to:
   a) Impress others and earn a living.
   b) Express yourself.
   c) Express yourself and add to the world.
   d) Earn as much money as possible and impress others.

5. In your work space, you have:
   a) Personal mementos and photographs.
   b) A few toys, personal mementos and photographs.
   c) Inspirational objects, toys, mementos and photographs.
   d) Only work-related materials.

6. Your business environment is like a:
   a) Bustling city. People rush about. There is little intimacy.
   b) Forest. It is quiet and allows for contemplation.

    c)   Home. People here care about each other.

    d)   Jungle. It's eat or be eaten.

7. When did you last encourage someone at work?
   a)   Last week.
   b)   Yesterday.
   c)   Today.
   d)   Not in a long while.

8. If you were the world's greatest at your job, how would you perform it differently?
   a)   Pay more attention to the quality of your work.
   b)   Increase the quantity of your work.
   c)   Do very little differently, because you already strive to do the best you can.
   d)   Do it totally differently.

9. During the day, you think about:
   a)   Tasks at hand, past disappointments and future uncertainties.
   b)   Mostly tasks at hand and some personal problems.
   c)   Tasks at hand.
   d)   Going home.

10. Which of these archetypes best describe you when you are at work?
    a)   Warrior. You battle all challenges and adversaries.
    b)   Magician. You create, invent, and make things happen.
    c)   Sage. You help, teach, and use wisdom to improve situations.
    d)   Dragon. You stay in a cave and breathe fire upon all those who bother you.

11. When was the last time you were creative?
    a)   Last week.
    b)   Yesterday.
    c)   Today.
    d)   At least a month ago.

12. Intuitive thinking is:
    a)   Something you'd like to develop for work.
    b)   Something you occasionally use at work.
    c)   Something you rely on all the time.
    d)   For flaky New Agers.

13. Your greatest fear is:
    a)   Being laid off and not finding another job right away.
    b)   Not having a calling.
    c)   Hurting others.
    d)   Not being admired or respected by others.

14. Think back to childhood. Are you still doing any of the things you loved most when you were young?
    a)   Yes, once in a while.
    b)   Yes, frequently.
    c)   Yes, you've incorporated some of your childhood delights into your vocation and hobbies.
    d)   No. You've outgrown those interests.

15. Think about some people in your past who caused you great pain. You:
    a)   Are less bothered by them now, but occasionally harbor angry thoughts about them.
    b)   Hardly think about them anymore.
    c)   Forgave them and learned from the relationships.
    d)   Frequently fantasize about getting revenge.

16. Work crises are:
    a)   Avoidable if you plan carefully.
    b)   Endurable if others support you.
    c)   Inevitable, but you have the strength of heart to weather them when they occur.
    d)   "Softened" by alcohol, drugs or food.

17. If you could work as someone else for a day, you'd be:
    a)   A movie star.
    b)   A motivational author/speaker.
    c)   A healer.
    d)   "Chainsaw" Al Dunlap.

18. Change:
    a)   Scares you.
    b)   Sometimes scares, sometimes inspires you.
    c)   Excites you.
    d)   Confuses and angers you.

19. When was the last time you had a great laugh at work?
    a)   Last week.
    b)   Yesterday.
    c)   Today.
    d)   A while ago, at a co-worker's expense.

20. Success is:
    a)   Public acclaim for a job well done.
    b)   Realizing personal goals.
    c)   Performing your best and making a difference in others' lives.
    d)   Fame, fortune and an appearance on "Oprah."

SCORING: If you answered honestly, then all your answers are correct. But if you didn't check off at least 15 Cs, you have to wonder whether you have the attitude you need to make a success as an entrepreneur, and/ or you have to start asking yourself how you can "C" better.

Downsides of Business Ownership

Against all expectations at the start of the decade, there's never been a better time to go into business for ourselves. According to Del Jones of *Money* magazine, it wasn't long ago that people who started their own businesses were not given the same public respect as doctors, lawyers, or heads of corporations even though they made millions.

"But it's a new era now," says Jones. "Suddenly, people see these entrepreneurs as trendsetters or gurus. They're being swamped with invitations to speak at colleges, where students hang on every word."

Jones writes, "Technology, financing...and especially public acceptance...have all converged to make conditions as ripe as they've ever been for entrepreneurs. Surveys show that most millionaires are in business for themselves. Long hours and heavy demands now come with any well-paying job. So, why not put in long hours for yourself?"

Don't answer too quickly. There is always a downside to every upside. Just ask Russ Karlen, who, after graduating from the University of Southern California, spent ten years owning his own construction business. He was extraordinarily successful.

"I made good money, but with 40 or 50 people working for me, and multiple jobs going at one time, there were always problems—a pool not installed right, a brick laid crooked. I was always on the job...all day every day. I ended up in divorce and never seeing my kids....I was miserable."

Investments

There is a consensus among business owners like Russ. For one thing, you will have to invest money, more money than you ever imagined. You will need solid capital, something that beginners in business tend to underestimate. Many launch their own business on the strength of their own personal savings. "It's enough," they think, "to get started." Then everything ends up taking longer and costing more than they had planned. If they can't borrow more from their Aunt Tilly they must pay from 18 to 20 percent interest borrowing on their credit cards or try to get an unsecured business loan from a bank that normally won't lend to anyone without substantial collateral. In other words, banks are only willing to lend money to people who don't really need it.

More Hours, Persistent Worries

"Another thing," Russ continues, "you will end up working much longer hours than you ever expected. I always put in more time than the guys who worked for me. It's just expected. And if anything went wrong, the buck stopped with me. In most cases, I was the one who stayed late to solve the problem.

"And vacations. You can forget carefree vacations. Exhaustion and fatigue seem to take the place of good old-fashioned rest and relaxation. I was always compelled to call back to the office checking on things. I carried the worries with me right onto the beaches of Hawaii or the golf courses at Carmel.

"Friday payroll was never an option. It had to be met whether the cash flowed in that week or not. And the job went forward even when the employees were out sick. Who filled in? I did.

"I got remarried to Linda toward the end of this phase of my life and she kept our books. Even though we were doing well, there were still

Surveys show that most millionaires are in business for themselves. Long hours and heavy demands now come with any well-paying job. So, why not put in long hours for yourself?

weeks she stressed about stretching our cash to cover equipment, materials, hidden costs, overhead, payroll, F.I.C.A., and unemployment taxes."

"Everyone depended on us," added Linda. "Our staff were like our kids. And the clients always wanted to talk to Russ, not anybody else...right in the middle of dinner."

Minority-owned Businesses

Business management and finances are tough enough with everything else being equal. If you're a minority, you can pretty much forget it when it comes to bank loans. Although minority-owned enterprises make up nearly 12 percent of the nation's business population, the Milikan Institute reported that in 1999, they received only an estimated 1 to 2 percent of the total equity capital invested in the U.S. (There are moves, however, to make more capital available to minority entrepreneurs. In March 1999, a growing number of influential leaders, including President Clinton, Federal Reserve Chairman Alan Greenspan, and the Reverend Jesse Jackson, were speaking publicly on the issue, calling for more equity investment in traditionally under-served communities and pondering ways to link those communities with investors.)

Whether the investing public will or will not be able to buy stock in minority-owned businesses (or some other form of government intervention), borrowing money will always be a struggle, no matter what your ethnic background.

Nevertheless, many immigrants find it much easier to start a business in America than in their home countries.

"It cost me $35 to incorporate, and I got the form within 24 hours," says Narenda Popat. "In India, it's difficult to even get the form...The United States is the best place in the world to do business."

Just ask the Vietnamese who fled their war-torn country a generation ago. Their kids are now storming places like Harvard and MIT and Cal Tech.

More Startup Businesses Going Under

Then, of course, there are people like James Oxendine. His tale is instructive but cautionary. Oxendine grew up in Dayton, Ohio, graduated magna cum laude from Ohio's Central State University, earned a law degree at Georgetown, and then topped it off with a Ford Fellowship in political economy at Clark Atlanta University. With that kind of background, he was able to get a good job managing a $1 million urban-problem-solving program at the Martin Luther King Jr. Center in Atlanta, revitalizing minority neighborhoods and businesses.

Then, at age 49, he decided to start his own community-development service. Easy, right? All he had to do was get some stationery printed and sit back in his low-overhead office (his living room) and wait for the phone to ring. He'd had some verbal commitments from people who said they planned to use his services as a lecturer, mediator, and bridge builder among banks and bureaucrats, and community-development groups. But the phone didn't ring. So he dipped into his savings to meet the expenses of his new company, The Oxendine Group, even though he was the only man in the firm. Sounded big, but the only one he was impressing was himself. His humblest moment came when a friend offered to buy his lunch because, she said, "You don't have a job."

Actually, he probably didn't mind if someone picked up his lunch tab. After three years and the depletion of his $25,000 in liquid savings, Oxendine was still making less than he had in his "job" job. The jury is still out, as far as Oxendine is concerned. He has survived four years now without much success but without sinking, either.

According to Dun & Bradstreet's press release of March 3, 1998, business failures are on the rise again after a three-year plateau. The number of businesses going under in the United States rose by 16 percent in 1997.

"The number of failures is now approaching the high levels reached in the recession of the early 1990s," reported Joseph Duncan, chief economic advisor to the Dun & Bradstreet Corporation.

According to Fugi Saito, an analyst for Dun & Bradstreet, of those businesses that do fail, 85 percent do so in the first five years. However, 70 percent of the businesses in Saito's 1995 study were still, like Oxendine, barely holding on after eight and a half years. It is perhaps noteworthy that Saito has now gone on to start his own business. Let's hope that he fares better than his case studies.

Exercise Caution

Deciding whether you want to go into business for yourself is a major decision. The Norwest Bank of Minnesota has come out with a set of questions that will help you draw conclusions that are right for you. This will be one of the most important decisions of your life, so you better be honest with yourself.

- Are you a self-starter? It will be up to you to develop projects, organize your time, and follow through on details.

- How well do you get along with different personalities? Business owners need to develop working relationships with a variety of people including customers, vendors, staff, and bankers...and professionals such as lawyers, accountants, or consultants. Can you deal with a demanding client, an unreliable vendor, or a cranky staff person in the best interest of your business?

- How good are you at making decisions? Small business owners are required to make decisions constantly, quickly, independently, and under pressure.

- Do you have the physical and emotional stamina to run a business? Business ownership can be challenging, fun, and exciting. However, it's also a lot of work. Can you face 12-hour work days six or seven days a week?

- How well do you plan and organize? Research indicates that many business failures could have been avoided through better planning. Good organization of finances, inventory, schedules, and production can help avoid many potential pitfalls.

- Is your drive strong enough to maintain your motivation? Running a business can wear you down. Some business owners feel burned out by having to carry all the responsibility on their shoulders. Strong motivation to make the business succeed will help you survive slowdowns as well as periods of burnout.

- How will the business affect your family? The first few years of a business start-up can be hard to balance against the demands of family life. There also may be financial difficulties until the business becomes profitable, which could take months or years. You may have to adjust to a lower standard of living or put family assets at risk.

This last point hits very close to home for me. From painful experience, I have learned that starting your own conventional business can be costly, in far more than just the financial sense. When my husband and I started our own company in 1998, of course, we had overhead—inventory, employees, office and equipment leases. We seemed destined for success and believed passionately in our cause. We had beautiful offices, 7,000 square feet in the Bank of America building, and were supported by a group of enthusiastic partners.

Although designated "equal" partners, some were willing but unable to make any investment. Others pledged to invest but, in the end, couldn't meet their full commitments. Every single partner had the highest of intentions and gave their best, but the responsibility of the company fell to us. After investing every bit of available cash into the business, personally guaranteeing everything we couldn't buy on credit, and borrowing another quarter of a million dollars, it still wasn't enough. When there was no place left to turn and no one else to carry on, the walls of our life came crashing down on us.

All of this was largely responsible for the loss of everything dear to me: our marriage, our family unity, and the company. We were in a business field in which we had expertise. We were determined and hard-working. But, we'd made other mistakes. Perhaps it was because of our zeal that we had not been cautious enough in making decisions. We obviously weren't thorough enough in our investigation of the financial requirements—the operating expenses as well as our sources of capital. We also found that Murphy's Law was alive and well—if something could go wrong, it did.

Somewhere in our determination to press forward despite all odds, my husband and I destroyed the most important element of our personal life. There is hope on the horizon for the company, now that a financially solid corporation has bought us out, but the marriage is gone.

If you are considering going into a conventional business for yourself, the kind that takes incredible amounts of capital…weigh it carefully, always keeping your life priorities clearly in front of you. No business is worth the devastation of a family or a marriage.

If you are considering going into a conventional business for yourself, the kind that takes incredible amounts of capital, please take time to weigh it carefully, always keeping your life priorities clearly in front of you. No business is worth the devastation of a family or a marriage.

In summary, if you are currently satisfied working for yourself in a traditional business, but just need to make some minor adjustments, do it. If, however, your business is running you, rather than the other way around, then stay open to explore how you might create a better work environment for yourself. There are other options—not the least of which is to become an entrepreneur with your own home business.

CHAPTER 4

Integration of Work and Leisure
Lifestyle: A Home Business

Now let's consider a new breed of business owners whose enterprises provide room for only one paycheck—their own. They're not pioneering new technologies or spawning the industries of tomorrow. They're not building empires or getting extravagantly rich, but in many ways, these solo operators are changing what it means to be in business by inventing new varieties of self-employment.

Some call themselves sole proprietors. Some call themselves consultants. Others refer to themselves as contractors or free agents, virtual employees or virtual-business owners. The electronically savvy, especially in Europe, profess to do "telework." I've also heard the terms, lone wolf, lone ranger, lone eagle, and soloist. Whatever name, most of these entrepreneurs share one thing in common: they work from home.

What Industries Work from Home?

According to *Inc.* magazine's *Almanac of Business Start-ups*, these were the top ten home-based businesses in 1998:
1. GENERAL CONTRACTING: 28,887
2. CONSTRUCTION: 21,697
3. COMPUTER SERVICES: 17,669
4. BUSINESS CONSULTING: 15,261

5. CLEANING SERVICES: 12,505
6. REAL ESTATE: 7,007
7. PAINTING: 6,518
8. CRAFTS: 5,437
9. TRUCKING: 5,279
10. MARKETING SERVICES: 5,028

I'm talking about a legion of individualists who are blurring the lines between job holding and business building. They are corporate mutineers, refugees, and asylum seekers. Most of these soloists found they could do business without the baggage—no employees, no capital, no equity, no overhead. Maybe part-time, maybe full-time. Maybe they were downsized out of a job, or maybe they just got sick of one.

Why Choose a Home Business?

Ellen Leanse, a 35-year-old mother of two young children, left her executive position at Apple Computer because she couldn't imagine raising her kids while working 80-hour weeks. Jane King, a veteran of several large financial companies, started thinking of a change when she found herself bringing her breast pump to business meetings after the birth of her daughter. Jody Severson, a 45-year-old political consultant from Rapid City, South Dakota, left the small advertising agency he had co-founded to unshackle himself from his 15 employees, paperwork, and the burden of having to manage anyone else at all. "I got tired of spending every Sunday night sweating payroll," relates Severson. "That loses its charm after a while."

These are representative of the courageous souls who have opted to take more control of their lives by leaving their companies and launching their own businesses. Many of them do not regard their ventures as short-term résumé fillers. Even among those laid off, downsized, or "re-engineered" out of corporations, self-employment can be as much an act of liberation as an act of desperation. These lone eagles are not throwaway workers but walk-away ones, tired of laboring away in organizations for stagnant wages, inflexible schedules, and obsolete promises about job security.

"The so-called security of a regular paycheck is an illusion, anyway," says Jody Severson. "Either you're answering what the market needs or

The successful businesses of the future will place more emphasis on time freedom, personal determination, and entrepreneurial latitude.

you're not. If you're not, you're doomed, whether you're in an office at IBM or an office in your basement." His years at the ad agency had cured him of any impulse to build another company. "As soon as you start a company, you've got higher overhead, you've got at least a 40-hour week, and you've lost the luxury of choosing the work you want to do. Running a company is just a race to keep the cash coming in, to cover that payroll. There's no freedom in that."

The Value of Leisure Time

Juliet Schor, an economist at Harvard Business School, sums up why people are trading in their employment for a home business in her noted work, *The Overworked American*. Today, leisure is more important than materialism. We've learned that acquiring "things" doesn't bring happiness. The successful businesses of the future will place more emphasis on time freedom, personal determination, and entrepreneurial latitude.

You may have heard about the American businessman who was vacationing in a small coastal Mexican village. While standing at the pier, he watched a small boat dock with just one fisherman in it. Inside the small boat were several large yellowfin tuna. The American complimented the Mexican on the quality of his fish and asked how long it took to catch them.

"Only a little while," the Mexican replied.

The American then asked why didn't he stay out longer and catch more fish?

The Mexican said he had enough to support his family's immediate needs.

The American then asked, "but what do you do with the rest of your time?"

The Mexican fisherman said, "I sleep late, fish a little, play with my children, take siesta with my wife, Maria, stroll into the village each evening where I sip wine and play guitar with my amigos. I have a full and busy life, señor."

The American scoffed, "I am a Harvard MBA and could help you. You could spend more time fishing, catch more fish, and with the proceeds buy a bigger boat. With the proceeds from the fish you catch with your bigger boat, you could buy several boats. Eventually you would have a fleet of fishing boats. Instead of selling your catch to a middleman, you would sell directly to the processor, eventually opening your own cannery. You would control the product, processing and distribution. You'd probably need to leave this small coastal fishing village and move to Mexico City, then LA, and eventually New York City, where you would run your expanding enterprise."

The Mexican fisherman asked, "But señor, how long will this all take?"
To which the American replied, "15-20 years."
"But what then, señor?"

The American laughed and said that's the best part. When the time is right you would announce an IPO and sell your company stock to the public and become very rich; you would make millions.

"Millions, senor? Then what?"

"The American said, "Then you would retire. Move to a small coastal fishing village where you would sleep late, fish a little, play with your kids, take siesta with your wife, stroll to the village in the evenings where you could sip wine and play your guitar with your amigos."

Who Chooses a Home Business?

Many Americans are reevaluating their priorities. They are taking a walk away from the commute, the pressure, and the harassment, toward freedom. What kinds of people are taking this walk? Statistics tell us a few things. *Inc.* magazine reported in 1996 that 53 percent of the proprietors of home-based businesses were male and 47 percent female. Their average age was 43 years. Around 44 percent were college graduates, and 85 percent were married. Fifty-four percent of them had children under 18, and their household income was fairly high, $55,100. Forty-six percent of them were in fields categorized as white-collar work, only 22 percent were blue collar.

Many of them started out as "consultants." This is a term many of us have chosen to save face about being unemployed after we've been ousted from a job. They're doing some of the same things they had done before for their old companies (or picking up on what their competitors were doing), but without the perks or profit-sharing. This turns out to be a good deal for the companies, who get temporary custody of blue-chip talent.

"We are running an infinitely more sophisticated organization as a result," contends Dale Winston, president of Battalia Winston International, a $7.5-million executive-search firm based in New York City. "By using independent contractors with years of experience—usually in companies much bigger than ours—we gain access to expertise and sophistication that was once the private property of large corporations. I get Fortune 500-caliber talent, but without the carrying costs."

Given the relentless pace of corporate downsizing, for the foreseeable future, the demand for such free agents should only increase. As companies large and small continue to atomize their operations and contract out more functions in pursuit of a more "virtual" structure and more real profits, the opportunities for those working on their own, out of their homes, will abound. So too will the urgent necessity of knowing how to navigate such a journey. With nearly half of all workers witnessing layoffs in their own workplaces, and at least one in five seriously worried about losing his or her job, few should ignore the flight plans of the soloists. We all may find sooner or later, to our shock or delight, that Lily Tomlin is right. "We are all in this alone."

Numbers Working at Home Growing

In the last decade, millions of Americans have left their jobs and started their own home-based businesses. From 1983 to 1997, the number of home-based workers grew from 6 to 32 million. By 1997, more businesses were started at home than on Main Street or on any other commercial street or mall. According to *Inc.* magazine, 705,000 home businesses began that year, compared to 610,000 businesses that located at commercial sites. It's a phenomenon that promises profound consequences for the economy, challenges the way we think about work, and makes us look back to America's roots. Less than 100 years ago, most Americans worked for themselves, and over 200 years ago, Thomas Jefferson envisioned a nation of independent merchants and farmers. Today's entrepreneurs are their heirs.

This trend wasn't as easy to spot a decade ago. "Ten years ago, if you were working out of your home, it was like you had some sort of disease," says Don Vlcek, a former vice-president at Domino's Pizza, who now works from his home in Plymouth, Michigan. Over the past ten years, home-based businesses have quietly begun shedding their stigma.

"Many, indeed, are actually coming out, if not out of the closet (a converted walk-in, perhaps?), then certainly out of a spare bedroom or the basement," says Vlcek.

Technology, the Internet, and Working at Home

Two major trends have helped to legitimize those of us who choose to work at home. One is the recent explosion in affordable and easy-to-use office technology. The other is the popularity and convenience of web sites. Anyone in any home business can compete on a level playing field with much of corporate America. No one really knows whether our home page or the faxed document came out of the equivalent of a Fortune 500 company or a one-person home operation.

Lyle Bowlin is one such example...and he lucked into it. On March 9, 1999, Thomas L. Friedman, a columnist for the *New York Times*, reported with glee on the success of Lyle Bowlin of Cedar Falls, Iowa, who spent $150 to put together a web site that put him in competition for book sales with Amazon.com. Friedman reported that Lyle was "running the whole operation out of a spare bedroom in his home." According to Friedman, Bowlin had more than 142,000 hits on his site from 40 different countries in less than 24 hours after Friedman had written about him in *The Times*, and 10 percent of the visitors to his site took the time to drop him an e-mail message.

"There is a whole group of people out there who like the idea of a 'little guy' competing against Amazon.com. People see Amazon.com as this big, impersonal thing," Bowlin muses. "They like the idea of dealing with a person they know actually exists. Even though their contact with me is over the Web, and it is through e-mail, they know when they contact

In the last decade, millions of Americans have left their jobs and started their own home-based businesses.

Two major trends have helped to legitimize those of us who choose to work at home: office technology and web sites.

me the answer is coming from a real person, with a real name." High tech is combined with human contact.

High Tech Combined with Human Contact

Friedman drew another lesson from Bowlin's experience.

"If you think globalization is overrated, you...ain't seen nothin' yet. The minute you start to do business on the Web, you now have to think globally. You have to think about your customers as global, your competitors as global, your readers as global, your suppliers as global, and your partners as global."

I also have a web site, yarnell.com. Shortly after it went on-line, my distributor began getting orders for books and materials from Australia, South America, and Europe. He didn't know where this was coming from. Since we've run no advertising, it didn't take us long to realize what was happening. The very existence of my obscure web site, also not advertised but relying solely on word of mouth, brought this about.

Bowlin's results were astounding. Friedman reported that this small entrepreneur had been doing a $2,000-a-month business, and that was mainly in the U.S. After the publicity boost that Bowlin and his web site got from the *New York Times*, he started doing $2,000 worth of business a *day*. And much of it was business from around the globe.

The Bowlin tale proves to me that the best business is still "people business." The Web brings people together without the need for oodles of middlemen. Look what's happened in "cyberspace" in just a few years. In 1995, there were 16 million Internet users, and 29 percent of them actually made on-line purchases. By the year 2000, we can expect to see 163 million people on the Internet, and 45 percent of them will be "buyers." According to the International Data Corporation, that represents nearly 75 million buyers spending a staggering total of $95 billion in on-line commerce by the year 2000, up from a mere $318 million in 1995.

The first World Wide Web site was launched in 1993. By 1997, 13 percent of all small businesses had their own web site. In 1998, that figure was up to 30 percent. By the year 2000, that number will climb to well over 50 percent. Once upon a time, a business was judged by the quality of its stationery. More and more, it's by the professionalism of its web site. In fact, most small to medium-size businesses don't even bother with pre-printed stationery anymore. They adapt it on their computer and print it out as needed.

As *Inc.* magazine has pointed out, no one can tell the difference between a corporate-based business and a home-based business. No one really knows whether that business is run by a man or a woman. In fact, I can guess that women will take to home-based businesses, with or without the help of computers or technology or web sites, like kids to an ice cream store. I know I have, and I've been doing it most of my professional life.

Freedom Through Home Businesses

Many women in the work force have begun to realize that the old *journey of the broke* we call a j.o.b. hasn't given us as much satisfaction or freedom as we'd once imagined. Many of us have experienced guilt because we haven't been there for our children as much as we've needed to be. For the first time in our history, the majority of babies less than a year old have mothers in the paid workforce. The fastest-growing segment of mothers in the workforce is precisely the one with the greatest child-care responsibilities—those with children under six years of age. Since 1960, these mothers have tripled their workforce participation.

Of the 8.5 million jobs created since President Clinton took office in January 1992, half were created at female-owned firms, according to Laura Tyson, chair of the President's Council of Economic Advisers. At the same time, the number of female-owned businesses has jumped 25 percent to nearly 6.5 million, or more than one-third of all U.S. businesses.

Why are women launching out on their own?

• *Barriers to advancement.* Nearly 30 percent of female entrepreneurs with prior private-sector experience cited glass-ceiling issues as the major reason they left corporations, based on a 1998 survey by an association of women's groups.

"There didn't seem to be a lot of opportunity for moving up," said Diana Lasses, who started her own financial planning firm in New

Providence, New Jersey, after quitting a corporate management job. "I felt like the opportunities weren't there anymore."

• *More flexibility.* Even though entrepreneurs toil long hours, many can choose when they work. "I can't wait for the day when I'm just doing my own business," said Tammie Chestnut, a 27-year-old woman out of Tempe, Arizona, in the process of launching a résumé consulting business. "I want freedom. I want to take the day off to spend with my child." The need for flexibility was cited by more than half the female business owners as a major reason for leaving corporate positions.

• *An entrepreneurial spark.* Many women feel that their entrepreneurial interests were stifled at corporate jobs. "As you get larger, it's really a struggle to think outside the box," says Lois Haber, CEO of Delaware Valley Financial Services in Berwyn, Pennsylvania, which uses a focus group to foster creativity. "You just want to get the work done."

Going out on your own is no guarantee of success. Hours can be grueling. Failure rates are high. In spite of this, more and more women feel that going solo is worth the gamble. Studies show that women are more likely than men to take greater risks. If we try and fail, we pick ourselves up, shake off the dust, and try again. Each failure brings us that much closer to a victory. According to a survey, 59 percent of male business owners polled are in a business closely related to previous careers, while 56 percent of the women own businesses that are either totally unrelated to previous careers or that revolve around interests or hobbies that had always been fun for them.

The shifts can be dramatic. Gail Johnson quit a job as a systems programmer to start Lasting Impression, which helps clients improve presentation skills and business etiquette.

"This was always my love," says Johnson, 50, from Lafayette, California. "It seemed appealing to be in charge and in control. You're out on a limb more and you have to wear many hats, but I love it."

Today's female entrepreneurs are more apt to be former managers and executives, reflecting women's advancement over the past twenty years.

"I kept thinking, 'Why am I making all this money for someone else?'" says Nina McLemore, who in 1995 co-founded Regent Capital Partners, an equity and debt investment firm, after being president of Liz Claiborne Accessories.

Wendelyn Martz was an urban planner in Upper Marlboro, Maryland, who took a leave of only three months after the birth of her son and raced back to work to finish a high-profile project just five weeks after her daughter was born.

She began to burn out. Her husband was working long hours, too, so all the duties at home landed on her shoulders. Something had to give.

"I thought, 'This isn't right. I'm cheating someone and I'm probably cheating everyone,'" she says. "I needed to be home." Finally, she resigned. But she wanted to continue her professional interests. For both personal and economic reasons, she needed work. "My whole world cannot be successfully reduced to just taking care of my children. I was trying to find that middle ground."

Martz found it by starting a home-based business designing and marketing greeting cards. Sales took off. Her husband lent his marketing expertise to the project, and today her Pathway Art can be found nationwide, from the Borders Books chain to the John F. Kennedy Center for the Performing Arts in Washington, DC. Her son, age six, even helps assemble orders and offers his comments on new designs.

Wendelyn Martz is not an anomaly. As women, we are gravitating toward entrepreneurial ventures and home-based businesses because the people in our lives count for everything, far more than money. A growing number of workers are leaving established companies to start their own, and becoming entrepreneurs by setting up home-based businesses. For many men and women, this is the best of both worlds.

Home-Based Businesses Good for Economy

New rules from the Internal Revenue Service will make it easier for everyone with a home-based business. For years, the IRS flagged for audit anyone who took a home-office deduction. Over a seven-year-period, the IRS reclassified 439,000 independent contractors as employees and collected more than $750 million in fines.

No more. Congress has changed all that. In 1999, as long as you use your home office on a regular and exclusive basis to administer and manage

> # I kept thinking, 'Why am I making all this money for someone else?'

your small business and you don't have another fixed location where you perform such duties, it qualifies as a home office. Our government finally realized that penalizing home-based businesses didn't make any sense. Not only are home-based businesses good for "working moms," but they're also good for the economy. Mrs. Field's Cookies, Estee Lauder Cosmetics, Lane Bryant, Stairmaster, and even Steinway pianos all started as home-based businesses.

Downside of Running Your Own Business

Having run a business from my home most of my professional life, I am a strong proponent. But I'd be remiss if I didn't tell you about some of the rocky paths that lie ahead.

Requires Money

It takes money to start a business, and raising it is difficult without a track record. The average franchise costs about $83,000 to start up. An established chain like McDonalds costs a half a million dollars plus a free and clear corner lot. One premise is for certain: all business cost more to get going than you had planned to spend.

Keeping Up by Yourself

There's another aspect to being an entrepreneur. It's called running the business. Despite their desire to leave the hassles of corporate management behind and focus on the job they love to do most, many who work alone also acknowledge that, their rhetoric notwithstanding, they have in fact become managers.

"It's something I'm still struggling with: the business of running the business. I've got to project cash flow, decide what equipment to buy, file the right tax forms, and still have time to bring in business," laments one entrepreneur.

No One to Show You

Many home business owners feel loneliness most of all. They don't have the camaraderie. There is no mentor to train them or take them step by step through the process of what to do. Consequently, all too many home businesses plug along doing just okay because of the lack of a clearly defined business plan or goal-oriented direction. Too little success means

> **As women, we are gravitating toward entrepreneurial ventures and home-based businesses because the people in our lives count for everything, far more than money.**

lack of cash flow. Too much success leads to the desire to hire help. Both represent challenges.

Feeling the Need to Hire Help

Those who work alone, at least the busy ones, unfailingly reach a point at which they must hire out much of the administration of their businesses. They pay others, often other soloists, to file, to bill, to manufacture, to maintain databases, to mail brochures, even to sell. If you don't hire out, you struggle trying to do it yourself and keep up with everything else. If you do, your employee(s) become part of your breakfast table and you worry about the cash flow.

Concern about Cash Flow

Entrepreneurs can't delegate an understanding of cash flow, and learning to manage cash can be the cruelest lesson. After years of predictable paychecks, entrepreneurs branching out on their own face a new and sometimes harsh reality called intermittent income.

"It can be feast or famine," says Ellen Leanse, who copes with the vagaries of cash flow by occasionally over-committing herself. "To make sure I won't have a gap in income later, I'll take on too much business now. You never have equilibrium."

You can go the better part of your first year without any income at all.

"It's the most degrading and awful thing," reports Leanse. "I was doing all this work, taking time away from my child, to get the business going, with no paycheck coming back to the family. It took months to get a client. And I felt demoralized most of that time."

Moonlighting or launching the venture part-time can ease the financial pressure.

"You should set up the business so you don't have to rely on it for sustenance during the first six to eight months," advises Leanse, who waited at least a year before she saw steady cash flow and even longer before she started to see reasonable margins. "In the beginning, you under-bill and over-work because you haven't convinced yourself you can really do this or that you ought to be paid well for it."

Jane King, a financial consultant, concurs.

"In the first couple of years, I didn't come close to matching my old salary. And I always had a pretty good price on my head." She was charging customers way too little, she says. But then, pricing wasn't much of a science. "I'd say a number and hope they didn't faint." Over time, after doing plenty of work for nothing, she lost her shyness about bolstering her own cash. "I was watching my customers' assets grow," says the financial planner. "And I realized, hey, my expertise must be valuable."

Summarizing Your Options

Working at home can be an answer to many of the objections to working in corporate America or even working for yourself from a commercial location. Let's summarize them now:

(1) Masses of workers are moving away from working for someone else for many reasons:
   a)   insecurity due to layoffs and downsizing
   b)   pressures and stress placed on those left to do the work
   c)   Baby Boomers are being replaced by Gen Xers working for half the pay with twice the energy
   d)   inequities for women and older managers in the work place
   e)   the stifling of talents
   f)   restrictions placed on earning potential
   g)   ineffective pension systems
   h)   lack of priority given to family needs

(2) You may choose to work for yourself, giving you many advantages over employment, but there is a new set of challenges for the business owner that should be taken into account, primarily due to:
   a)   the failure of so many start-ups
   b)   the business taking more money than you allowed
   c)   the difficulty of acquiring unsecured loans, especially if you are a minority

d) the work requiring more time than you want to give it

e) the fact that you can never get away from the business—you carry it home every day and even take it with you on vacations

f) cash flow worries, especially when payday rolls around

g) the never-ending expenses for equipment, materials, hidden costs, overhead, payroll, F.I.C.A., and unemployment taxes

h) the fact that when there are problems, clients want to discuss them with you and no one else

i) the business running you rather than you running the business

(3) More and more people today are electing to go into a home-based business, and you may choose to be a part of this trend. But, depending on the type of business you decide on, there are still a few issues with which to contend:

a) even a home business requires some money

b) you have to fill many different roles all on your own

c) you have no one to show you exactly what to do

d) you feel the need to hire help before you can afford it

e) if you have employee(s), they become part of your breakfast table

f) you worry about cash flow to cover even modest overhead

g) you still have no retirement plan

Home-Based Business Without the Downsides

So haven't I just shot holes in every viable alternative? Actually, no. There is still another option open to professionals and business people in today's world. If you went down the checklists I've provided and found yourself facing some or many of those dilemmas, then you may be open to considering another option. What if...

a) you could have a business of your own

b) you could work at home

c) it didn't require a vast amount of start-up cost

d) it requires no employees

e) you are in business for yourself but not by yourself

f) you inherit an experienced team who train you

g) you have an unrestricted earning potential

h) you can create a passive, residual income

> # You could be one of the new entrepreneurs giving rise to the emergence of a new culture in our society, replacing the confinements of traditional employment with the autonomy of a home-based business.

i)   you can determine your own schedule and prioritize your own life events

j)   you now have the leisure to contribute yourself and your resources to organizations and activities that are reflective of your values?

Of course, you must be willing to work hard and stay with this option long enough for success to take hold. Just like every profession, there is a learning curve. You will need to devote the first phase of your business to apprenticeship, advanced education, and refinement to gain mastery over this new option.

If you have eliminated working for someone else as an option, you are a candidate. If you have already experienced working for yourself, and are tired of measuring your success by what you gave up to get it, you are a candidate. If you are attracted to the idea of a home-based business, but want to avoid the downsides, then you are also a candidate for the new profession emerging in today's world—a profession that embraces lifestyle freedom, personal fulfillment, and long-term financial stability for the 21st Century. You could be one of the new entrepreneurs giving rise to the emergence of a new culture in our society, replacing the confinements of traditional employment with the autonomy of a home-based business.

CHAPTER 5

Residual Income and Time Freedom
Through Network Marketing

This emerging profession is best known today as network marketing. I can hear you now. "Oh, that! I know everything I want to know about that—enough to know I don't want to get involved."

Keep an open mind just a bit longer. Unquestionably, network marketing has been a greatly misunderstood industry. But it is on the verge of discovery, just waiting to be mastered by thousands upon thousands of new professionals.

In the past, due to a general lack of understanding, the multi-level marketing (MLM) industry has stirred up a great deal of controversy. Some think it is a pyramid, a predatory business that is, at best, quasi-legal. They decry it as nothing more than a get-rich-quick scheme in which those at the top make money and the Johnny-come-latelies lose out. On the other hand, there are Fortune 500 companies lining up to open networking divisions or manufacture goods for these young growth businesses. Companies such as Citibank, MCI, IBM, Toyota, Xerox, Texas Instruments, General Motors, Chrysler, Ford, General Electric, Gillette, Colgate, Whirlpool, Hotpoint, and Coca-Cola have distributed some of their products and services through network marketing. Now some of the newer

Network marketing is fast becoming the next major profession of the new millennium.

entities, including Netscape and Oracle, are moving toward this channel of distribution.

There are scores of people who have faced the same decision you may be encountering now, and you will read about some of them throughout these chapters. Their stories will candidly describe the upsides and the downsides, the gratification, and the challenges of this industry. They will share their soul-searching scrutiny of the industry and the process of their own discoveries. I invite you to read these stories, weighing all sides of the issues, so you too can make an informed decision based on facts and not hearsay.

Creating a Healthy and Well-Balanced Lifestyle

Where can serious entrepreneurs who value their own time and worth find the ultimate solution to both in one business? Network marketing is fast becoming the next major profession of the new millennium. It's also the only profession that allows serious business people to generate residual and mammoth earnings while simultaneously preserving a well-balanced lifestyle utilizing all aspects of the wellness wheel:

Inspiration/Spiritual
Finding your sense of self
Joy
Meaning
Enthusiasm

Nourishment/Physical Health
Nutrition
Movement
Touch, sound, light
Silence

Mental Health
Awareness, inner wisdom
Mindfulness
Attitude
Frame of mind

Learning/Education
Life as a learning experience
Understanding
Truth, reflection
Teaching others

Community
Contribution to others
Contribution to earth
Multicultural
Non-polluting

Recreation
Spiritual value of work and play
Creativity
Relaxation
Rejuvenation and refreshment

Loving Relationships
Family
Couples
Forgiveness, acceptance,
compassion and trust

Career
Making a difference
Financial security
Lifestyle desired
Attracting value-driven people to your team

These new entrepreneurs want everything life has to offer and might very likely subscribe to a philosophy that says one of the truly unfair things about life is the way it ends. You struggle to make something of your existence on earth and then you die. They would suggest that the lifecycle is all backwards.

You should die first, get the ugly part out of the way. Then you live in an old-age home where you're pampered. You get kicked out when you're too young. You get a gold watch when you finally go to work. You spend your adult years creating a legacy through your work until you're young enough to enjoy your retirement. You do drugs, alcohol, you party, and get ready for high school. You go to grade school and become a kid again where you think McDonald's is a four-star restaurant and M&Ms are better than money 'cause they melt in your mouth. You run a lemonade stand with your friends. You lie carefree in the grass looking up at the clouds, seeing all kinds of people and shapes. You become a little baby, completely pampered. You go back into the womb where you spend your last nine months floating in warmth and comfort...and you finish life as a beautiful orgasm. Much better....

While most business leaders in our industry advocate using and duplicating a single system, there are many different levels of competence and aptitude that make up an effective organization builder. Networking businesses benefit from the multitude of experiences and breadth of the wellness wheel enjoyed by those joining the industry. There is no aspect of your personal or professional experience that will be superfluous in this business.

In my own case, I have run the gamut in my life, from Roman Catholic nun to elected public official, from teacher to talk show host, from wife and mother to business woman. Every one of those roles has gone into the building and supporting of my organization. No previous responsibility, however seemingly insignificant, is without application. No dream is too grand. No aspiration too massive. No cause too weighty.

What Is Network Marketing?

Network marketing is a form of distribution of products and services that, through word of mouth promotion, uses the power of duplication of effort. Unlike conventional marketing, which generally has a few representatives responsible for large volumes of sales, this form of marketing has large numbers of representatives responsible for a small number of sales. It is a form of direct selling in which the distributors are compensated on a multi-level basis as opposed to the traditional single-level pay plan.

At this particular time in history, when traditional business offers so little security, network marketing introduces a system in which common people can invest a small sum and, through sheer tenacity and determination, rise to staggering levels of financial reward and personal freedom. And this can be done from home! Seventy percent of all direct sales distributors do this business from home. You avoid the usual pitfalls of running your own traditional business: commuting through traffic, payroll, cost of employee benefits, advertising, overhead, bookkeeping, and accounts receivable.

The industry has evolved considerably over the years. It began as a home-based business focused on one-on-one direct sales. While still a home business, it transitioned into a business more focused on building an organization of sales people, each of whom is responsible for a small amount of sales. Today, it is moving toward a high-tech business that utilizes the computer, the Internet, e-mail, voice mail, and fax-on-demand, sophisticated telephony, and a multitude of electronic media, including audios, videos, CD-ROMs and DVDs. These various forms of technology are used as a form of educating rather than selling to prospective business associates.

Along with our industry's development and maturation has come a certain sophistication. Marketing reps are moving away from merely sifting through huge numbers of prospects and returning to the original spirit of this industry: building on their own personal relationships. The larger your list of personal contacts, the more likely you are to establish your business.

By whatever name you call it—multi-level marketing, network marketing, network distribution, referral marketing—our business truly is about "relationship marketing." It is building strong, solid, lifelong business and personal relationships with those who join you, and are seriously committed to working with you to build their businesses. It is

> **Network marketing is a form of distribution of products and services that, through word of mouth promotion, uses the power of duplication of effort.**

your magnetism as an ethical person and knowledgeable leader that will make others want to be a part of your organization. It is the spirit you inject into your group and the dynamics of your bonding that will build lasting relationships.

The true strengths and benefits of network marketing come from long-term commitment to one company. Starting with one company, switching, and starting again is what hurts the reputation of our industry. I predict that the coming millennium will see much more stability. Those who establish enduring, long-term relationships within their organizations will be the ultimate winners.

Earning Enormous Income while Transforming Lives

Steven Campbell's entrepreneurial penchant began while attending college at Brigham Young University in the late 70s. About the time that President Reagan initiated a program offering tax credits to property owners who insulated their homes, Steve found a niche market and started the Ther-Max Corporation, a little company that specialized in home energy-conservation products.

Steve can't do anything in a small way. He broke sales records in Utah by creating a door-to-door sales campaign. In 1980, he recognized an even better opportunity when California introduced its Low Cost Financing program, offering additional state tax credit to energy-saving homeowners. The best part was that the improvements could be financed through customers' utility bills over eight years at zero interest. He educated homeowners about these federal and state tax credits and payment plan through his door-to-door promotion. Nearly all of them felt it affordable and sensible to insulate their homes.

By the second year, he had sales in excess of $4 million, more than four times greater than his closest competitor. Steve's "little collegiate business" was soon ranked 57th of the top privately held companies by the *Orange County Business Journal*. After eight years, with the challenge and newness gone, Steve sold the business, becoming a millionaire at the age of 26.

In 1987, something happened that would permanently alter the course of Steve's life. He had a benign brain tumor. A successful surgery left the right side of his face paralyzed and his right ear deaf. Given his physical challenge, Steve knew that he didn't want to have another

> ## By whatever name you call it—multi-level marketing, network marketing, network distribution, referral marketing—our business truly is about "relationship marketing."

business that entailed six office locations, FICA, payroll, health insurance, workmen's comp. etc. It was in 1990 that Steve was introduced to network marketing by Craig Tillotson and Craig Bryson, two superstar network marketers.

"Based on my one experience in business, I thought the only way to get ahead was to work 12, 14 hours a day just to outwork your competition," he says. "I was young and willing to do that. Every time someone had approached me on network marketing, trying to introduce me to a better way, my attitude was 'show me'... So I couldn't have been more skeptical about network marketing until the day the two Craigs stopped by my house to talk about their company. The only difference was that these guys were making the money. When I saw a copy of Craig Bryson's check in June 1990 for $399,154.35, I became a believer. And when I saw that check had gradually escalated each month from $188,396.11 in January, I lost sleep. I was used to thinking in big dollars, and finally someone had presented this to me in a way that I could relate to." According to *Sports Illustrated*, Michael Jordan's contract with the Chicago Bull's was $3.1 million, the eighth highest paid basketball player in the U.S. that year. And here was someone who was going to out-earn Michael Jordan selling skin care, of all things!

Steve jumped into the fray of that company's growth and, working full-time, broke company records. In his first month, he found 12 people who planned to pursue a leadership position with the company. Working closely with them, ten of his distributors "broke as executives," which means that they fulfilled the necessary requirements to become an executive in the same month that he himself reached executive status. Because of their accomplishments, he skipped all the other steps and emerged in the second highest achievement level in the company. By most people's standards, Steve was set for life. But by his own measure of success, he was still not making the kind of money to which he was accustomed.

Weighing his strengths against his two mentors, he could see only one difference—they had gotten involved in the company six years sooner than he. "I'm basically one of these guys who loves pioneering and gets bored quickly when it becomes routine. So I took the next six months flying around the U.S. and Canada looking at network marketing companies. But it was ultimately a friend, Kelly Thayer, who introduced me to the company that met my criteria. Where you get involved in the chain really doesn't matter. What does matter is the timing. I wanted a company that had survived the early challenges of start-up but had not yet grown too large. I found it more difficult to present the opportunity when millions of people had already heard about it. It was so much easier for me to introduce a new company that people were unfamiliar with, but one that had a recognized and trusted name and product line."

Steve once again gave his all. Prevailing over the after-effects of his brain tumor, in five years he built an organization that was generating nearly $100 million in annual sales, out of his Provo, Utah home, with no overhead and no personal liabilities. But what he is most proud of is that five others emerged in his organization who earned over $100,000 a month in commissions, and innumerable distributors who earned that much a year.

A Pioneer Who Loves the Chase

Steve has a true pioneer spirit. He loves the chase and gets tired of the routine, even if it is a $100,000-a-month routine. Once again the thrill of building was gone and he found himself restless. In April 1997, he sold his networking business and joined a start-up network marketing company to serve as its founding distributor. Drawn by the excitement of beginning another venture and attracted to the up-and-coming service industry, Steve violated his own "don't get involved in a start-up" rule for one reason: this company was backed by Richard Marriott, high on *Forbes* magazine's list of the "World's Wealthiest People." Steve observed what happened to another service-oriented network marketing company three years earlier. As a publicly traded company, it was generating $30.8 million in sales in 1993; by 1996, the Wall Street Journal touted this corporation as the fifth largest long-distance carrier in America with sales of $1.4 billion, and it was all done by word of mouth, by friends telling friends.

Steve asked himself, 'How was this possible?' He came to the conclusion that it was because people weren't being asked to make a lifestyle change. "People use their phone every day. They used it yesterday, they're using it today, and they're going to use it tomorrow. No matter how tough the times, everyone pays his or her phone bill. Consequently, there is no stocking of products and no huge monthly requirements to meet.

"To my way of thinking, it was ideal for part-time people, who make up, by far, the largest percentage of networkers. Most people are either not generating enough income or don't have enough time freedom, or both," he says. "Because of today's business environment, workers are changing jobs multiple times. What most of them want is not to make millions of dollars, but to have a safety net, a kind of backup plan if something should happen to their job, where they can work out of their home and create a small residual income. I think it was in *USA Today* where I read that 64.9 percent of all households (that's usually a two-person income) make less than $3,000 a month. And only 2.8 percent make over $100,000 a year. If that's the case, then what a difference it can make to help people earn an extra $500 to $1,000 a month."

On fire with a new crusade, Steve generated almost $700,000 in income in his first 12 months with his present company.

"What I love about this industry is that I can do anything I want whenever I want and for whatever reason I want. If I choose to help someone out financially or contribute to some charitable cause, I can do that. But what really gives me a rush is to see the changes that have occurred in other people's lives who have joined me in business. To see a single mom able to stay at home with her kids, or to have the mailman working part-time in my organization now making more than he does at his full-time job...makes me feel good to know that I have been able to help change so many lives."

Personal Relationships the Key to Success

It was in December 1985 that Russ and Linda Karlen joined their network marketing company. They leaned on each other for support. When

> **Most people are either not generating enough income or don't have enough time freedom, or both.**

she was ready to quit, he talked her into staying, and when he was fed up, she convinced him to give the business one more month. At first, they did everything wrong, not really understanding how the business worked.

"There was a time that Linda was begging me to quit, weekly if not daily," Russ recalls, "because we weren't making enough money to make our life work. I remember her crying, but I blocked it out. I would give her a hug and go right back to work. If you have a dream and a goal in life, you have to be so focused that nothing distracts you from achieving those goals.

"When I look back, I think about the sacrifices that we made, along with all the time that we put into the business, until we finally figured out that it was a business of duplication," says Linda. "With all of the ups and downs, it took us nearly four years of trying a lot of different approaches before we finally got it right."

In April 1988, I flew down to Orange County to meet with the Karlens. I was seriously looking at the business and he was the most experienced upline on the team. I spent the day between their beach and their patio just observing Russ while he talked on the phone to prospective distributors. I soaked up every word, studying how he worked and whether I could see myself doing this. I was not an easy close. I had hundreds of questions, concerns, worries, and fears. I was a single parent, in transition professionally, and with no income at that moment. Failure wasn't an option I could entertain. This business *had* to work! With their help, I could begin to envision myself actually building an organization. Russ helped me see the business side of it, which was what appealed to me.

To this day, I owe my involvement in this industry to Russ and Linda Karlen. I left with Russ committing to work with me every step of the way, and he kept that promise.

The rest of that year was a kind of apprenticeship for me. But by 1989, our company clearly had momentum. Company sales grew from $2 million to $10 million a month, an increase of 500 percent in 1989. Through March 1990, Russ and Linda's organization, of which I was a small part, produced for them commission checks that escalated from $10,000 a month to almost a quarter of a million dollars monthly. It was one of the most exciting periods I've experienced in the industry. Russ, too excited to sleep, would be on the phone with us early risers at 4:00 a.m. Our friendships bonded. Our bank accounts grew, our worries dissipated, and our spirits were filled with exuberance. So, I finally got it… this was network marketing!

The Karlens have one of the largest international organizations in the company today, but their greatest volume is still generated in the United States, or as Linda puts it, "our own back yard." She feels that network marketing is an industry built on relationships, and this is really difficult in the international arena. Russ and Linda built internationally strictly through relationships. They began through the Asian community in California and then let them take it internationally.

"My philosophy," reflects Russ, "is to work with a couple of people at a time and help them build their business. Like a father who has kids, I want them all to make it. In my heart, I know that I have the power and knowledge to help them succeed, and the motivation will never stop. Actually, one of our distributors is our own son. Eric, at 24, has been in the business for a year and half and is now making nearly $18,000 a month."

Because they were able to sustain each other through the tough times, Russ and Linda are now living a happy and healthy life. "Why wait until you're too old to enjoy your money and your life with your family and friends?" quips Linda. "You need to have dreams and goals written out, and then strike them off the list as they are accomplished. It's a wonderful feeling."

Russ and Linda reside in their dream home that overlooks a golf course in Las Vegas. They enjoy sharing the guest wing of this home or their home in Palm Springs with friends. Brittany, their daughter, loves to tell distributors that her dad has traded in his business suit for a swimsuit. On any given day, if you stop in to see the Karlens, you're likely to find Russ on the phone by his Olympic-plus size pool, next to the waterfall, working with one of his new "kids."

"We have everything, but money is relative," he says. "What keeps me going is helping others achieve their dreams and goals, and experiencing the joy of sharing a product that we know will change peoples' lives."

Living the Life of Time Freedom

Richard Kall is one of the true legends of the network marketing industry. Behind the large-framed, tough-talking, soft-hearted man, there was always Carol, a low-keyed, even-tempered woman who, through all the vicissitudes of life, provided constant stability to this dynamic man.

Twenty years ago, Richard was a successful real estate investor and insurance broker. He and Carol were creating a beautiful family life together, raising their three girls. Recalling that fateful day on which his life took an entirely new direction, Richard realizes that he clearly took the road less traveled, and as Robert Frost said, it has made all the difference.

He needed to get his muffler fixed. As Providence would have it, his neighborhood mechanic sent him clear across town to get the needed part. Standing at the cash register collecting the money, wiping the grease off his hands onto his trousers, the young manager asked a question out of nowhere: "Are you making all the money you want to make?"

Richard drove a nice enough car. Where did that question come from? If his demeanor weren't quite so sincere, Richard might have given him a flippant response, but instead he simply answered, "I do all right."

"But do you have all the freedom you want so you can do whatever you want whenever you want to do it?" persisted the young man.

"No one can do that," Richard replied. "What are you talking about? You work hard. You support your family. Who has that kind of free time, anyway?"

"Actually, I know some people who have all the money and the free time they want. We're having a meeting tonight at one of their homes. I could get you in if you'd like to come."

Most people would be thinking, what could a kid like this possibly have to teach me about making money? He's working in a muffler shop talking to me about having free time? But not Richard. He drove home unable to shake the conversation. After explaining it all to Carol, he said, "Hey, why don't we go to this meeting and just see what he's talking about?"

"Richard, we already have plans to go to see Bette Midler. We've had these tickets for the last three months."

"I can't explain this, but I just have to go see what it is."

Giving those valuable tickets away, on that momentous May night in 1979 Richard and Carol Kall found themselves at an MLM meeting. It was the first time Richard had ever heard of the concept of building a distributor force and leveraging your income. Fascinating! Why not? For the next several months, Richard gave his new business everything he had, working it into his already busy schedule while keeping up his real estate investments and meetings with insurance clients.

After investing countless hours and tireless energy, he and Carol were acknowledged for reaching the first "pin level," but it wasn't good enough by Richard's standards. He was outraged at himself for believing this was a viable way for a serious businessman to create a leveraged income. If he couldn't make it work better than this, he thought, no one could. Agreeing with her husband, Carol responded, "Ours will be the first 'riches to rags' story. We were doing fine before we got into this business."

"You're right, Carol", Richard agreed, "we're going backwards. We have to give it up, but I feel like I'm losing my right arm. If I never find this again, life will have really cheated me. I believe so much in the concept." In all, Richard tried seven MLM companies, but one by one, each one fell by the wayside. In each instance, Richard always fell back to the profession he knew and understood.

While interviewing an insurance client, Richard learned of the 46 pounds she'd shed on a new weight-loss program. Deliberating whether he wanted to dial the number she'd given him or not, he tucked the scribbled note into the cellophane of his cigarette pack.

"Oh well, what the heck!" Richard rationalized. After a few failed attempts at getting the number to ring through, he threw the number away along with the empty pack. Then he accidentally kicked over his trashcan by his desk, and there on the floor was the infamous number. Okay, okay, Richard thought. I'll try the number one more time. He quickly learned that it was a diet plan being sold through, of all things, multi-level marketing. He was excited.

For the next year and a half, Richard was off and running with his new MLM company. It was the perfect combination of a product that would show immediate results, coupled with an income potential that would excite anyone. Richard far surpassed his wildest dreams for making money.

In the early 1980s, what Richard Poe calls the Wave Two phase of multi-level marketing, network marketing companies struggled fiercely for their own survival. Before long, Richard found himself without a company to represent. At first, he and Carol were devastated. But now Richard had the network marketing bug, and once it is in your blood, you are infected for life. He could never go back to traditional business. He had a taste of being at home with Carol, taking her to matinees mid-week, and being there when the girls came home from school.

In October 1985, Richard joined what would be his seventh network marketing company. From a folding card table in the bedroom, Richard worked harder than he'd ever worked in his life.

With the support of Richard and the leadership of a handful of loyal pioneers, the company grew from sales volume of less than a few hundred thousand a year to over a billion annually today.

He thought back to that resolute young muffler manager who had started all of this and wondered if he himself had accomplished this wonderful time freedom he had introduced to Richard. Reversing the tables, Richard finally sponsored the young man in this company.

In 1987, Carol experienced a recurrence of an earlier diagnosis of breast cancer. Richard could not conceive of life without her. From the second diagnosis on, their life was lived in episodes of despair, then hope. One moment she was in serious condition; the next she was miraculously in remission.

Many families experience such tragedy. A key difference here was MLM. How else could Richard have taken off the time to travel with her in and out of the country seeking cures, to the Bahamas, Texas, England, Mexico, California, Santa Domingo? Whatever it took, if any cure for cancer existed anywhere in the world, Richard would find it. His determination was not undermined by the need to make a living—he did both.

As Carol's struggle for life continued, their daughter, Laura, who was about to graduate from college, came to her parents after having looked over the job market and interviewed at prestigious firms.

"I've finally made my decision," she told them. "I want to join you both in business. I want to sign up on your front line."

"But, Laura," her dad objected, "you're just a kid. You're only 22. You don't have any mature contacts. And the few you might have had, we've already signed up."

She would have to build her business the hard way—through cold contacts. Graduating magna cum laude with a bachelor's degree in business from the State University of New York at Binghamton, she was ready to do whatever it took. Laura had grown up in network marketing. She was as infected with it as her father. Nothing else excited her. Like any other distributor, with no special favors from her father, she began running ads and inviting people to her home for a business opportunity presentation.

Richard, Carol, and Laura were a phenomenon in network marketing. They were frequently on stage together at company conventions speaking about the lifestyle this opportunity had afforded them as a family. "Free-

> The big picture of network marketing...is never just about how much product you can go out and sell. It's about learning to establish a network of leaders, in which dozens of people can network with hundreds of people, and that can turn into thousands of people, each doing a little—using a little product, selling a little, and networking a little.

dom, Family and Fun" by Richard Kall was an audiotape that I will always remember as one of my all-time favorites. When Richard lectures, he commands an audience.

"When Carol had been so sick," Richard professed while addressing the convention, "I won't ever forget receiving a call from the company president offering his support. Every month, wherever we were, our check would arrive, whether we'd been able to devote time to our business or not. Where else can that happen but in an industry like ours?"

Over the decade of Carol's battle with cancer, Richard and his family learned what really matters in life is time together. They traveled the world together and took one memorable trip to visit us at our home. Richard and Mark cooked exotic meals in the kitchen, while Carol and I watched *The Nun's Story* in the library. As their daughters gradually grew up and married, Richard and Carol enjoyed family events, grandchildren, and especially the quiet times alone living between Westport, Connecticut, in the summers and Boca Raton, Florida, in the winters.

Today, Richard is working closely with his daughter Laura, who is highly regarded in her role as president of Global InterNetworks, an organization that consists of hundreds of thousands of distributors moving millions of dollars of products via the Kall network. "The big picture of network marketing," Laura explains, "is never just about how much product you can go out and sell. It's about learning to establish a network of leaders, in which dozens of people can network with hundreds of people, and that can turn into thousands of people, each doing a little—using a little product, selling a little, and networking a little. And for my family, that has turned into hundreds of thousands of representatives around the world." Richard doesn't actively sponsor anyone anymore, but he works daily with any distributor who calls. He believes in giving back what the business gave him—total freedom.

In the spring of 1997, Carol died in Richard's arms with her children gathered around. Thanks to the freedom of network marketing, Richard was able to spend incredible time with Carol during their 15-year bout with her cancer.

"People married five hundred years," Richard said in a choked voice, "couldn't have had any more than what we had together."

PART II

Aspiring Entrepreneurs Discover a Home in Network Marketing

"Between tomorrow's dream and yesterday's regret is today's opportunity."

—*E.C. McKenzie*

CHAPTER 6

Choosing the Industry
and a Specific Company

A sound decision emerges from the interfacing of relevant knowledge, clear vision, credible models, and well-grounded intuition. Throughout these pages, you are being given the opportunity to weigh the issues, hear from the top people in the industry, and read the stories of numerous people whose backgrounds may be ones with which you can identify. You will meet people who faced challenges and expressed skepticism that may sound very similar to you. The real question to ask yourself is this: *Will the track you are now on take you where you want to go?* If the answer is yes, then continue on that path to pursue your personal mission. If the answer is no, then is it possible that this industry could provide you with the means to achieve your goals and fulfill your vision?

Is the Industry Right for Me?

The night the Gulf War began, you may have seen this man interviewed on television by Dan Rather. He has been quoted in *Time*, *Newsweek*, *U.S. News & World Report*, *The Washington Post*, the *Wall Street Journal*, and other major publications. His 26 books have sold over 3 million copies in

15 languages. "An old friend and advisor to George W. Bush" is how the February 1999 issue of *U.S. News & World Report* describes Doug Wead. With the exception of a five-year sabbatical when he served in the Bush administration, Doug has studied, written about, and worked in the network marketing industry for the last 30 years. He has filled auditoriums and soccer stadiums in Poland, Hungary, France, Turkey, the United Kingdom, Australia, Indonesia, and the United States with eager network marketers. But let's turn the clock back 30 years as he describes his inner turmoil in deciding whether to get involved with network marketing.

"For me the very real problem was not physical at all. It wasn't money, it wasn't people, it wasn't product, and it wasn't time. For me, the challenge was entirely between my ears. It still is, incidentally. For me, the early struggle was only philosophical. Of course, I can do it. Anybody can do it. The question, the very real, nagging, haunting question was: Should I do it? Is it right? Is this what I am supposed to be doing with my life?" Doug remembers.

"Nothing is more wearisome and draining than self-doubt. Nothing is more effective at stripping off the fine edge from everything you say or do. Nothing can empty your emotional gas tank quicker. Network marketing, which we see as such a sensitive machine, easily influenced by attitudes, was not a bit impressed with my emotional and psychological drama. It only seemed to crunch numbers like a mindless calculator. The secret for me, I was to learn, was simply to survive and then plod on. Above all, I couldn't quit. Over time, as I slowly fed this monster, it grew and grew exponentially.

"'Believe. You have to believe,' they kept telling me. I didn't even have to do that. Two times two equals four. You don't have to believe it. It is four anyway. And my business grew—in spite of myself."

Now residing with his family in Dallas, Texas, Doug has watched the evolution of the industry over three decades and feels that in some ways it

---

The very real, nagging, haunting question was...Is this what I am supposed to be doing with my life?

---

is both easier and riskier for people who come out of a professional background today to join this industry. The risk is that, because of the MLM boom right now, there is a proliferation of companies and you can select the wrong one. You need to take a serious look at the people involved, their track record, their expertise, and look for diversity of products or services.

"One thing that hasn't changed is that this industry is still based on relationships," Doug maintains. "Now you just have to figure out how to use the technology of today without losing the personal touch of building networks through relationships."

But it wasn't until Doug found his *why* that it became clear that network marketing was the right vehicle to take him where he most wanted to go with his life. And with the money he made through his business, working alongside Pat Boone and Cardinal Bernard Law, Archbishop of Boston, he co-founded what is today one of the world's premier relief organizations, Mercy Corps International. Last year it distributed more than $73 million worth of medicine and famine relief to troubled areas of our world.

One significant step in deciding if the industry is right for you is determining your ultimate life goals and then examining whether the industry is in concert with your objective. If so, then it only remains to select the right company.

Criteria for Evaluating a Network Marketing Company

Jim and Candy Webb are a professional couple, he with two degrees in architecture and she with one in economics, and an MBA in finance. They had felt trapped in the very circumstances that they had created, ending up with fourteen-hour days, stress-filled lives, and no long-term financial security unless they were willing to invest many more years of the same.

"We had a dream for lifestyle and financial freedom that we gradually came to believe could best be achieved through network marketing. It took us two tries, but we are now where we belong."

Along the way, both Jim and Candy have been corporate trainers and speakers at national conventions for two major companies. Jim has become a noted, serious student of the industry, and has reviewed and examined in detail several hundred companies, evaluating leadership, products, compensation plans, support and timing for judging the potential for individual success. He offers this advice:

"One of the most important criteria is to evaluate the integrity of the owners: where have they been? What have they done? What were their successes or failures in other Network Marketing companies or business ventures? Next, what do the field distributors offer by way of integrity, leadership potential, and experience?"

"I recommend a company that does not push a lot of 'front-end loading,'" adds Candy, "the kind that gets distributors in over their heads should be a concern for the novice to this industry."

"Today's savvy company uses interactive marketing techniques to create a completely new paradigm," Jim explains. "In this system, the customer or potential business partner interacts with demographically targeted information before they ever contact the independent representative. We're products of this system which quickly gets to the nuts and bolts of networking.

"Our advice to our prospective business partners is not to make the mistake of thinking your present time commitments, resource limitations, and other road blocks need stand in the way of your success. We started at a time when we had no time, just a burning desire. That's the bottom line!"

As recognized trainers and speakers, the Webbs reside in Granite Bay, California, a rural area just north of Sacramento, working out of their beautiful three-story home right on Folsom Lake.

"Sometimes I don't think people realize what fun it can be to work with your partner. Husband and wife teams can be so effective," Candy muses. From a monetary standpoint, they were always successful in their past careers. "But now," Jim comments, "I much prefer working for myself, choosing my friends, and building an organization with people I enjoy being around."

The difference is that now, along with the money, they have full control over their lives. Candy advocates to other professionals: "You have a choice: choose freedom."

Selecting a Compensation Plan

"The compensation plans should be simple, fit on one page, and talk in percentages of real dollars," advises Jim Webb. "You want a plan that pays commissions on full wholesale dollars, not on personal volume (p.v.), which represents a lesser percentage of the actual dollar value. It is better to be paid 10 percent on one full dollar than 15 percent on an item that

> ## Our advice...is not to make the mistake of thinking your present time commitments, resource limitations, and other road blocks need stand in the way of your success.

carries a p.v. of 50 cents on the dollar. Another thing to avoid is a plan with a punitive measure. A punitive measure means that if you are unable to keep in step with the distributors in your organization, you will lose them."

The four most popular types of compensation plans are: breakaway, uni-level, matrix, and binary. The following is a summary to help you understand these plans and their basic differences:

The Breakaway Plan

The breakaway plan has come to be known as the most traditional and, for networkers who succeed in building large organizations, the most lucrative. When leaders emerge meeting the basic requirements as set forth by the company, they "break away" from their upline executives, thereby forming their own organization with multi-levels of distributors. In a breakaway plan, leaders receive a commission on unlimited levels generated by their own circle volume and, based upon the number of "breakaway" leaders on their frontline, they are paid a commission on a designated number of levels of their breakaway groups. Even though a larger percentage is generally paid on the circle volume, the real money is made in the massive numbers generated by those leaders who form breakaway groups.

The Uni-level Plan

As designated by the company, the uni-level plan essentially pays commissions on a specified number of levels of distributorships, as opposed to the plans that can run to depths of 20 or more. A uni-level formula has no breakaway system. Because the uni-level is not as lucrative as other bonus programs, it is more often used in combination with another plan.

The Matrix Plan

Next is the matrix plan, which is inherently limiting as a compensation plan by its very definition. Let's consider the 3 x 7 matrix as an example. It would fill up in this manner: you are on top and have three on your frontline. Your second level is 9, third is 27, fourth is 81, fifth is 243, sixth is 729, and seventh is 2,187. Your entire organization, if it filled up, would compensate you for a total of 3,279 people. Many leaders have ten to a hundred times that many people in their organizations. It's literally a case of converting an unlimited opportunity into a limited income position. Most matrixes carry too small a dollar requirement in each position; consequently, they tend not to pay out enough.

What's worse, for others to succeed requires a fairly significant stretch of imagination. Let's pretend that everyone on your seventh level has a sincere desire to succeed in filling up each of their matrix organizations. That would require a company of over two million distributors. The problems now arise, because for people to succeed on that seventh level would require the equivalent of the entire populations of China, the U.S., and Germany to fill up the matrix. Although often promoted as "all you have to do is get three," be prepared in a matrix plan to personally recruit enough associates to fill up your first four or five levels and you'll likely prosper.

The Binary Plan

Finally, the premise of the binary is that all you need to do is sponsor two frontline individuals, who are called your profit centers. Once you've got your two, teach them both to duplicate what you've done, and so on until, poof! You're rich! Not in most cases. Many of the binary plans I've reviewed require a distributor to balance the sales volumes of both sides of his organization. If left on their own, each tends to grow at a radically different pace. The distributor needs to focus constantly on adding enough quality people to either or both sides in order to keep volumes in balance. Otherwise he is paid only on the lower of the two sides of his binary-shaped organization.

In matrixes and binaries, some would have you believe that you need only sponsor a few frontline networkers and you are on your way to unlimited wealth. No matter what type of compensation plan you have, it simply isn't true. Successful leaders sponsor large numbers to find the few who will emerge with the leadership necessary to build large organizations.

The Hybrid Plan

As you explore compensation plans, what is becoming well received is a hybrid plan, combining two or more of the above systems. One currently popular plan contains a front-end uni-level, back-end breakaway, plus what is called an "infinity bonus" that pays a small percent to the next generation equal to your level of achievement.

Finding a Stable Company

"Dream builders"—that's how Joe and Sandra Hornsey see their role in life. They speak from experience, too.

"People who are 35 years of age or older normally have enough bumps in life that they've quit dreaming," Joe reflects. "Today so many people have had their dreams stolen so many times that many believe they don't deserve recognition, financial success, or happiness."

The Hornseys joined their network marketing company in March 1995 after a devastating and harrowing experience with another MLM company. Having achieved top levels with their previous company and even selected to serve on a prestigious International Training Team, their hopes for a fulfilling life dimmed as the company fell into financial difficulties. They were forced to give up their home in San Antonio and move into a rental. Sandra took on two full-time jobs just so she and Joe could survive.

"Having already received one big 'bump,' I was interested in how financially sound the company was and the integrity of the management and staff," Joe says. "Sandra was more interested in the products."

Company stability became the key for the Hornseys in the search for their next company. "Respect the word of others, even very successful distributors, but investigate yourself!" That's Joe's philosophy.

Here's Joe's checklist for researching a network marketing company today:

1. **Products:** Are they unique? Do they work? Do they have a market?
2. **Company:** Are the owners debt-free? Do they manufacture their own products? What is the caliber of the management staff?
3. **Momentum:** Is the company growing? If so, how long has it been growing? (You don't want to catch a company during a down cycle.)
4. **Market Potential:** Is there room for growth in the market area of your interest or has the company reached a saturation point?

Has the company expanded, or does it have plans to expand into the international market?

5. ***Cash flow:*** What percentage of the wholesale price is returned to a distributor? Is it easy for the new distributor to earn money with the company? Does the compensation plan encourage the development of leaders? What type of compensation plan is it: binary, matrix, uni-level, breakaway or hybrid plan?

6. ***Timing:*** Is the company a new start-up? Has the company reached the saturation point? (Ideally you want to find a company somewhere in between these two zones.)

Joe and Sandra sponsored into their present company satisfied that this group met the criteria. In less than a year as distributors, they replaced their lost earnings, and when Joe's income reached $10,000 a month, Sandra was able to leave the workforce to join Joe full time. With commission checks now averaging over $50,000 a month, they have moved to a beautiful home in a gated community in North San Antonio. What brought about this phenomenal turnabout? The Hornseys believe that success, high achievement, and advancement come as a result of teamwork. Joe designed a Success Training System that targets the beginning distributor or the advanced professional and leads them through a step-by-step program to master the intricacies of the industry:

1. ***Share the products and business opportunity with new prospective associates:*** This can be through advertising, word-of-mouth, mailing letters, postcards, tapes, co-op advertising, the Internet, or a combination of all of these.

2. ***Qualify prospects with a short interview:*** Find out if they are looking for your type of business opportunity or products.

3. ***Provide information:*** You may want to give them cassette tapes, videos, literature, or a web address in order to assist them in evaluating your products or business.

4. ***Follow-up within five days:*** Answer their questions and overcome their objections.

5. ***Close the sale:*** People become involved with network marketing for two basic reasons: they want the products at wholesale or they are looking for a home-based business opportunity, or both. Find their need and fill it.

Choosing a Company that Fits Your Skills

In addition to points already mentioned, you will want to select a company that meets as many of the following criteria as possible:

- If the commodity is a consumable product, is it used by a large segment of the population? Are these products which create extraordinary results for their distributors and only require customers to redirect their spending, not completely change their behavior?
- Does the compensation plan pay, at the very least, to the fourth levels, preferably more? Is it based on accurate or inflated product prices?
- Is the company in good standing as a member of the DSA?
- Is a 90-percent refund policy offered, based on the shelf life of the product?
- Is a penalty code in place to discourage an illicit shift of a distributor (and their entire downline) from the original sponsor's front line to a brand new sponsor?
- Is it a visionary company with long-term objectives for introducing global expansion and new product lines?
- Does the company either supply training and recruiting materials or have an approval process for distributors who supply them?
- Is a corporate printout of distributor data supplied monthly?
- Does the company have a competent corporate legal staff?
- Is this a debt-free company or does it have solid financial backing?
- Has the company been in business at least two years, and does the leadership have a strong network marketing background?

Tony Neumeyer was first introduced to network marketing when his construction company in North Vancouver, Canada, went bankrupt. Tony, then active in the real estate business, had already tried several networking business ventures with limited success. Before he joined his present company in 1992, Tony was determined to find a successful network marketing opportunity.

"Even though the others cost me more money than they made me, I knew the concept was solid," declares Tony. "I knew people who were multi-millionaires from their network marketing businesses. My problem was obvious to me—I had made poor choices in the companies I selected."

This time he researched what was required for a successful business opportunity:

- the company's history
- the record of successful management
- the quality of the products
- the pay plans
- the timing and development of products, and
- the all-important issue of team support for teaching and implementing the system.

Once he used these criteria to find the right network marketing company, Tony made use of the same skills for network marketing that had made him successful in real estate:

1. *Consistency:* Talk to people every day! He identified a long list of friends and associates and began phoning them every day, five or six days a week. He wanted to attract people not by arm-twisting, but by extending the offer to build residual incomes together that would provide them both with a quality lifestyle.

2. *Has a "franchise-like" system:* One that is so duplicable anyone can step into it and be successful if they put in the effort. You can show others what to do but you can't do it for them. In the early days, Tony found he sometimes wanted success for people more than they wanted it for themselves.

3. *Follow-through:* Once you have given your prospects the information they need, you must be there to answer their questions and give them direction as to their next step.

4. *Only count productive time:* "When I was starting out, the only time I counted as work time was the time spent talking with people. The rest was my 'self development time,' which is also very important for success."

5. *Devote most of your time to those actually working:* The rule is that you should spend 80 percent of your non-prospecting time with the people who are really doing the business and 20 percent with the rest.

6. *Match your effort to theirs:* Your new distributors must take responsibility for themselves. As they start to spend more time at the business, you spend more time with them.

7. *Never stop learning:* Tony reads books and listens to tapes continually and considers every "turn down" a learning experience rather than a failure.

Select an Effective Team

Once you have prioritized the criteria that will help you select the right company for you, then choose the organization you want to join. Network marketing is, in every sense of the word, a team business, and, yes, your team does matter.

For Wayne Paulson, it all began in 1995 when he took a course in his hometown at the University of Illinois at Chicago. A graduate of the University of Illinois, Wayne was impressed that his alma mater was offering such a course, and after 20 years of owning his own business, he was open to a life transition.

Wayne's family thought he was going through a mid-life crisis, or, perhaps less worrisome, that he had merely hit his head on the spiral staircase in his home. Maybe it was a kind of mid-life alignment. At the age of 51, Wayne sat down with his family and talked openly about his passion in life and the kinds of things he wanted to do with the rest of his life.

Wayne selected a ten-year-old company backed by a 42-year-old pharmaceutical-grade manufacturing facility. He was drawn not only by the quality, but also the integrity and consistency, of the corporate management. He appreciated the fact that the marketing system was designed to allow for a phenomenal cash flow and that the company had an established track record in the multi-level marketing arena. He felt reassured that if anything should happen to him, it was a business that would protect his family.

Wayne was a businessman who evaluated the worth of each consultant's business in his organization as having an intrinsic assessed dollar value. The larger their organization, the greater its worth on the open market. Wayne began to work with individuals to help them understand that their business could be transferred, either sold or passed on to their children. A network marketing business is a real business…without the overhead and encumbrances of conventional businesses.

Wayne offers this advice to anyone looking to make a career change:

"I strongly suggest that you take a course in multi-level marketing to help you grasp the basics of the philosophy of the industry. This will also provide you the necessary criteria for selecting a network marketing company and a sponsor. Think of it just like you would when going on a career interview. There, you would ask questions about the company, about

> ## A network marketing business is a real business...without the overhead and encumbrances of conventional businesses.

your prospective co-workers, and about the work environment. With a multi-level marketing company, it is really no different. You will want to ascertain that you have a reliable and trustworthy corporate team, products that you can extol from personal experience, and, equally important, a sponsor and/or an upline team who is supportive of your needs, and gives you the assistance you require."

Interview your prospective colleagues. You want to know that there is someone upline on the team who has generated a good income and others who are willing to offer you support. Evaluate their training and duplication system, their efforts, and their financial returns. These factors are critical to the success of your business.

Network Marketing Is Teamwork Building

As the electronics warfare officer on a B-52, Roland Fox knew the meaning of teamwork. Each member of the crew carried the responsibility for the safety of everyone on board. Fox's job, in particular, carried great responsibility as their survival was dependent upon his ability to evade enemy radar and missiles. The team leadership skills he developed in the Air Force have served him well as a successful network marketing distributor.

Shortly before retiring Roland experienced his first network marketing presentation, and was overwhelmed by the concept.

"I thought I'd died and gone to heaven. I couldn't believe that someone would pay me for just recommending high-quality products to other people."

In 1973, Roland retired as a major and planned to find a civilian job to supplement his military pension. He was still intrigued by network marketing, and over the next decade, he looked into more than 24 opportunities. Out of those, he actually joined six companies which, without exception, failed and cost him money.

Yet, Roland still believed that network marketing was the vehicle that could provide the lifestyle he desired. In 1983 he was approached about a fledgling company marketing oral hygiene products.

Roland and his wife, Virginia, rose to Worldwide Master Director, the top position in their company working from their Spokane, Washington home.

The key to Roland's ultimate success was the same as in the Air Force: "I work closely with leaders who are creating a team. The team is everything. If you have a good team, you can accomplish any milestone. An individual can lead a charge, but without the team, that individual's effort is meaningless."

The New Model of a Network Marketer

John Kalench was introduced to network marketing more than 20 years ago. He had founded a medical brokerage business that specialized in the distribution of innovative orthopedic products. While his company was doing well financially, John felt a void. There was little personal fulfillment in his work.

"The first night that I was presented the concept of network marketing, I fell in love with it and have been in love with it ever since," he says. "The thing I connected with was that, for the first time in my life, I was taught a method of doing business that made complete and unconditional sense to me. My success was totally dependent upon how many people I helped become successful."

Over his first nine years in the industry, John built prosperous networks with three successive companies. Unfortunately, each one eventually went out of business. After putting so much of himself—his hopes and dreams as well as his name and credibility—on the line with each company, he still loved the business but felt let down by the companies he had chosen.

In February 1987, he founded Millionaires in Motion, Inc., based in his hometown of St. Louis, Missouri, to provide education and training to all network companies. He wrote several acclaimed books. *Being the Best You Can Be in MLM* is recognized as a step-by-step guide to building the business. *The Greatest Opportunity in the History of the World* tells the story, going back more than 50 years, of how network marketing started, where it's been, where it is today, where it's headed in the future. *Seventeen Secrets for the Master Prospectors* is a leadership book dealing with the philosophies and attitudes of the master prospectors in this business. The company, under John's leadership, has grown today to be recognized as one of the premier independent training companies in the network marketing industry. And John himself has personally coached tens of thousands of distributors. After more than a decade of traveling all over the world teaching people about the power of network marketing, John knew that he and his company had made a valuable contribution to the world. But he was reaching a time in his life when he no longer wanted to be running a conventional business.

With his wife five months pregnant with their second child, he was diagnosed with pancreatic cancer. It came out of nowhere. When he came out of surgery, the doctors were pessimistic and preparing his family for the worst. John's office was inundated with cards, letters, faxes and phone calls. Literally tens, if not hundreds, of thousands of people all over the world offered their prayers. Three days later, the pathology report came back saying that he was clear; they had caught it all. He is in that very small 3 percent of pancreatic cancer patients who survive.

"I am convinced," he says, "that I manifested that pancreatic cancer because I needed a signal to tell me that it was okay to put myself and my family first. Having gone through the health issue, I knew the time was right and the networking world would understand."

John's list of criteria for evaluating a network marketing company?

(1) He preferred an established company; he had no interest, at this point in his life in a start-up.

(2) He wanted a company with people in management and upline whom he could trust, who spoke the truth and delivered on their promises. If the management doesn't have honesty and integrity, nothing else really matters.

(3) He wanted products that were innovative, proprietary, and added value to the end consumer. His belief has always been that the more passionate distributors are about the genuine benefits offered by their product or service, the greater chance of their becoming successful.

(4) He was looking for an existing support system. He didn't want to start building a business and also have to build the infrastructure.

My success was totally dependent upon how many people I helped become successful.

Network marketing will help you transform your life and countless lives of others—forever!

He wanted everything in place for his team to be free to devote their energy to being productive rather than creative.

(5) He insisted on a compensation plan that was proven. He feels a "stair step breakaway" is the fairest and most rewarding compensation plan for those who are willing to work.

John became the fastest distributor in North America to achieve Diamond status with his company. And of all the people he personally sponsored, he had known only two previously, one of whom was his sister. Exemplifying the highest integrity, he did not feel the need to assemble his group through his industry contacts. John is a product of his own teaching over these many years through Millionaires in Motion and is living proof of its effectiveness.

We can either choose to coach and cheer people on from the sidelines, or we can get out on the field and score. After 11 years of valuable coaching, John Kalench has chosen to get into the game.

"Right from the beginning, I recognized network marketing as an opportunity for anyone to discover what is inherently possible," he says. "This industry has the ability to bring out the best or the worst in people. If distributors make the decision to submerge themselves in the process, seeing the industry as an opportunity to get in touch with the good within them, and focus their attention on what they can contribute to the lives they touch, it is inevitable that they will prosper, and prosper tremendously. There is almost a spiritual quality to network marketing. Contrary to popular belief, ours is not a transactional business, it's a transformational one. For those who are ready and willing, network marketing will help you transform your life and countless lives of others—forever!"

CHAPTER 7

Qualities Essential to
a Networking Professional

Network marketing is a unique business. To be successful in it, one must encounter the full spectrum of human experiences, much as Ralph Waldo Emerson has described: "To laugh often and much; to win the respect of intelligent people and the affection of children; to earn the appreciation of one's critics and endure the betrayal of false friends; to appreciate beauty, to find the best in others; to leave the world a bit better, whether by a healthy child, a garden patch, or a redeemed social condition; to know even one life has breathed easier because you have lived. This is to have succeeded."

Networking is the antithesis of the traditional workplace. Rather than delegate, in our business you lead by example. You want what you do duplicated by even the least qualified among the people in your organization. Rather than meaningless meetings and memos, you communicate by voice mail, e-mail, and teleconferencing. Unlike traditional business, where you are taught to emphasize your strengths and successes, network distribution teaches you to share your vulnerabilities as well—the circumstances leading to your hitting bottom. Rather than commuting, you work from home. Rather than competing with associates, you work side-by-side with them. A qualified worker under your supervision is not a threat to you in network marketing, but your most important asset.

Be Open-Minded

Getting into and maintaining a groove in our lives is common. Everyone does it. It takes extraordinary courage to get out of this "comfort zone" even if you're miserable.

Between the known world and the uncharted territory lies a great abyss of fear which few people are willing to explore. Rick Matheney openly shares the process of his own passage into the unfamiliar but enticing new world of network marketing.

"High school, college, Vietnam. Through all the growing years I had a clear vision of my future work," he says. "Learn a business and then start my own. Travel, meet interesting people, share ideas, give back something. The time slipped by quietly and quickly. But somewhere along the way, I lost my driving vision."

Rick's first job after the Army was in sales. He learned quickly that people buy what they want, not what they need. The money was good but the routine was not. So he advanced to a more professional level, as a sales rep for a large apparel manufacturer. When his territory began to build, his boss insisted he move 300 miles to another city. He traded good money for good location.

By the late 70s Rick was in the restaurant business, loving the idea of socializing while earning a living. But it wasn't long before he found himself working until 2 a.m. six days a week. His dream of travel had been reduced to a one-week vacation each year.

"For the next 15 years my spirit was not fully into the mortgage business, the building business, nor even my most recent, the golf course development business," he says. "It was only after my partner decided to stop our involvement in the middle of a golf course project that my vision came rushing back to me at warp speed. In October 1995, at age 47, I looked into the mirror and didn't like what I saw: aging Boomer trying to live up to someone else's ideal of success."

The idea of residual income had been in the back of his mind since he bought his first water filter from a friend in 1988. For weeks, he had considered possibly getting involved with that company. But the timing wasn't right. By the early 90s, he had two other friends, one with a phone service and one with a skin-care line, each doing well in network marketing. He tried their products and had the usual dreams of earning millions in their companies. But the passion was missing.

> Getting into and maintaining a groove in our lives is common....It takes extraordinary courage to get out of this "comfort zone" even if you're miserable.

Reading through the newspaper one day, he saw another one of those hyped-up classified ads touting six-figure incomes your first year.

"I knew it had to be a networking ad," he says. "This time, something drew me in. Maybe all the years of financial struggle? Maybe the dreams of being debt free? To this day, I believe it was my attitude that was beginning to change. Fifty was staring me square in the face and easy paths, tried and true, leading to dead ends were no longer in the way. I had read all the stories: housewife turns home-based business into millions; college student earns more than her professors by networking out of her dorm room. My thoughts were if they can do it, I can too!"

Security vs. Risk

Rick acknowledges that the hardest thing to overcome was the paradigm shift from the security of what he knew to the uncertainty of what he didn't. He was earnestly trying to reprogram his brain from the years of build-up: get that degree, find a company, dress the part, play the political game, join in the good ol' boys network, and move up the corporate ladder. He wanted to tell himself that it was okay to let go of all of that and seriously consider this type of business.

"I made a pact to give my all to this new venture for one full year, no turning back, no 'wimping out,' giving a 100 percent effort. Never mind that I hadn't a clue as to how to build this type of business."

Rick experienced some important lessons early on in his networking business. He went anywhere and everywhere his business took him. He sometimes drove up to 300 miles one way for weeks, catching a few winks in his car when he couldn't drive anymore.

"You get back exactly what you give out," he says now. "If you treat your MLM business as a business, it will respond like a business. If you deal with it like a hobby, it will grow accordingly."

Rick's goals were clear. This business venture with all the camaraderie, the leveraged income, and the residual potential would become a replacement for all the traditional businesses of his past and future. With that affirmation driving his vision, he set out to learn this business, choosing travel as his medium. Why? Because he wanted to see the world.

"The first year was awesome. I made the trek from coast to coast, meeting wonderful folks along the way. I used talents I hadn't called upon in years. I was able to give a little back to those who had helped me on my life's journey. And, oh yeah, I blew right past that notorious six-figure threshold without noticing too much.

"Dream with me for just a minute," he encourages. "Imagine traveling across this great land of ours on your own schedule. You have no alarm clock screaming for you to blast out of bed each morning. You can afford to stay at any hotel and eat in any restaurant you choose. You can purchase clothing and extras without too much notice of the price tag. While you are at your leisure, thousands of people are putting thousands of dollars in your bank account each month."

This not only describes Rick's life, but the lives of thousands of others in MLM companies around the world. Though a native of Charlotte, North Carolina, for the past two-and-a-half years now he has actually lived in hotels and continues to travel to build his business in new areas. He doesn't have to do this. He chooses it because he loves it. How many times in our life do we have the chance to see the world on our own schedule and build an enormous business at the same time? As Rick says, "The challenge of transforming my mindset has served to diminish my fears of a mundane future and has set me free forever."

Rick Matheney is finally living his vision. He owns his own business, is traveling, meeting interesting people, sharing ideas, and giving something back. But, best of all, he is helping others who lost their vision, find it.

> If you treat your MLM business as a business, it will respond like a business. If you deal with it like a hobby, it will grow accordingly.

The Courage to Persist

Ken and Karen Long might have been any small-town couple. He was an eighth-grade teacher and coach and she taught piano in rural Oregon. Ken was nominated for the Fox Television teacher of the year the same year he received a $4,000 pay cut because of the economic crisis caused by the "spotted owl" controversy. After 20 years as a teacher, suddenly these inequities hit home. In an effort to compensate for the pay cut, Karen added more piano students until she was up to 54 each week.

"It was exhausting," she says. "All I did was work. Ken and I had no life. On top of that, our older son was at the university and the tuition payments that third year were the straw that broke our financial back. We had robbed every 'hidey hole' in our home and were just barely keeping our heads above water.

"Ken's sister, Peggy, knew our plight and, deviously, asked to borrow some money as she had just lost her job. It was February, and we decided to take money from our furnace fund (our ancient furnace was on its last legs), figuring that we had made it through the worst of winter. She called to say she received the money and had just gotten us started in a new business she had discovered. We were excited that she had found an answer for her situation, but were furious about her decision to include us. We told her we wanted our money back and she assured us there was a full money back guarantee. We all agreed she would make the 1,400-mile trek to explain this face to face, and that we wouldn't do anything 'rash' until then. Though we were excited about her coming to visit, the two of us made a private pact between ourselves not to get into any business. Period!"

The pact melted away after they looked over what this sister had to show them. It wasn't easy getting started. They felt terribly ineffectual at first. Their frustration over this only increased their self-doubt. Yet they persisted even while they watched others quit, some when their success was only a few months away.

"Once, while in a long-distance race, Ken pulled a muscle at mile 12," Karen recalls. "Through sheer determination, literally putting one foot in front of the other, he finished. We hit that mile 12 in our networking business. And we finished exactly the same way, with our upline and team members cheering us on. Without the encouragement, support, and reassurance from them, we would never have made it."

Ken and Karen's lives weren't altered drastically as a result of their success. They still live in the same small town of Lebanon, Oregon, in the same house, but life is a whole lot easier. Gone was the Chevette for a luxury car that made driving a true joy. The ten-year-old mini-van was replaced by Ken's recreational vehicle for hunting. Ken planned a fly-in fishing trip for his kids and his dad. Karen purchased a new grand piano and took her 80-year-old parents to Finland for a two-week trip. That represented a life-long dream come true.

It was nothing short of utter devastation when their network company of seven years went bankrupt. They found themselves at a serious cross-roads. Would they stay in networking or find regular work again? Having had the taste of what this industry can do, they found a new network marketing home that would keep the brother-sister team together. They knew that nowhere but in networking could they continue the kind of life they had, surrounded by a supportive group of people who shared the belief that you only win by creating other winners.

Your Back Against the Wall

Sometimes it is when your back is totally against the wall that you discover your real strength. That is the story of Danette Johnson, a young girl only 19 when the story begins.

Imagine a teenage girl fleeing a welfare home and a life of shattering violation and mistreatment, a young woman afflicted with dyslexia and destined for a marriage that would steal her dignity, money and credit. Forced onto the streets, she lived out of a car, homeless and hopeless, with nothing and no one left.

"I remember feeling like I should just end it," she says. "But I was afraid that I couldn't even do that right."

She was talking to other girls about wanting to lose weight, and mentioned the program that she tried to buy with a bouncing check after her runaway husband stripped her account. They insisted on knowing more. She called the woman who received the bounced check, and told her about the girls.

"She suggested that I become a distributor. I said 'No way, I'm not going to become a distributor for any MLM company!' She insinuated that I needed to figure out how I was going to cover that bounced check. I quickly reconsidered.

"Everyone laughed at me for doing MLM, but I just stayed focused. Gradually, I watched my monthly check grow from nothing to $6,500 to

> ## Sometimes it is when your back is totally against the wall that you discover your real strength.

$10,000. On December 7, 1990, I was living out of my car. By December 7, 1991, I was able to make a substantial down payment on a beautiful home in Northern California, furnishing it with all the nicest things I could find."

Dani and her new husband, Hans, started their own company, but soon discovered that the stress wasn't worth it. Giving that up to join another MLM enterprise, they found peace of mind doing what they passionately loved: working with and training people to become financially independent; changing their lives emotionally, mentally, physically, and financially. Over three years, working part-time, Dani and Hans earned over $700,000. Now living in a beautiful 4,000-square-foot home in Pleasanton, California, these two young people are raising a family with God, family, and business as their priorities, in that order.

Some of the best success stories of this industry come from people like Dani, who had absolutely no options left. If this is your situation, be encouraged. Experience has shown that having your back against the wall is more of an asset than a detriment coming into this business—not a physical advantage, not a head start, not even the benefit of timing. Your advantage is that you have to try harder. This is one place in life that, with consistent effort, it is possible to succeed in a reasonable amount of time starting with nearly nothing.

Believing in Your Company and Products

From his earliest teens, Ladd McNamara wanted to become a doctor. Dedicating 12 years of his life, sacrificing family time, sleep, and even a little of his sanity, while incurring a $100,000 debt, he embarked on a career in obstetrics and gynecology with one of Atlanta's premier medical groups. He and his wife, Susan, had just given birth to their third child, and eventually they would have their fourth. Feeling guilty for wanting to be an attentive father to his children, yet, knowing that many, if not most, weekends, evenings, and holidays would be spent at the hospital, Ladd was tormented. Added to this, Ladd was chronically sleep-deprived, fighting commuter traffic, run ragged by insufferable office and hospital schedules, and managed health care was lowering his income.

"It was my mother's perseverance that got me started in network marketing early in 1995. She informed me about her company's nutritional product line, insisting that they could potentially help a lot of my patients. Like most of the physicians I knew, I had no appreciation for the importance of a high-quality, balanced vitamin and mineral program. And marketing through a networking system? That did it. I told my mother, 'Stay away from all those scams.'

"Pressed by her to try the products, my wife and I noticed some immediate health benefits, and we were encouraged enough to use the products ourselves; but there was no way that I would ever get involved with the business. 'No self-respecting physician,' I thought, 'would ever lower himself to get involved with such a degrading business.'

"I agreed to give my mother exactly one hour to explain this ridiculous business. What an hour! I began to grasp the true meaning of network marketing."

But then his self-questioning began: what would people think of him? That he failed at his practice? That he was just greedy? Some might even consider him unethical. But he overcame his fears and, much to his wife's dismay, enrolled.

"At first, I had only a few patients with such ailments as arthritis or chronic fatigue syndrome try the products to test their results. I was absolutely stunned when all these patients came back within a few weeks reporting astounding results," he says.

"Even without earning commissions, based upon what I had witnessed, I would be recommending these products. But what made it even better was the fact that I was earning enough to pay for my products and then some. In the first few months the checks were initially $100 per week, but they quickly grew to $200 and then $300 per week. I had not learned to concern myself with prospecting serious business builders, as I was making a comfortable salary in medicine. I certainly would have liked to find people who wanted to build an organization, but I thought I didn't have the time to work the business at a level that could bring in a six-figure income. So I would be happy with the small checks I was receiving."

His medical-practice partners, however, weren't happy. They didn't agree with recommending vitamins and minerals to patients. Where was the medical evidence? Then came the ultimatum: "If I didn't stop selling vitamins and minerals to my patients, I would have to leave the practice!"

He was making $200 to $300 a week as a networking distributor and $145,000 per year as a second-year practice partner. Two weeks later he was out of a job, having been unceremoniously dismissed.

With a bank loan and a deep-seeded belief in his products and company, Ladd began seriously studying the industry and business techniques. The time and money it cost for training in network marketing was nothing compared to the time and money it took to become a doctor. At times, he wished that he could rewind those 12 years of his life, the sacrifices and pain of his medical training, and start over with network marketing. Soon his checks began to grow. After two and a half years, working part-time while still holding down a solo medical practice, he earned over $2000 per week. At this level he was able to drop the most difficult and stressful part of his medical practice, obstetrics. He works only three days a week, has no nightly pages and is sleeping regularly.

For physicians like Dr. McNamara, an earnest belief in the products is the key to their success.

A Personal Growth Life Journey

A commercial pilot since 1975, George Iddon has made a profession of travel. Once he discovered network marketing, he traded his high-paying, high-stress career for an equally high-paying but low-stress career in the convenience of his home in Point Roberts, Washington. With his wife, Julie, he now travels for the sheer joy of it when they journey about the globe building their business.

"Up until the early 90s, I was happy with my profession. I had grown accustomed to a certain lifestyle and had no idea of the 'turbulence' ahead when deregulation for the aviation industry hit, and the airlines began cutting back employees, hours, salary, and benefits.

"One day in 1993, a flight attendant came into the cockpit and showed me a cellular phone, which I had been looking to purchase. Because of deregulation in the telecommunication industry, he suggested that there would be opportunities for the average person to get into telecommunications."

What irony! Deregulation of one industry was his ruination, and deregulation of another opened new possibilities. While dabbling in the business of selling discounted long-distance services, George discovered *Upline* magazine, an industry publication that literally answered all of his questions. Soon George had all of his downline members subscribing to *Upline*, which provided the resources they needed to do their business.

"One of the best things about network marketing," says George, "is that you're never tied down to your geographical location. You can work your business in Florida in January and February, spend July in Chicago, August in Alaska—it really won't matter. You can follow the sun."

George doesn't boast that he makes an enormous income from this business, but he and Julie live a fabulous lifestyle.

"I enjoy traveling again and have made some wonderful friends along the way. I love the fact that Julie and I work as a team and as equals. A lot of people don't have such a partnership, and I feel very fortunate in that respect. In fact, I don't think this business should be called 'network marketing'—it should be a personal growth life journey, because that's exactly what it is. It's not the end result that represents success; the journey itself also matters."

If you want to enjoy success, only today's achievements can be counted on to produce it.

Team Play Vs. Solo Practice

When network marketing first came his way, Tom Entwistle had been in private practice as a chiropractor in Bristol, Connecticut, for six years. He enjoyed his profession, made an excellent living, and was well respected. But in 1994, he began to see some unsettling changes in his profession. Managed care was beginning to make itself felt and suddenly the future didn't seem as secure as it had only a short time ago. Tom soon found himself working longer and harder, and still slipping back financially.

It was about that time that a fellow practitioner mentioned that he had found a possible way out from under the thumb of managed care. He urged Tom to be open-minded enough to take a look.

> One of the best things about network marketing...is that you're never tied down to your geographical location.... You can follow the sun.

"The power of leveraging offered by network marketing seemed very attractive, but I was still not convinced that it could be done in a time-efficient way," he explains. "I couldn't afford to have it interfere with my practice, and I refused to give up time with my family. I was told that this business could grow with serious—but part-time—effort. I was really skeptical, but soon found out why that was true."

Ever since opening his practice, Tom's income had been dependent on his own effort. Intellectually, he could see that network marketing offered him a way to leverage his time and income through a growing organization. What he didn't see right away was the power of leveraging that came from utilizing his upline. By the very act of joining his company, he immediately had access to a proven business system and six experienced business partners who, by virtue of being in his upline, had a vested interest in his success. They went to work for him, training him, answering questions, and offering invaluable coaching.

"Their assistance in making initial presentations and training those people who joined me right away made all the difference," he notes. "All of a sudden I was no longer in a solo practice, at least as far as my networking business was concerned. I couldn't put a price tag on their knowledge, expertise, and willingness to work. I didn't have to; it all came with my signature on the application.

"After a year, my network business was doing well enough for me to cut back my hours. I put some of those hours back into my business and the results were self-evident. My strong six-figure income from this incredible industry has enabled me to put my practice up for sale. I will soon be able to devote a full-time effort to my network marketing business. Of course, my definition of 'full-time' is now defined by me, not by insurance companies. My initial objection to taking on this business was my lack of time; the end result of my decision to participate is unlimited time-freedom and the resources to enjoy it!"

Necessary Apprenticeship

Experience is often something you don't acquire until just after you need it. This is especially true for successful professionals, like Marc Barrett, who joined our industry without initally grasping the differences in approach between traditional business and network marketing.

In the beginning, despite a successful track record as a real estate investor, nothing, absolutely nothing, worked for Marc in his first few months

> My initial objection to taking on this business was my lack of time; the end result of my decision to participate is unlimited time freedom and the resources to enjoy it.

after joining our industry. Trying desperately to fit the square pegs of traditional business into the round holes of our industry, Marc hit a brick wall. It wasn't until he allowed himself to be trained, and assimilated the unique aspects of network marketing, that the business began working for him.

Marc Barrett was a businessman through and through. He conducted his meetings in an office wearing three-piece suits and dazzling people with his lengthy presentations filled with facts and statistics and interesting data about our industry, our company, and the market share of our product.

Marc had cleared his first million in real estate by the time he was 28. He had made and lost $4 million by the time he was 37. Trying to stave off bankruptcy, he poured what cash he had left into commercial buildings. But it was futile. Marc lost his commercial properties, his money, even his house, and was financially set back to where he had been 20 years earlier, except now he had a wife and three children to support.

His wife, Laura, who, through the earlier years, stayed home with the children, took matters into her own hands. She found a network marketing skincare company and rather quickly built her way to executive status.

"I was convinced that she had been duped," Marc says. "As she got more involved, I started looking over her shoulder and examining the materials, because I didn't want her to get mixed up in something illegal."

What Marc discovered was just the opposite.

"I started seeing the potential for leverage. I saw people selling products, recruiting distributors, and having the potential to develop income streams of several hundred thousand dollars a year."

Unable to agree on a common approach, Laura stepped aside and let Marc take over where she left off. Marc Barrett was a proud man. After all, he'd made, and lost, millions in his short lifetime. The losses had shaken his confidence. He knew (at least he thought he knew) that he

114

could rebuild it all. But, for the second time, he found himself nearly paralyzed. Nothing that he was doing was working. He couldn't even duplicate his wife's success.

"Four months in this business," he thought, "and I still haven't recruited my first distributor."

Marc looked around for successful distributors in the company who could coach him. Rumor had it that a guy named Mark Yarnell out of Austin, Texas, had signed up 30 people in his first month and cleared $15,000 in commissions by his fourth month in the business. By this time, the Yarnell monthly commissions were reputed to be four times that amount. Yarnell was directly upline from Marc Barrett, so he had an immediate financial interest in seeing that Marc did well.

He decided to give Yarnell a call, but his pride still held him back from seeking the comprehensive help he needed. The only part that Marc retained from that short call was the advice to take out ads in local newspapers.

At last Marc's phone was ringing, but something was still wrong. Marc would bring his prospects into his office, impress them with facts and figures, and they would listen politely through the whole two-hour presentation. Then they shook his hand and left, never to be seen again. He still had not sponsored a single distributor.

Changing the Approach

A few weeks later, Marc was back on the phone with Yarnell. Yarnell acknowledged Marc for the incredible businessman that he is. No one would question that. But few others could do what he did. And apparently, based on Marc's track record, he had yet to find a single person who even thought he could. The Yarnell system for presentations takes into account that prospects are not only looking at the business, but how you're doing the business. They're saying inside their heads, "Can I do what he's doing?" In the case of Marc's prospects, the answer was "No." They took one look at his fancy office, his designer suit, and his polished presentation and concluded that they couldn't duplicate it. Marc's approach seemed too expensive and too difficult for others to visualize themselves doing.

Yarnell's advice to Marc was to adopt a simplified approach: (1) use a prospecting video instead of doing all the talking; (2) dress casually, sport coat and jeans, rather than a suit; and (3) work from home and shut down the office. When Marc hung up the phone, his head was spinning. There was so much to learn. But for the first time, he was genuinely open to being coached.

"The office was the hardest habit to break," admits Marc. But he did it and to his surprise, he began sponsoring distributors excited about joining his team, right from his home. The video he used was one produced by Yarnell himself, who was wearing blue jeans, suspenders, and a three-day-old beard. When people saw it, their reaction was "If this guy can do it, then it's all over but the shouting. We're rich!"

Marc had excellent presentation skills, but he followed Yarnell's advice and stopped trying to give his own pitch. He would just sit people down, plug in the videotape, and let them watch it. After one such presentation, Marc's prospect, a CPA, turned to him and said, "I just want to know one thing. Can I get that tape and can I do what you are doing?"

At long last, after nearly six months of going through innumerable prospects, Marc Barrett was back in business.

"In my mind, the goal was to recruit 12 top-notch salespeople and train them to a high level of proficiency. This is exactly what I would do if I were setting up a real estate office," Marc remembers. "Eventually I would see each of them moving $30,000 to $40,000 worth of product per month."

Marc finally understood that he was working the business backward. Network marketers don't try to find a small group of people to move a large amount of products. Our mission is to get *a whole lot of people to do a small amount of sales volume*. Network marketing is a business of providing high-quality products and services through person-to-person relationships. Marc dropped all of his preconceived ideas about marketing. Thanks to Yarnell, he no longer worried about his professional look or office. He dressed casually and invited prospective business associates to his little rented house on the beach.

"In the last year," says Marc, now living back in his hometown of Denver, "I personally sold about $5,000 worth of product for the entire year, which is about $300 to $400 a month. But my business organization has generated an average of $20 million in sales volume per year over the last three years."

The good news for professionals joining the business today is that you have advantages that were not available to Marc during the Wave Two era. With the advancement of technology, professionals are able to utilize conference calls and satellite broadcasts. They have access to multi-media training programs, internet web sites and e-mail, voice or fax-on-demand, virtual office systems, follow-me phone lines, and a multitude of other

> Network marketers don't try to find a small group of people to move a large amount of products. Our mission is to get a whole lot of people to do a small amount of sales volume.

electronic devices that have completely revolutionized the network distribution industry. A magnificent opportunity awaits those joining the industry today: a new and engaging industry geared to challenge your creativity and provide unimaginable rewards.

CHAPTER 8

Frequently Asked Questions
about the Industry

Like any new and unfamiliar industry, network marketing inevitably raises certain questions and concerns. Turning to some of the most successful people in the industry, let's hear how they address these commonly asked issues.

Isn't Network Marketing an Illegal Pyramid?

All structures essentially are pyramids: the government, religious organizations, the military, corporate America. So how do these pyramids differ from network marketing?

Kathleen Deoul has been in a "pyramid" all of her life. She worked her way up the corporate ladder only to hit the glass ceiling head on and realized she could never make it to the top of the corporate pyramid working for someone else. So she started her own company where she was the apex of the pyramid, only to have to deal with daily commuting, the reality of employees, payroll, bank loans, mortgages, tax issues, and a myriad of other problems so fundamental to a corporate pyramid.

During this period, Kathleen remarried and, to cap it all off, at the age of 42, she gave birth to her only child. What could be better? But, during the pregnancy she was afflicted with a disease of the muscles and connective tissue which relegated her to a life of constant agony from the neck down. She couldn't sleep, was in constant discomfort, and eventually even walking became an agonizing experience. She commuted 120 miles round-trip each day in severe pain, collapsing at home each night, taking all kinds of medications that created their own problems. She lasted for nine years, getting progressively worse, undergoing six surgeries, walking with air splints and canes, and praying for a miracle. That miracle came in the form of magnetic products that transformed her life, literally overnight. Suddenly she didn't hurt anymore. She could walk without suffering and once again had the energy of an 18-year-old!

"But I found myself in a 'good-news, bad-news' scenario," she says. "The good news was I had gotten my quality of life back with magnetic products, and I couldn't wait to share them with everyone I could think of. The bad news was that they were sold via network marketing, and I wanted nothing to do with that! Most network marketing companies go out of business leaving you with a garage or basement filled with products you can't sell. And it is, after all, one of those 'pyramid things'! I decided to become a distributor just so I could buy the products wholesale, without any intention to build a business. I simply felt a strong motivation to share the products with others who may need them.

"Little did I realize that others who used my products would have similar experiences to mine and would want to share the products, too! Twelve months later I received a $4,200 check. It was that check that taught me my first lesson in network marketing. It made me see the power of 'leveraged time.' I didn't earn that money all by myself. It was all the people in my small organization who were simply duplicating what I was doing. They put that check in my pocket."

She had been commuting that 120 miles a day for 13 years and it had taken quite a toll. She was gone in the morning before her daughter left for school, arriving home in the evening too exhausted to do anything. She was not able to go to her daughter's after-school games or rehearsals, or have "quality time" with her husband. They lived in a newly built dream home, but she was hardly ever there.

"Now, with energy to burn, and that $4,200 check to make me realize that working out of my home could be the solution to the lack of balance

> # I didn't earn that money all by myself. It was all the people in my small organization who were simply duplicating what I was doing.

in my life, I announced to my husband that I was going to sell my company," she says. "Six months later, my monthly check generated from working out of my home was $16,000, and I sold my company. The rest is history."

One of the greatest satisfactions for Kathleen is that many leaders in her organization are now approaching, and some have already surpassed, a quarter-million dollars in annual income. Kathleen is finally in the "ultimate pyramid," a flexible one! She is at the top, once again a CEO, but her earnings and her ability to influence others are limited only by her own beliefs, ambitions, and her capacity for dreaming. Free of glass ceilings, employees, and other burdens, she has achieved the wealth and freedom to lead a truly balanced life. So can similarly motivated members in her organization, all of whom have their own respective pyramids.

Don't Only the People at the Top Make Money?

In an illegal pyramid scheme, this is true. As an example, you are asked to send out a chain letter asking 20 people you know to send one dollar to the person whose name is at the top of the list. Each, in turn, will send out 20 letters to people they know, asking each of them to invest one dollar that will go to the next name on the list. Each new grouping invests their respective dollars with the hope that this chain will last long enough for their name to get to the top of the list. Clearly, in that type of a pyramid structure, only the people at the top make the money.

Multi-level marketing's approach is in sharp contrast to the so-called pyramid schemes. Ours is a business that distinguishes itself in two ways.

First: in a legitimate pyramid sales company, there are generally 45 to 60 percent profits available for commissions, which represents distribution costs. The rest goes toward company profits and manufacturing expenses. There is a limit to how many levels down a company can afford to pay out. It might remunerate five levels at 10 percent each or eight levels at 6 percent each. But there is a limit to how much or how many levels the company can accommodate. Some newer companies today are coming out with software programs as their product line. The value of this is that there are no manufacturing costs beyond the initial setup. Without this added expenditure, they can afford, if they choose, to compensate the distributor at a higher percentage. Some pay as high as 65 to 70 percent, retaining 30 to 35 percent for company profit and overhead.

Second: a real product or a real service must be distributed. All legitimate network marketing companies have a product or service that is sold. Field representatives are compensated on sales of the company's products or services. They do not receive commissions for selling training materials and other items related to the establishment of their business. All compensation in a legitimate network marketing company is based on the sale of the company's products or services. If you agree that the market cannot be saturated as long as new people join the business and new products are introduced, there is no bottom to this type of pyramid structure.

Doesn't Most Everyone Quit?

Network marketing is a business that demands effort. It is some of the hardest work most of us have ever done. The difference is that it has an approximate four-year business plan instead of a 40-year one. In the early stages, for the labor put forth, we are paid very little. It is at this stage that most people quit. Those who persevere and stay with the program long enough for success to take hold are compensated extremely well for a gradually diminishing output of exertion.

It took Suzie Kaster, a successful corporate realtor, and her husband, Duff, a practicing dentist in Las Vegas, Nevada, about three and a half years to go from network marketing skeptics to two of its staunchest advocates. They credit a leadership seminar they attended highlighting a "four-year career plan" as the start of their conversion.

> Network marketing is a business that demands effort.... The difference is that it has an approximate four-year business plan instead of a 40-year one.

> ## For years, MLM distributors were 90 percent women. Today...men...represent about 35 percent of network marketers.

The breakthrough came first for Duff while Suzie was still resisting. "But," Suzie explains, "when I saw the power of the geometric progression, I knew that we could achieve our lifetime career goals in four years instead of thirty; and best of all, the approach to the business of introducing without needing to persuade prospective distributors really fit my personality."

"I think the final turning point came long after we were both full-time distributors," Duff recalls, "when Suzie and I were in Key West lying on a hammock at sunset. I said, 'I wish we could stay longer.' And Suzie's response was, 'Why don't we?' And for the first time in my life, I couldn't think of a reason."

Suzie remembers the struggles of that first year in their new profession, with three or four appointments each night. In contrast, recalling the November they could afford to send 14 of their relatives to Hawaii on vacation, the quality time they now have with each other and their family, she says: "I just want people to know how valuable that time is."

Most people don't have the patience to persist through the early stage. So most people do quit. Network marketing is not a get-rich-quick scheme, but a work program. However, if the products are satisfactory, some wanna-be-business builders continue, and renew each year, in order to have access to wholesale products for their own use, or perhaps for a few customers. These may quit the business but continue placing orders for years to come.

Isn't This Just a Part-time Woman's Deal?

For years, MLM distributors were 90 percent women. Today the numbers of men joining the industry are significant; men now represent about 35 percent of network marketers.

For the first 35 years, MLM represented, both in perception and in reality, a means for homemakers to pick up extra pocket change selling soap, plastic wares, vitamins, cosmetics, toys, and other household items. They did home parties or simply sold by word-of-mouth. By the mid-80s, that began to change. The downsizing of corporate America had a lot to do with it. Whatever the cause, husbands began paying more attention to what their wives were doing. With their backs against the proverbial wall, they could see the potential. What if…this were treated more like a business? What if…a larger sales force could be brought onto the team? What if…we could create a franchise-like system of duplication? And so "Wave Three" came into its own. I predict it will not be long before there will be an equal number of men and women in network marketing.

How Practical Is Network Marketing?

"Network marketing is nothing more than a distribution operation," points out Ridgely Goldsborough, of *Network Marketing Lifestyles* magazine. "To me, it is the most effective and efficient distribution business ever created on this planet. Clearly, distribution is one of the great businesses for the next ten to twenty years."

Paul Pilzer, author of *God Wants You to Be Rich*, believes that the key to wealth no longer lies in manufacturing existing products.

"For most people seeking wealth in the 90s," he told me at the beginning of this decade, "the greatest opportunities lie in the distribution sector of our economy."

In the 60s, Paul pointed out, manufacturing and distribution accounted for equal portions of the retail cost of an item. But in the 90s, the cost of that same item has been lowered by as much as two-thirds. Production costs have been substantially lowered. Although distribution costs have also fallen, they now constitute the larger portion of the cost. Approximately 80 percent of the price of a retail product today is due to distribution costs. For that reason, Paul explained, the big opportunity now lies in finding ways to distribute products less expensively.

After Paul's initial introduction, through Mark Yarnell and myself, to the power of distribution through networking, Paul created an alliance with Amway, the oldest and largest network marketing company. Retail-

> For most people seeking wealth in the 90s…the greatest opportunities lie in the distribution sector of our economy.

ing, direct mail, and other conventional ways of distribution failed him completely. Every penny of his $8 million in revenues from sales of his CD-ROMs is generated today through network marketing.

Don't Commissions Drive Up the Product Cost?

If a network marketing company pays commissions four levels, six levels deep, doesn't that just drive up the cost of the products? Of course it does. But does that mean that the products that go to the consumer are more expensive? No. As network marketing companies add costs to pay the distributors, they take away costs by cutting out some of the traditional distribution costs. This form of distribution cuts out the national and regional distributors, the local wholesaler, the advertising budget, and the overhead of a retail store. Network marketers cut the distribution costs by going directly from the manufacturer to the consumer. These savings are then conveyed to network marketers in the form of a compensation plan.

How Exactly Are the Products Distributed?

Network marketing is really relationship marketing. The vast majority of the nearly $100 billion dollars of products and services moved through the estimated 31 million distributors worldwide is by word of mouth, the oldest and most effective form of advertising. Product volume is created for the distributors through a variety of ways:

Promotional Volume

The products are ordered, often in multiple packages, as a first step to introduce to those associates looking at the business. This type of volume propels your business into a quick start. The danger is that distributors, all too often, get lulled into a false sense of security believing that they are building a stable, growth-oriented business. Promotional volume can disappear as swiftly as it surfaced.

Wholesale Consumption

If your personal contacts like the products after buying them, they will likely continue to use them, especially if they can receive a discount. This is what creates long-term stability in your organization and ultimately creates passive, residual income. You can never successfully build a network organization with promotional volume only; unless this trial, exploratory volume converts to real volume, you have an organizational structure built on sand.

Referral marketing is a concept just catching on that treats both distributors and customers the same. If an individual is interested in ordering the products on a regular basis, she may do so (at a fixed price set by the company) either as a customer or as a distributor. The only difference is that the distributor is entitled to build a network while the customer will order the products only for personal use.

Life Force International is one multi-level marketing company that is a strong proponent of the referral form of marketing. Wayne Hillman, founder of Life Force, told me:

"One of the objectives in multi-level marketing is that, in order to meet requirements for benefiting from the compensation plan, distributors must meet quotas each month by purchasing the products at wholesale and selling them at retail. With referral marketing, as it is used in our company, there are no quotas. The distributors simply network with their friends and invite them to contact us, and the company takes it from there. We answer their questions, mail them literature, and, if they so choose, send them out the product. By this method, we are better able to control what is said about the products. If a sale is made, the referring distributor is compensated on a multi-level pay-out plan."

Retail Sales

This represents the standard wholesale to retail mark-up, the difference of which is paid directly to the distributor. Traditionally, these retail sales have been the heart of the direct sales industry. While retailing distributors will always be a part of the network of an MLM organization, there is a definite movement today toward developing a division for business builders, even within old-line companies.

However products are distributed, they are typically marketed through conversations with friends. By far the vast majority of distributors for Avon, Shaklee, Tupperware, Mary Kay and other single-level (as opposed to multi-level) companies rely on party plans and one-on-one relationships as their primary means of distribution. Business builders, those building an MLM organization, tend to focus their "networking" on the business opportunity itself. They will generate retail customers among those declining to join them in the business.

Do I Have to Retail Products?

Remember the mission of network marketing. It is having a lot of people doing a little bit of sales volume rather than having a few people producing a large volume. This is not a business of delegation, but one where each of us does our part and leads by example. So the answer is yes, you are expected to do your part if your goal is to be paid commissions. A minimum sales quota of $100 to $500 monthly volume is typical to qualify for your commission. As described above, this may occur through conversations with family and friends or with those who say no to the business opportunity but want the products.

Why Emphasize Contacting Family and Friends?

New networkers are encouraged to begin their business closest to home. Why? Because it is effective and it is duplicable. Family and friends are forgiving if your presentation is not as polished or professional as it might later become.

If every new associate to our industry avoided family and friends, we'd be miniscule in comparison to the size we are today. Most new distributors are inexperienced at sales. Asking them to begin by calling on strangers and teaching their people to do the same would stifle business-building possibilities considerably. Remember, this is a business built on duplication. What you do others will duplicate.

From the earliest days of MLM, an overriding philosophy has prevailed: network organizations are built on personal relationships. While there have been innumerable changes in the industry over the years, that principle has remained consistent. Distributors have always been encouraged to build their business with family unity in mind. Husbands and wives have been encouraged to work together, reaching out to other family members, parents, children, brothers, sisters, and friends who have spouses, parents, children, brothers and sisters, and friends. The "family tree" concept is a proven system that has made network marketing what it is today.

How Do You Find Brokers and Agents?

The way you attract other distributors to your network marketing organization is exactly the same as if you were starting any other kind of business. If you start a new company and need an assistant, a sales rep or a board of directors, where would you go to find them? Most often you start with people you know. Maybe you turn to people you've worked with in the past. Family members who are in transition or frustrated or people with whom you went to school are possibilities. You would also ask for referrals, and spread the word that you are searching. You could hire executive search firms, run ads in newspapers and on the Internet. All of these methods work for traditional business, and they work for network marketing as well.

With his background in direct sales and management, Peter Mingils began looking at industry bottlenecks.

"A friend of mine once said, 'If you're not advertising your business, it's a little bit like winking in the dark,'" Peter reports. "You know you're doing it, but no one else does. A professional understands this."

Many MLMers will turn to proven techniques that have worked for them in past professions. These can be very effective. There's the post-card or letter-mailing program (which now includes e-mail). Or you can send a direct-mail package (perhaps an audio with a letter).

"In my company, PM Marketing," Peter says, "we specialize in making calls for people initially. We qualify the people first and then they can buy the screened list and work the leads of those who have already been pro-filed. This is a great way to get your people going when they get stagnant." (See the Resource section at the back of this book for more information.)

How Do Some Networkers Earn Such Huge Incomes So Fast?

It is the compensation structure that most boggles people's minds for better or for worse. It is often both the stumbling block and the break-through of this industry.

Tim Sales knows something about working under pressure. A former diver with the U.S. Navy Underwater Bomb Squad, his job was to secure hotels, automobiles, and boats for Olympic athletes, the President, and foreign dignitaries.

When Tim was first introduced to the network marketing industry, he didn't have the usual objections. With the risks he had already taken in life, this seemed about as perilous as a walk in the park. He saw an ad in *The Washington Post*, received a video, attended a meeting, and immedi-ately saw the possibilities.

From the very beginning, Tim treated his business like a profession. Like a Navy diver, he worked at mastering each component of the busi-ness and executing it precisely. He felt other professionals coming into the business would want solid facts to assess. Somehow there must be a better way to deal with the objections his people were confronting. After years of grappling with this, Tim "decided to create a generic, third-party product that would defuse the 'killer' objections, and give network marketers back their pride." The result was *Brilliant Compensation*, a best-selling industry video that addresses these "killer" objections.

Tim describes four main principles to look for in choosing a profession in today's world. The opportunity you consider should be positioned for (1) a huge and expanding business; (2) a unique and consumable product; (3) trends and timing, such as health, youth, education, retirement, security, savings; and (4) its ability to create leverage.

What Is Leveraging?

Tim's *Brilliant Compensation* offers one of the more brilliant explanations of leverage I've heard.

"Let's say that I'm a real estate broker and I hire an agent named Robert. Robert goes out and sells a building and earns a commission on the selling price of the building. Why do I, the broker, earn a percentage when it was Robert who sold the building? Well, I did some of the advertising; I trained Robert; I had the initiative to go get my brokerage license in the first place; I put up the risk; I did a lot of things. It is valid that I earn my money. But Robert doesn't work for me as an employee. He just hangs his real estate license on my wall. A broker and agent have the same amount to gain from the sale of a home. So it is a form of leverage for the broker.

"There is a flaw in this leverage situation. The broker can have multiple agents, but the agent cannot. The broker has leverage; the agents don't, until the agents do what most brokers dread. What happens when I, the broker, have been really effective at teaching Robert to be a good agent? What is Robert going to want to do in a couple of years? Be his own broker, right? Is this good for me? No. Because as soon as he becomes a broker, two bad things happen to me: (1) he breaks away from me and I lose him as an income source; (2) worse than that, he's now my competitor whom I trained. He knows all my good stuff. By the way, this doesn't just happen in the real estate industry; it happens in every industry. If you are a business owner, how many people have you trained that are no longer working for you? And it gets worse.

"Let's say that Robert is now a broker right down the street. What will he do now that he's a broker? He'll go out and hire his own agents. And let's say one of his agents is Linda, who will eventually also want to be a broker. So now, she too becomes a competitor whom I indirectly trained in addition to Robert whom I directly trained. I am responsible for having created a chain of competitors whom I trained.

"What if we did a whole new paradigm shift? This is where this becomes brilliant. Let's say instead that I am going to empower Robert to become a broker. I want him to become a broker from day one. See, the only way that you and I can retain a leader is to provide him with the same opportunity for growth that we have; hence, an opportunity where everyone has the same amount to gain. From day one, I am going to encourage Robert to be a broker. He doesn't break away from me and become my competitor. Rather, he shifts from agent to broker, which now allows him to sponsor his own agents. To create an incentive (for me) to always help Robert and his agents, I'm still going to earn a percentage of what he and his agents sell. After all, I trained him. I put up the risk. And all those reasons I mentioned earlier. Now the percentage I earn should be a lot smaller than when he was an agent. But I should still earn a percentage. That is my incentive to keep working with him.

"Now some people would say, 'Isn't that one of those pyramids?' What is people's perception of a pyramid? The people at the top make all the money and the people down below do all the work. Let me explain why this is not a pyramid and why the people at the top do not necessarily make all the money. It is not the geometric shape that people have a problem with. This is probably the shape of your family tree, the shape of our government. To the architect, it is the strongest structure known to man. Every organizational structure known to man is this shape. So the shape isn't the problem. It's the misperception that the people at the top earn all the money that is the problem.

130

> # Why should only one person get compensated for the efforts of the entire organization? From the perspective of a network marketer...everyone should benefit equally from a leveraged opportunity.

"Let me illustrate that for you. At the top you have a CEO, chief executive officer. Does the president under him earn more money than the CEO? How about below the president? Do any of the vice-presidents earn more than the president? No. Let me ask you this question, and I want you to really think about it. What would happen if some of the vice-presidents made more money than the president? Talk about total confusion. This whole process is called delegation. Each level of the corporation earns less income. The reason presidents can tell the vice-presidents what to do is because they make more money. The reason middle managers can tell the staff and employees what to do is that they make more money. So the corporate structure is people at the top make the majority of the money, and people at the bottom are paid less. The CEO of any corporation earns off the productivity, or is leveraged off, of everyone in his or her corporation, whether that CEO personally hires everyone or whether someone else in the company hires them. The CEO, and only the CEO, earns on multiple levels of that company."

How Can Leveraging Work for Me?

Why should only one person get compensated for the efforts of the entire organization? From the perspective of a network marketer, that doesn't sound fair. In our mentality, everyone should benefit equally from a leveraged opportunity.

Brilliant Compensation then shows how effective leveraging can be.

"What is the maximum number of hours you can work in a day? 24 hours, right? So if you didn't sleep all day for a whole day, you could actually put in 24 hours. If you didn't sleep for a whole year, you could put in 8,760 hours per year. But that is the maximum number of hours you could work in an entire year."

Tim and his partner have 56,000 people in their entire organization worldwide. Let's suppose that they all worked only one hour out of a year. That's 56,000 hours that he is being paid on. For most people to earn on 56,000 hours of work, they would have to work 6.4 years without any sleep to put in the same amount of hours that he could in one leveraged hour per year. Now let's consider something really ridiculous. Let's suppose that all 56,000 people worked one eight-hour day in a year. That's 448,000 hours he is being paid for. It would take most people working over 51 years for 24 hours a day to make what he makes through one leveraged day out of every year.

"The model that I am suggesting as brilliant," concludes Tim, "is where you as an individual are given that same opportunity to earn on multiple levels of brokers and agents, just as the CEO of a corporation is.

"Network marketing is the most ethical business I have ever seen in my life," Tim concludes. "And the reason I say that is because my success and your success are forever intertwined if I sponsor you. I can't change that. I can't fire you. Nor would I want to. So it is far better to be sponsored into a network marketing 'pyramid' than hired by a corporation. Network marketing companies are making so many dollars available to distributors that it has now become a true profession."

Won't the Market Eventually Be Saturated?

This is one of the greatest misunderstandings of the industry: the fear that the last people to sign up won't have anyone left to sponsor. The reality is that people and products change too quickly for any company to ever reach market saturation. I don't know of anyone who doesn't have a TV, and yet they are among the hottest selling items today. Someone will always want a new one, a bigger one, an extra one, or one with more bells and whistles.

The advertising world has taught us that there is a dramatic difference between exposure and participation. While a large number of people may hear about something, only a percentage will buy it. By the time everyone in the entire world has been exposed to a concept, there is always a new assemblage of people who forgot they heard it, or just moved here, graduated from school, lost their jobs, or changed their minds.

> # Network marketing companies are making so many dollars available to distributors that it has now become a true profession.

Mark Yarnell cited a humorous example in *Success* magazine in September, 1993.

In 1975, the Federal Trade Commission (FTC) sued a lingerie MLM called Ger-Ro-Mar as a deception pyramid because of the "inherent inevitability of eventual market saturation." The FTC calculated that "if each participant in the plan recruited five new distributors a month, in a mere 12 months the number of participants would exceed 244 million." But the judge in the case ruled in favor of Ger-Ro-Mar, rebuffing the FTC with the following: "We...agree that the prospect of a quarter billion brassiere and girdle hawkers is not only impossible, but frightening to contemplate....However, we live in a real world, not a fantasyland."

CHAPTER 9

Working at Home with Family
and Creating Extended Family

In the past, MLM has been known to antagonize families and cause rifts between closest friends; in some cases it has even come between husbands and wives. Network marketing of today is developing a reputation for uniting families on a much deeper level and in fact creating extended families.

MLM Brings Families Closer

Every family has a central player. In the Valenty family it is John, whose entrepreneurial spirit displayed itself at an early age. By the time he was nine years old, John was making several hundred dollars a month running a lawn-mowing service for the neighbors. Bored by school, he was the kid in the classroom that teachers couldn't figure out how to reach. He didn't like school but loved to learn. At age 15, he became interested in personal development. He started learning from Zig Ziglar, Og Mandino, and Jim Rohn at this very early age. He bought and ran a car-detailing franchise in high school and managed to out-earn some of his teachers. Dropping out of school after his junior year to focus his full attention on his business, before long he found that he was grossing more than $250,000 a year.

But by the summer of 1995, continually pouring more and more money into the business, John's debts and expenses were far outweighing his income. At age 22, he was no longer feeling successful at all. John had accumulated over $100,000 in high interest debt and no matter how many hours he worked, he couldn't seem to make a dent in it. Since working more hours was not a solution (he was already working all of the hours he could), he felt he had no choice but to find his next entrepreneurial adventure.

It is not difficult to understand where John got his drive. His mom, Janet, was one of the first women to earn a six-figure salary as a corporate executive in southern California. She and Steve Stanfield, who was an executive with a large clinical lab when they met, resided in a comfortable, middle-class home, where Steve's two young children from a prior marriage had come to live with them. Janet's job was stressful and demanding, and left little time for her to be a stepmother to Steve's children. When Steve became a victim of corporate downsizing, Janet had to continue her grueling schedule for the family. By the summer of 1995, she felt that "the light at the end of the tunnel was an oncoming train."

It was during this period of transition and deep dissatisfaction for both mother and son that John was introduced to a network marketing opportunity. Janet was circumspect, concerned about John's growing debt. She knew her son well enough to know that, once he focused on a new business, it would be the end of his old one. She was right.

John's brother, Michael, was incredulous at this new venture. "When are you going to stop fooling around and get a real job?" he teased his brother. Michael was the pragmatist in the family, planning a career as an electrical engineer.

But John was not discouraged by his family's reaction. He knew he would have to prove himself before either of them would take his latest risk-taking seriously.

"I wasn't going to be like so many people who set themselves up for failure by applying more value to their family's disapproval than they do to their own decision-making ability," John recalls. "I didn't try to persuade my mother or Michael to do the business with me. I just told them my goals and plans and invited them to join me when and if they felt comfortable."

Plunging enthusiastically into his new business, John was faced with the common challenge of being broke and in debt. Every penny he could squeeze out of his automotive business immediately went towards his looming debts.

John made one of the most difficult decisions in his life: to throw all his energy and focus into network marketing. Knowing there was no turning back, John went for it with all the enthusiasm and energy he could. "Knowing that at any given moment I was only a couple of payments away from bankruptcy, I didn't let anything or anyone get in the way of success," John says.

At the time, John didn't have enough money to eat, let alone advertise or buy supplies. His solution was to leverage his time with other people's money. His first recruits were reluctant to jump in the business full time, so John offered to help them by working leads for them while they were at work. "They paid for the advertising, and I worked the leads night and day."

John was convinced that he could sponsor hundreds of people if he could just get enough marketing pieces to the right people. His excitement about lead generation sparked a few people to join his downline. Some of them invested in direct marketing supplies on the promise that John would help them work the leads they generated. Within 30 days, John was sending out audiotapes, fliers, fax broadcasts, placing classified ads, and, of course, engaged in a multitude of business presentations. After hundreds of hours on the phone, John drew his first commission check, for $136. With over $300 in long-distance telephone bills alone, it would be easy to conclude that his new venture was not faring well.

John could see where this was leading, whether anyone else could or not. He poured even more of himself into his business, and the next month received a check for over $2,000 as 300 people purchased products from his organization. The growth pleased him, but his bills were piling up fast. He had to build faster in order to stay ahead of his creditors from his previous business. He set a new goal of bringing in 700 new distributors throughout his organization for the next month, a goal that he openly shared with his mother and everyone in his group. Visualizing this goal, John's next month's check vaulted to $8,200. Janet knew by this time that her son was on to something and began actively reaching out to the rest of the family, including her mother, Helen, and her son, Michael, both of whom reluctantly signed up. In the early months of 1996, John's downline grew at an unbelievable pace.

Within five months, John became the number one earner in his company and his mother was the number two earner. Janet's mother, Helen, was living on a fixed income with Janet's father, Henry, in a remote little town in Washington State. Despite her resistance, she found herself submerged in business. Never having sold anything in her life, she was surprised to discover that she actually enjoyed talking to people about these nutritional products.

Helen brought her other daughter, Barbara, into the business. After a fall that left her emotionally devastated and physically challenged, Barbara gained a new lease on life.

"It was a tremendous boost for me, psychologically," Barbara says. "Suddenly I was reaching out to help others, instead of asking them to help me. This is a wonderful business in that you only help yourself by helping others. I went from being in a down mode to being eager every morning to get out of bed and get started."

Even Michael, the shy brother and "doubting Thomas," gradually transformed into a confident businessman who engendered the respect of his downline. It was a very special moment of celebration in the Valenty family the day that Janet was making enough to quit her corporate job. It was another rewarding milestone for John when his father, Jack, signed up after holding out for nearly a year and a half.

Then came Shelleen Egelhoff, a single mom with a three-year-old son. Raised with entrepreneurial parents and discovering on her own the parental and financial constraints of working in a corporation, Shelleen was determined to find an income source that would allow her to work at home and raise her son. It was Shelleen's mother who first became interested in John Valenty's company and made an appointment to meet him. Shelleen decided to go along and agreed to take notes for her mother.

"During the drive to San Diego, my mom told me that John was famous for breaking sales records. He was the new guru of the industry. What she failed to tell me was that he was only 23. So when this guy answered the door in a T-shirt, sweats, and bare feet, I asked him if his dad was home. My mom was mortified."

Despite his youth, John gave them enough information to convince them to sign up with the company and join his team.

Building her business on a shoestring, in the first 45 days Shelleen earned a commission of just over $500. Using John's business strategies, his ads, and his phone scripts, but doing the business entirely on her own, within the next three months she built her income to $4,500 while caring for her son. The next time she ran into John, her business was expanding

> # The Valenty family has earned nearly $9 million of combined commissions over the last three years, with John himself earning $2.9 million in a single year.

and she had just been "pinned" an Executive Diamond Team leader, earning a commission of just over $8,400 that month. By the time her check reached $10,000, John asked her out on a real date. Their love and business blossomed together, and, five months later, when she achieved $20,000 in monthly commissions, he asked her to be his wife. If it were anybody but her upline, she might have thought he was marrying her for her money.

Today, John and Shelleen have all of their own family and a colossal extended family in their organization. Their team has generated nearly two-thirds of the $411 million in sales for their company, of which $220 million has been paid out in commissions among their part-time and full-time team members. The Valenty family has earned nearly $9 million of combined commissions over the last three years, with John himself earning $2.9 million in a single year. Shelleen's distributorship personally earned her over $250,000 in a single year before she and John were married. Not bad for a couple of kids in their 20s!

Although they've earned millions, John and Mike Valenty are still working harder than ever, pursuing their dreams once again as a family. They've founded Earnware Corporation, which is a technology-based company designed to help entrepreneurs and networkers reach their fullest earning potential through phone messaging. (To learn more about the Earnware technology, see the Resource section at the back of this book.) Through their company, John, Janet, and Mike are able to share their direct marketing experience with thousands of networkers throughout the industry. It is their deep-seated belief that they not direct anyone to any specific networking opportunity because they believe in the power of networking in general, not just in one specific company.

The Valenty family story truly is a lesson of family values—working together, building together, and becoming closer as a family.

The Second Generation of Networkers

Warren and Mary Nelson are familiar with the price of success in the corporate world. Before entering the field of network marketing, Mary was a $10 million producer, earning a six-figure income, with a top real estate firm. Warren, who holds an MBA from Harvard Business School, was a top-level executive for an electronics company.

It was Mary who was first introduced to network marketing through a colleague realtor.

Mary was open to looking at new alternatives. During her last year in real estate, she worked 274 days in a row, including holidays. Initially, Warren only looked into the business to prevent Mary from making a mistake.

"I had gotten used to her six-figure income, so I thought I'd poke holes in the concept of network marketing. But very quickly I saw a compensation plan that rewards people who are willing to work, distributing better products at better prices."

Within 12 months, working just part-time in 1990, Warren's corporate salary had been matched by his network marketing commission, so he made the decision to go full-time. Soon after, Mary retired from real estate to join him.

The Nelsons now have the time freedom they've always wanted. They work from an office in their Lake Mills, Wisconsin home, that overlooks its own beautiful lake, as well as from their cabin at Lake Tahoe, Nevada.

"Before getting involved in network marketing, I had no tax write-offs," explains Warren. "So I decided that snow-skiing trips where I could meet prospective business partners were going to be part of my business expense and tax deduction. Having invited my then 12-year-old son to join me, he was sitting in the back of the room during my network marketing training sessions soaking up the information. When we got home, he offered to run around the neighborhood and make retail sales, if he could keep the profits. By the time he was 16, he co-signed with his grandmother so he could have his own distributorship.

Today, the Nelsons' son, Matt, and daughter, Beth, are both putting themselves through college with the income they created through their own network marketing business.

Matt is the first student I've known who is pursuing a B.S. in network marketing at the University of Minnesota.

Choosing Success and Our Children

The biggest reason Connie Dugan chose a home-based business was her children. Long before becoming involved with network marketing, Connie Dugan was already a home-business owner; she owned a successful temp agency for dental hygienists. Though the hours were grueling, the business allowed her to run it from home where she could care for her baby. When she and her husband, Richard, had their second baby, she sold the business and started a new life with her family on Hilton Head Island, South Carolina. After looking at over 60 businesses and having three negotiations fall through, the couple began to have second thoughts about investing their entire savings into another business that may or may not be successful.

Connie was looking for something that would complement her previous professional work but would not risk the life's savings that she and her husband had accumulated. In 1990, Connie discovered the network marketing company with which she would spend the next decade. She came across a classified ad in a dental hygienist magazine: "Earn what you're worth. Work from your home. Flex hours, unlimited earning potential..."

Her greatest concern was that this kind of business would be perceived as unprofessional. She continued to be apprehensive until she received literature from the company and found a glowing product endorsement from a dentist who was one of her largest accounts from her former temp agency. "I thought, 'If he shares that dream and vision, why can't I?' So I took the leap."

Looking back, Connie finds several elements contributed to her success. She treated her home business like big business, structuring her schedule and plugging into every available technology. She wrote an annual business plan with quarterly milestones and received consistent help from mentors along the way. She became a student of the industry, examining the systems of all the top leaders. And, perhaps most importantly, she invested in her own personal development.

"To the degree that I improve myself, I will be a magnet for leaders to be attracted to me. And because of the personal growth I've experienced, I am a more powerful person today," she says.

Connie subscribes resolutely to the belief that success is directly correlated to how well we develop our life skills of communication, listening, accountability, compassion, setting goals, and follow-through. Part of Connie's personal mission is to be an example to other women in this industry.

"Network marketing can free women from the captivities of life, and I intend to partner with as many women as possible to share that message and that possibility.

"Over the last 10 to 20 years, I have been in touch with so many women who are in the corporate rat race, trying to work their way up the ladder. You wouldn't believe how many of them have been extremely disappointed, frustrated, maybe even in lawsuits over the fact that they are so often viewed by their bosses or companies as not being able to pull off mother-hood and be in business at the same time. They've actually been bypassed when advancements or opportunities came up in their companies because they were contemplating having a baby, starting to look pregnant, or nurs-ing. In network marketing, there are successful mothers all over the place. I believe we are collectively counteracting the stigma we face in the cor-porate world, because the truth is that women can work at peak and be great mothers."

Connie's message to women is an uplifting one:

"We can make it in this business. We can reduce the stress in our lives. We can have babies earlier, we can stay at home, and we can make way more money in networking than we can in the traditional workplace. I think that a lot of success in network marketing is building relationships, and women are just naturals at that. As women we often shortchange our-selves and forget to realize what amazing innate life skills we have. Those very life skills can make us rich in every sense of the word in network marketing."

> As women we often shortchange ourselves and forget to realize what amazing innate life skills we have. Those very life skills can make us rich in every sense of the word in network marketing.

Renewed Meaning to Time with Family

Tom Bissmeyer was taught the old-school method of success: get a good education, work hard, and keep your record clean. Graduating with a master's degree in Business Finance in 1985, he was recruited to be part of the capital acquisition team for a large real estate development company. After his group received a miniscule bonus for bringing in over $100 million in financing in one year, Tom decided to start his own speaking, training, and consulting business. He soon found himself working seven days a week and traveling in excess of 250 days a year. From a financial perspective, it was great, but from a family and life perspective, he felt bankrupt.

"I remember hearing the first words from my daughter over the telephone and learning about her first steps the same way, important events that, no matter how much money I made, could never be replaced. I missed them and it hurt. When my wife, Lynne, delivered our second child in 1992, I took off for three weeks to be with our young family. The whole time I felt pulled. My family needed me and I wanted to be there, but I lost over $40,000 in income because I wasn't working. I felt like I couldn't win."

It was while facing this quandary that Tom began to look at network distribution. He had been exposed to the industry over the years and had the perceptions that many professionals have: pyramid scheme, scam, massive failures, damaged relationships, not a salesperson, etc. He decided to base his decision on facts, not preconceived notions. The more he read and learned about the industry, the more he realized that network marketing was his escape hatch and his ticket to having the lifestyle he wanted.

"It offered me everything. I could work part-time and, when I was ready, I could then move into it full-time. It could afford me a leveraged income— one not dependent solely on my efforts," he says. "It offered unlimited income potential, knowing, of course, that it would take hard work to make it to the top. It offered a flexible schedule that I could design around my consulting/speaking business and my family. I could choose whom I would work with. The start-up capital was very low. I could work out of my home and utilize the skills I had already developed. And, most importantly, I would own it. There was no other business that I was considering that would offer all this."

He entered the industry of network marketing in the spring of 1993.

"At first I had the normal fears that most professionals have when they begin this business," he recalls. "What are my family and friends going to think? How will my colleagues look at me? Can I do it? What if I fail? ...

Et cetera. At first, some people thought I was crazy. My wife wasn't all that excited either. But I knew that if I didn't initiate some changes in my life, I would still be in the same place five years from now."

Tom's motivation was strong. The fact that corporate America was on a downsizing trend furthered his determination. The last thing he wanted was to be 55 years old and have a company tell him that he was no longer needed. For Tom, going into network marketing was no riskier than trying to make it to the top in corporate America.

"Today, I enjoy everything I set out to do," he says. "My income this year will approach seven figures and I fully anticipate that it will double in the next 24 months. Corporate America was never going to pay me this kind of income. However, the money isn't the part that I am the most excited about. Recently, I had an experience that reminded me of what my networking business really meant to me. Lynne was on the computer e-mailing some friends; our daughter was at my desk doing her homework; our son was drawing on my white board; the dog was lying in front of the fireplace; and I was doing a conference call for one of my distributors. Money can't replace what we, as a family, experience at these times.

"By taking that leap of faith, I learned an important lesson: the most painful thing to experience in life is not defeat, but regret. My life is on an entirely new and better course because I dared to step out of my comfort zone. And now I have the privilege of helping countless other profession-als do the same."

Creating Family through International Friendships

Mary Lou Wilson is a septuagenarian enjoying her "golden years" with a lifestyle devoted to building relationships. Although she has been in-volved in the networking industry for more than 20 years, it wasn't until January 1991, already past retirement age, that Mary Lou first heard about the network marketing company with which she is now affiliated.

"Had I known that I would have found my 'dream job' only nine years ago, after a lifetime of career choices, I probably would go back some-where around the year 1980 and just hang on for the ride!" she says.

As a young girl growing up in New England, Mary Lou Wilson learned the value of hard work. When she was six years old, her parents were divorced. By age ten, Mary Lou began working in a vegetable factory to help her mother support herself and her three children. These early expe-riences prepared Mary Lou for the business world, where she worked as a

> I knew that if I didn't initiate some changes in my life, I would still be in the same place five years from now.

financial advisor and owned and operated one of the largest show-dog kennels in the world. It was there that she met her husband, Bob.

"We alone are the masters of our own destiny, so the choices that we make are the threads with which we weave the fabric of our lives," mused Mary Lou. Bob, a retired airline pilot who survived no less than 55 combat missions in World War II, was not particularly eager at first. But today he is pleased to be involved in the business with his wife.

"Those early days consisted of lots of cold-call selling as I set out each morning armed with my personal testimonial and a station wagon filled with boxes of Nature's Tea," she says. "Events began generating a momentum of their own as I improved the well-being of others and helped thousands of people improve the quality of their lives. I became fascinated with learning and the more knowledge I gained, the better I became at building an organization. When my company opened for business in Japan I was well prepared."

Japan, the most successful country for network marketing, even above the United States, is definitely a critical market. Fortunes can be made in that one country alone.

With the launch of this exciting foreign market, Mary Lou sponsored three people on her first level and worked diligently with them to sign up a group of 379 distributors, who expanded over the following three months to a downline of more than 15,000 Japan-based distributors. Nine months later, in March 1999, that number had tripled.

"I was intensely driven by my desire to show people that being a woman in my 70s was no barrier to this kind of accomplishment," she says.

"My philosophy is centered around the value I place on my first level distributors. They are the real assets of the business. Without them, we have nothing. I consider it a privilege, along with good business sense, to hold their hands and go the extra mile, always letting them know how much I appreciate them and their efforts. I am extremely grateful to do something which allows my wonderful husband and me the financial freedom to enjoy so much and bring so many wonderful people into our lives."

Today, Mary Lou has about 60,000 distributors in her organization moving just under $5 million of product throughout six different countries. She has co-authored with Dr. Gordon Pedersen, the book, *Seeds of Life,* a self-help approach to natural alternatives using vitamins, minerals, herbs, and food supplements.

"Network marketing allows common people to produce uncommon results. Even at the age of 70, it is not too late to seize the number one position in a company. If I did it, others can do it. We put our faith in the company and its products, but it is the friendships that actually make it grow."

Extended Network Marketing Family

Growing up a war orphan in World War II and serving as an infantry squad leader in the Marine Corps during combat in the Vietnam War, Frank Keefer finally found a secure home and family in network marketing. Wounded in action, he was commissioned an officer for combat leadership. An Honors alumnus from the University of Baltimore, Frank completed four years of undergraduate studies in two, graduating at the top of his class. With such distinctions in his favor, employment opportunities should have been readily available for him. But with anti-war sentiment still strong at the time, it took more than 50 interviews to land a job as a high school teacher. Then came divorce, ten years raising his children as a single parent, and finally meeting his new wife, Gingie, whom he describes as the love of his life.

Frank was intrigued by network marketing's emphasis on leverage and timing, two elements that Frank had learned were critical to financial suc-

> Japan, the largest market for network marketing, even above the United States, is definitely a critical market. Fortunes can be made in that one country alone.

cess. One of his strongest beliefs is in the critical importance of selective sponsoring.

"As we strive for professionalism and more favorable public acceptance as a legitimate business, we can no longer afford to litter the countryside with MLM casualties and failures," he says. "By association, every distributor who fails, hurts us as an industry and collectively indicts us all as scam artists. Success for many network marketers, not just a few, will do more than anything else to enhance the industry image and place us in the forefront of product and service distribution where we belong."

At his very first meeting, Frank poses the single most important question of the entire interview to his prospective business partners: "What do you really want to do with your life?" Whether a follow-up interview ensues rests on the conviction of their answers. Frank's strategy was to identify 12 leaders who in turn would commit to helping 12 others do the same.

"I'm in the business of developing self-reliance, building leaders, and creating duplication of the process."

His basic philosophy is that successful sponsoring is a process rather than an event. Through a series of appointments before an application is ever filled out, Frank takes each prospect through those tasks necessary for success. Based on the outcome, he and his prospective partner then decide whether they want to join forces in business.

Working in the networking industry since 1988, Frank Keefer is a sought-after speaker and author of *Let's Get Down to Business* (1990). Stricken with health problems two years ago that forced his retirement, he is now serving as CEO for the magazine, *Network Marketing Lifestyles*. Of his numerous accomplishments, Frank is most proud of the fact that his networking organization enjoys some of the highest commissions in the company, producing millions of dollars per year in actual bonuses. Through this industry, Frank has created his own family and has been able to help many others achieve their dreams.

His many life experiences have taught Frank what truly counts in life. His relationship to his wife is his number one priority.

"While we enjoy the lifestyle, Gingie and I have learned that we'd trade it all if the cost was time away from each other and our families. With our networking business, fortunately, it's simply not an issue."

> The family is still the basic unit of our society.
> Network marketing not only understands that,
> but from its earliest onset has refined its very
> structure around this principle.

These family stories are at the heart of the power and effectiveness of network marketing. This is where corporate America has failed us culturally. It has forgotten that the family is still the basic unit of our society. Network marketing not only understands that, but from its earliest onset has refined its very structure around this principle.

CHAPTER 10

Finding a Sense of Purpose

and Leaving a Legacy

You may have heard about the two shoe salesmen who were assigned to check out the outback of Australia as a possible location for a new branch for their company. Within the first 24 hours the first rep called back.

"Forget it! Don't even think of expanding into this part of the world. These people don't wear shoes."

Another couple of days passed before the second agent was heard from.

"We've got a gold mine here," he shouted into the phone. "You won't believe it. Send every shape, size, and color. These people haven't even heard of shoes yet!"

There will always be both kinds of people who look at our industry and respond in much the same way.

"It's a pyramid scheme!" cry out the non-believers.

"It's a cash cow just waiting to be milked!" exclaim its supporters.

The facts are the same; only the outlook varies.

Attitude Is Key to Success

People fail in business not because success isn't possible, but because they can't picture themselves achieving prosperity through that particular medium. Usually fear holds them back: fear of failure, fear of what others might think, fear of approaching people, even fear of success. Learning to exercise control over our own attitudes is the key to life. When a marriage ends, we can choose to embrace the notion that we have been abandoned or that we have been released. When a business partnership is brought to an abrupt closure, we can elect to adopt the outlook that we have been rejected or that we have been freed to go on with our life. Both viewpoints are open to us. The power is within us to choose our own attitudes. Sometimes it takes time to transition from the negative to the positive. The sooner we assume a confident belief about ourselves and how we will approach any situation, the faster we can move into a productive realm.

Disappointments come readily in this business. Our attitude has to be one of appreciation for all the good that comes and not be held captive by the letdowns that inevitably go with network marketing. In some ways, we need to develop the trust of a child. Like the boy playing Little League who told his dad as he arrived late that they were behind by 14 to nothing.

"You don't seem too discouraged!" his dad replied.

"Discouraged?" the boy asked with a puzzled look on his face. "Why should I be discouraged? We haven't been up to bat yet!"

The Art of Visualization

How do you evolve from the reality staring you in the face to the vision of how you want your life to be? Begin by visualizing the outcome long before it ever happens. Say to yourself, "It's possible that this positive outcome could happen...even though it isn't happening now." Think in the future tense and visualize the goals as already having been accomplished. Permit yourself to feel the feelings as if the dream were happening now. Focus more on the end result, and don't let your mind get bogged down with how it will happen. The only thing that can suppress growth is if you

> People fail in business not because success isn't possible, but because they can't picture themselves achieving prosperity through that particular medium.

are locked into your present reality so strongly that your vision of what you really want cannot overcome it.

It is normal to feel this battle waged within your psyche: reality versus vision. No, vision versus reality. As long as reality is on top, growth is stifled. When vision wins out, change is effected.

How do you keep the vision stronger than the reality? With affirmations. An affirmation is a trigger tool, a statement of belief written in present tense and repeated as if the goal were already an accomplished fact. This is not "airy fairy" make-believe. The principle and efficacy of affirming your vision has been validated by such people as Dr. Albert Bandura of Stanford University, by Lou Tice of the Pacific Institute in Seattle, by Dr. Charles Garfield at the Performance Sciences Institute at Berkeley, and by Dr. Lou Tartaglia of the Tartaglia Mind Institute.

Here's how it works: You visualize the new, and believe vehemently that what you see is possible. You can actually see yourself there. You gradually become dissatisfied with the way things are and begin to shed your former behavior. Affirmations keep you focused on your vision and on track to pursue your life's purpose.

Real Life Problem Solving

Visualization does not take the place of good old-fashioned, down-to-earth problem solving. If there are real hurdles to be faced, work through them. If you need a babysitter, hire one. If you need to take a part-time job or drop one, create the necessary structure or space in your life. If you need to carve out time by giving up something else, just focus and do it.

It is like the story of the Arabian sheik who died and left his sons his entire estate, consisting of 17 camels. To his eldest son, he bequeathed one half of his estate, to his middle son, one third, and to his youngest son, one ninth. Puzzled as to how to carry out the wishes of their father, they turned to their father's best friend, who served as the executor of the estate. A man of modest means, the wise man offered to lend his only camel to the bereaved sons as a means of resolving their dilemma. Now, returning home with the additional camel, the heirs were now in possession of eighteen camels. To the eldest among them, they assigned one half of the estate: nine camels. To the middle son, they assigned one third: six camels. To the youngest, they assigned one ninth: two camels. Nine plus six plus two totaled 17. With one remaining camel, they returned it to their father's most kind and judicious friend.

When tangible impediments stand in the way of pursuing your purpose, do whatever it takes to rectify them. Utilize the art of visualization with affirmations to keep you on track with your purpose.

Define Your Purpose

Have you given much thought to your preeminent life purpose? What I mean by that is a definition I have developed over the years:

Your Preeminent Purpose is your primary, ultimate, lifetime objective toward which all life's experiences lead, the accomplishment of which determines your true identity, the importance of which supersedes all other endeavors, giving overall direction to your life.

So many people, including the acclaimed Stephen Covey, author of *The Seven Habits for Highly Effective People*, are now endorsing our industry as a way of life. "Network marketing has come of age. It's become undeniable that it has become a way to entrepreneurship and independence for millions of people."

In a recent interview, when asked which aspects of the seven habits network marketing distributors needed to focus on the most, his response was, "I would say, habit number two: 'Begin with the End in Mind.' Develop a personal mission statement or a clear sense of purpose, a sense of your values." Of all seven habits, even Covey sees being driven by a purpose as the most critical.

Network marketing is a profession intended to provide us with the means to achieve our end. It is not designed to absorb our entire life for the rest of our life. Rather, it is a vehicle that, for many of us, after a few years of intense effort, provides the time and financial freedom to pursue our real life purpose.

It is all part of a magnificent telescope that allows us to bring into focus our long-range goals, then our shorter-term goals, then the specific mission we are undertaking, and finally a business plan for making our venture serve our ultimate purpose. As we implement our daily action plan, always within our distant vision is our reason for enduring the hardships and daily challenges that we will inevitably face in our business. Everything we do should focus on our major purpose in life, and all of our goals support us in the effort to become the kind of person we wish to be.

> So many people...are now endorsing our industry as a way of life.... "It has become a way to entrepreneurship and independence for millions of people." — Stephen Covey

80% Why and 20% How

Continually in search of a medium that would fulfill his purpose in life, John Busswood, soon after his graduation from the University of British Columbia, followed his entrepreneurial spirit into a career in real estate. It was the right choice, and for the first few years he excelled. Then in 1982, the shocking recession came with its 22-percent interest rates. Almost overnight, John Busswood was financially and emotionally devastated. As an interim solution, he fulfilled his boyhood dream of serving as a firefighter.

During this time, his searching spirit came alive again. He and his wife, Sherrie, began looking for alternatives that would support the lifestyle that they so desperately desired. One standard guided their choices. John knew he had to be his own boss. Sherrie, from a successful corporate marketing background, also felt the desire to be self-employed and responsible for her future.

"The first time I learned about network marketing, I was dragged kicking and screaming, to a meeting," John recalls, "and I had absolutely no intention of getting involved! But staying open-minded and learning the truth about it, Sherrie and I realized we didn't have a better alternative to achieve our vision. And just maybe network marketing could be a vehicle to help us do the things we really wanted to do in life. Unfortunately, a year later, we realized in our naïve enthusiasm we had not chosen a legitimate network marketing company, and we ended up losing a great deal of money. We had to sell our spacious, newly-renovated home and move down to a smaller dwelling."

Having been bitten by the MLM bug, and believing in the power of the industry, John and Sherrie decided to try another network marketing opportunity. It too failed them. So they began studying what gives a network marketing company longevity. They found what they considered three key factors:

(1) A company must have great products that work.
(2) The company should be well managed by experienced people who have expertise beyond working in corporate America.
(3) The compensation plan should be fair to the new person as well as the experienced network marketer.

Sherrie and John found a company that met all three criteria. But they faced several challenges when they first started building their business: getting out of their comfort zone, talking to enough people, participating at meetings, and getting more involved. As they found themselves getting more involved, they were naturally further out of their comfort zone. It was a cyclical, self-development process. As they grew, so did their business.

"In a few short months," recalls Sherrie, "we were making more money than we'd ever seen. Our lives changed dramatically. It was when John's monthly bonus check exceeded his annual income as a firefighter, he knew it was time to leave the department and concentrate on this business full-time."

"I'm certain that the key to our success was our persistence," John acknowledged. "We also knew that the only way to get some of the friends we valued involved was to go out and make it happen for ourselves first. There was no question in our mind that the only way we could lose in this business was by quitting.

"The business is 80 percent 'why' and 20 percent 'how.' If you can find a strong enough 'why' with your distributors, they become self-motivated; they can do the business for themselves and they'll have a reason to find out how. If you don't dig down inside a person and find out their reason to get up in the morning, and their reason to pick up that telephone, they're simply not going to succeed at this business."

Determining What Is Really Important in Life

Imagine, hypothetically, that you have just come from seeing your family doctor. After getting a second opinion, you learn that you have a terminal illness and are given no more than five months to live. Would you make a change in your life? Would you, perhaps, quit your job, spend more time with the people you love, travel more, or make amends with someone? Be honest with yourself. If you really believed, right this moment, that you had only a five-month guarantee, would you change anything at all about your life?

Now, leaving the hypothetical world and coming back to your real world...do you have a five-month guarantee now at this very moment? Why wait for a life-threatening crisis to make wanted changes in your life?

Stop waiting until you finish school, until you go back to school, until you lose ten pounds, until you gain ten pounds, until you have kids, until your kids leave the house, until you start work, until you retire, until you get married, until you get divorced, until Friday night, until Sunday morning, until you get a new car or home, until your car or home is paid off, until spring, until summer, until fall, until winter, until you are off welfare, until the first or fifteenth, until your song comes on, until you've had a drink, until you've sobered up, until you die, until you are born again to decide that there is no better time than right now to go for the things in life you really want.

Vivian Thompson owned Financial Seminars, a successful business in the San Francisco Bay area that generated a six-figure income consistently over the 12 years that she owned the business. Although she enjoyed her work, she began to feel that she was on a treadmill and if she slowed down or stopped, so would her income.

"In 1991, an event occurred in my personal life which had a major impact upon me. My only brother, to whom I was very close, died instantly of a massive heart attack while scuba diving," she remembers. "He had no apparent warning. He was only in his 40s, appeared to be in good health, and was in the prime of his life. I was so devastated by the loss that

> If you really believed...that you had only a five-month guarantee, would you change anything at all about your life?...Why wait for a life-threatening crisis to make wanted changes in your life?

155

I was compelled to do some serious soul-searching about what really matters in life. Is it being so busy with work and having our life so out of balance that we have no time to enjoy it with the people we love?"

While still anguishing over her personal loss and searching for answers, she read an article by Dr. Charles King and one by Mark Yarnell in *Success* magazine that changed her perspective on network marketing. Her perception had been that it was a business where you sold products door-to-door, added on to your house to hold inventory, made little or no money, and lost all your friends. Not long after that, she received a network marketing call from a person she knew who had a Ph.D. in business. Her first thought was, if he is doing this, maybe I should at least take a look.

"I joined in January 1994 and, after two years of part-time effort, I was able to sell my seminar business," she says. "Now my networking business is my primary source of income and I have completely replaced my previous income. My time is flexible and this business has given me the freedom to move to Lighthouse, Florida, where I can begin a new life. This is an extraordinary business, with many opportunities for personal growth. But my greatest satisfaction comes from the impact this business has had on my health and the health of so many friends and associates, and the income stream, both primary and secondary, that I have been instrumental in creating for them as well. What they say about this business is really true: if we help enough people achieve their goals, we will inherently achieve our own as well."

Take the time to discover what is important to you and make the life adjustments now, before a life-threatening crisis occurs in your family.

Deciding Your Priorities

One day an expert in time management was speaking to a group of business students and, to drive home a point, used an illustration those students will never forget. As he stood in front of the group of high-powered overachievers he said, "Okay, time for a quiz." Then he pulled out a one-gallon, wide-mouthed mason jar and set it on the table in front of him. Then he produced about a dozen fist-sized rocks and carefully placed them, one at a time, into the jar. When the jar was filled to the top and no more rocks would fit inside, he asked, "Is this jar full?"

Everyone in the class said, "Yes."

Then he said, "Really?" He reached under the table and pulled out a bucket of gravel. Then he dumped some gravel in and shook the jar, caus-

> ### If we help enough people achieve their goals, we will inherently achieve our own as well.

ing pieces of gravel to work themselves down into the space between the big rocks. Then he asked the group once more, "Is the jar full?"

By this time the class was on to him. "Probably not," one of them answered.

"Good!" he replied. He reached under the table and brought out a bucket of sand. He started dumping the sand in the jar and it went into all of the spaces left between the rocks and the gravel. Once more he asked the question, "Is this jar full?"

"No!" the class shouted.

Once again he said, "Good." Then he grabbed a pitcher of water and began to pour it in until the jar was filled to the brim. Then he looked at the class and asked, "What is the point of this illustration?"

One eager beaver raised his hand and said, "The point is, no matter how full your schedule is, if you try really hard you can always fit some more things in it!"

"No," the speaker replied, "that's not the point. The truth this illustration teaches us is this: If you don't put the big rocks in first, you'll never get them in at all. What are the 'big rocks' in your life? Time with your loved ones? Your faith, your education, your dreams? A worthy cause? Teaching or mentoring others? Remember to put these *big rocks* in first or you'll never get them in at all. So, tonight, or in the morning, when you are reflecting on this short story, ask yourself this question: 'What are the 'big rocks' in my life?' Then, put those in your jar first."

A Desire to Own Your Own Life

Having spent the better part of her adult life in and around formal education, Peggy Long has invested the past seven and a half years in network marketing. Raised poor in Chicago as a minister's daughter, her parents always impressed on her the importance of going to school and getting an education. This advice culminated in two-and-a-half masters degrees and a $40,000 tuition debt, which she hoped would bring her security and earn an income worthy of her effort. Peggy spent 30 years building her earnings to a six-figure income. A single mom to two sons during much of this time, she never had the kind of personal freedom she needed in this important role. In 1992 she was downsized from a "secure position" and found herself at age 49 wondering what she would do next.

"I made an internal commitment to myself that I would never ever work for someone else again," she states emphatically. "I was committed to spending summers with my family and friends on our island in Canada. I had heard of network marketing for years, but was such a 'doubting Thomas' that I wouldn't look at, much less touch, anything that closely resembled this kind of pyramid stuff."

Her dad asked her to look at a network marketing company with whom he had just became associated. She said, "No way, Dad," until he asked the magic question, "Do you trust me, Peggy?" Trust is a central theme in Peggy's life. She put aside her prejudices and placed her faith in him and began to see the world with new eyes. The concept of leveraging her time with the efforts of others made sense to her.

Without a coach, she plunged forward, the first year earning $7,000. Obviously she couldn't live on that.

"I came so close to quitting four times, actually," she recalls. "But out of allegiance to my word that no one would ever own my calendar and paycheck again, I just kept taking one more step in spite of the setbacks."

Despite the fact that she was forced to take out all her savings, cash in her IRAs, borrow over $40,000 from family and friends, and hold numerous garage sales just to generate the needed income to keep going, she never developed a poverty mentality.

By the second year in her network marketing business, she was earning $215,000 while driving a new Lexus and living in a beautiful home provided her by the company. Finally, Peggy had the time freedom and lifestyle she always knew would come. Living between the Sonoran desert outside Scottsdale, Arizona, and a family island in Muskoka, Ontario (Canada), she earned over two million dollars in six and a half years.

"So how did all these wonderful changes occur? I became a student of this incredible industry," she explains. "I attended seminars that helped me model the most successful leaders in our industry. I read, listened, and watched every resource material I could get my hands on. I invested and believed in myself. It is especially rewarding to witness the personal growth, expanded leadership, and improved communication that we all inevitably experience, allowing us to live life with passion," she relates.

In her book, *Like a Rock,* Peggy embraces these values, teaching and supporting others to become a leader of leaders through hands-on coaching.

"Now that I have experienced the fun as well as the powerful and lucrative aspects of the network marketing industry," Peggy concludes, "I could never go back to traditional business. I love being part of a team-oriented, integrity-based business that allows me to take full charge of my life, both now and in the future."

Leaving a Legacy Through Network Marketing

You may recognize his face. You've seen him on television and in the movies. He has acted in over 16 films with such legendary stars as Burt Lancaster and Clint Eastwood and he has guest-starred in more than 300 television shows. Jonathan Goldsmith no longer waits around for casting calls. Now he is the one placing the calls as he builds his network marketing organization and helps others do the same.

"My professional life was always dependent on the whims of others," he says. "I wanted some measure of control over my life, but with acting, I never had it. Network marketing allowed me control over my own destiny."

Most professionals don't consider other options at the height of their career. Jonathan was first approached about the network distribution industry by a lawyer who represented a major motion-picture studio at a time when he was between acting jobs. As soon as he realized he was being "prospected" and where this conversation was leading, he interrupted his friend by saying, "Look, I have no money. I can't sell anything. I hate business..." To which his attorney friend retorted, "Hey, big shot, I haven't seen you on television lately."

That was Jonathan's introduction to network marketing, something that he had previously thought of as a joke on the late night show where a bunch of amateurs would make money on their friends, sucking them into some kind of scheme.

Jonathan rose quickly in the company, becoming one of its first presidential directors.

"For the first time in my life, I found a way that I could be at the helm of my own ship."

It was a metaphor appropriate for Jonathan, because as his acting career wound down, he lived on his boat moored in Marina Del Rey. But this moment of distinction didn't last.

Within three years the company went under.

"I ended up sitting on the back of my beautiful boat, my pride and joy, realizing that I had nothing left, and was once again uncertain what to do."

Rather than giving up on the industry, Jonathan sold his boat, and for the next few months lived in an unfurnished apartment sleeping on an L. L. Bean camping mattress. With an unwavering belief in the power of MLM, he joined another company. Here he put 720 people into his organization within the first three months, becoming one of its five divisional heads throughout the world.

"I was on my way back from a meeting in San Francisco when I heard the news about the death of Caesar Chavez, the head of the United Farm Workers and one of my heroes. He was lying in state in the little, dusty town of Delano out in the middle of the agricultural belt in the San Joaquin Valley. Joining with hundreds of others from all over the country, I finally got to the head of the queue where I could offer my respect to this man who had sacrificed his life making strides to improve the lot of his people.

"I looked out over his body and there, working in the field, stooped against the wind and heat, were rows upon rows of laborers. It was at that moment that it really hit me what we have to offer people. No one should have to spend their lives toiling like animals if they don't want to. They don't have to live in desperation and without hope. We were not born to live as mules in harness to anybody else."

Now fully grasping the power and the magic of this industry, Jonathan and his partner started their own network marketing company dedicated to environmentally safe water-saving products that would effectively sell themselves.

"Those drawn to our company came from all walks of life. For the most part, they hadn't been to Ivy League schools but were people driven by a burning desire inside of them and a strong sense of dissatisfaction with their present circumstances. Reaching out to all people, regardless of their backgrounds, became a kind of crusade for me. Network marketing was far more than a money-machine; it became a means to help others reach their goals."

Today Jonathan is beginning again. With the steadfast support of his wife, Margo, who quietly administers the business, Jonathan is back where he feels he can truly be a contributor, "laboring in the field." Traveling the country in his camper, he feels he can inspire other "laborers" to stop standing on the sidelines watching life go by. Rather, it is time to join in the parade, to be proud of what one does, and celebrate life's possibilities. Like Caesar Chavez, it is here that he knows he can best leave his footprints on the earth, forging a path for future generations to follow.

From Overworked Physician to Healthcare Missionary

Neal Secrist was a flight surgeon with the U.S. Air Force who kept up two other emergency medicine practices on the side to pay down over $100,000 in medical school loans. Searching for a way off the treadmill, Neal started two additional home-based businesses only to fail and lose a few thousand dollars before being introduced to network marketing.

"Quite frankly, had I not been shown this business by someone that I had a lot of respect for, I wouldn't have ever taken a serious look," he says. "I have always been somewhat skeptical of these types of operations. But I was impressed with Richard Epley. After all, he was a Ph.D., college professor and a highly successful real estate broker, investor, and national seminar speaker. So as a favor to him, I agreed to check it out. Secretly, my real intention was to expose this charade, but as I began to do my medical research, I discovered that the products were for real."

Neal's next challenge was time. Between his active-duty responsibilities and two other practices, he was already working more than 70 hours a week.

"I stumbled about my early days and months in the business making almost every mistake possible. Much to the happiness of my wife, Kim, after six months I started to see results in the business. After two and a half years part-time, we were generating checks between $5,000 and $8,000 a month. I started wondering what would happen if I put more serious energy into this.

"Now, five years later, working out of our home in Wichita, Kansas, with full-time effort, we are bringing in a solid mid-six-figure income, more than triple what I made as a physician. I still practice medicine one morning a week...because I want to and not because I have to. Best of all, I have more time for my family and to do what I've always wanted to do: missionary work delivering healthcare to the deprived areas of the world. I still come home to find a check in the mailbox which, quite often, has even increased."

Personal Growth, Spiritual Fulfillment

In network marketing, Betty Sung, a Chinese emigrant, saw the potential to be her own boss on her own terms. On May 1, 1988, Betty and I joined the same company that distributed a line of skin care products. Because of the life-changing nature of this event, it was a special day for both of us. My religious background and Betty's strong spiritual penchant bonded us. Over the years, through her divorce and mine, we have preserved our friendship.

Betty is shy when talking about her accomplishments, but I can tell you that her success has been nothing short of sensational. A year after joining the company, she had already attained the distinction of reaching the highest pay level in the company. In time, Betty began traveling to Asia to help our company expand and become a truly international company. Through hard work, self-discipline, leading by example, assuming responsibility, and respecting each person in her group, Betty built one of the largest network marketing organizations in the world, and deservedly has been inducted into the Network Marketing Hall of Fame.

Many people fail in this industry. Betty thinks it is because they do not know the true meaning of network marketing.

"Ours is a people business," she says. "It is a way to help us change ourselves and our lives."

Network marketing is much more about personal growth than about money. There is no standing still in life. If you are not growing, you are already in a process of deterioration.

"By our example," Betty continues, "others will follow suit, generating a strong, stable, loyal group of people. And it is through them that we begin to generate a good income."

Betty is the epitome of someone who subscribes to ours being a business of building relationships, lifetime relationships. She truly loves and cares about her people. More than 200 leaders in her organization have

> I have more time for my family and to do what I've always wanted to do: missionary work delivering healthcare to the deprived areas of the world.

> People today are looking for a business that is honest. As we continue to attract these kinds of people, we can be assured that our industry will last forever.

reached the top of the pay plan and are living their dreams. This spirit is spreading throughout the 300,000 distributors in her organization, stretching to 27 countries.

Betty has changed the lives of many people as she goes from country to country working with her primarily Asian groups. Choosing to live in a simple hotel suite in Taipei, she commands deep respect as a person who is in the process of deepening her wisdom, discovering her serenity, and continually striving to learn and grow as a person. She enjoys the process of traveling and teaching these concepts to others.

"People today are looking for a business that is honest. As we continue to attract these kinds of people, we can be assured that our industry will last forever," she says.

Network marketing offers a true sense of purpose, unlimited altruistic options, and, if we continue to exercise the values that mean so much to us, it can be an industry that exudes fundamental integrity.

PART III

The Evolution and Expectations of the Network Distribution Industry

"Creative leaders look ahead, learn from the past, and turn their whole vision toward the wider context of present realities."
—*Warren Bennis*

CHAPTER 11

From Single-Level to Multi-Level Marketing: 1941-1979

History gives us a perspective and prepares us for what is to come. It helps us understand the philosophy and basic principles upon which the future is built. Multi-Level Marketing has evolved over the past six decades. Although it has struggled for acceptance and credibility as a legitimate method for marketing products and services, over the years it has remained surprisingly true to its fundamental beliefs in personal relationships, human dignity, promotion of worthy causes, freedom, and family values.

Network Market and Direct Selling

"Direct selling is the sale of consumer products and services in a face-to-face manner, away from a fixed retail location," explains Neil Offen, President of the Direct Selling Association (DSA). "If you line up Avon and Amway side by side, they are both direct-selling companies by that definition. However, Avon traditionally has been single-level and Amway multi-level. Multi-level marketing is a form of direct selling having a compensation system where commissions are earned not only on your own personal sales but on the overrides and bonuses of the sales by those who have been recruited by the people that you recruited." It is simply a way of organizing a direct-selling business.

For participants, apart from the rewards of making personal sales, it offers additional benefits based on the sales of others they have sponsored and whom they train and motivate. A network marketing business is, in effect, a mini-franchise with a low entry cost. Anyone with good organizational skills can build a substantial network marketing business without having to risk their savings or take out a distressing loan from their bank. It is a business you can start with an investment as low as the cost of a business license.

The ratio of single-level versus multi-level direct sales has dramatically changed over the years. Today, more than 80 percent of all direct sales people are moving their products through a multi-level system.

Multi-Level Marketing vs. Pyramid Schemes

One of the most frequently misunderstood issues is the difference between an MLM business and a pyramid scheme. The Federal Trade Commission Consumer Alert offers this distinction:

"Multi-level marketing is a way to sell goods or services through distributors. These plans usually promise that if you sign up to be a distributor, you will receive commissions not only on the sales of goods or services sold by you, but also on the sales of the people you recruit as distributors.

"Pyramid schemes have a similar structure, but a completely different focus. They concentrate on the commissions you earn just for recruiting new distributors, and generally ignore the marketing and selling of products or services.

"Most states outlaw pyramiding. The reason: plans that pay commissions for recruiting new distributors inevitably collapse when new distributors can't be recruited. When a plan collapses, most people—except perhaps those at the very top of the pyramid—lose their money."

Ed Wainscott, an attorney who has represented network marketing companies since 1984, explains the core issue. "What regulatory agencies are looking for is, very simply, whether you in fact are working with a legitimate business that has legitimate products. Is it being consumed or used

A network marketing business is, in effect, a mini-franchise with a low entry cost.

by an end user? As long as distributors are actually going out and marketing a real product or service, they shouldn't have any legal problems. It is those who go out and say, 'Oh, it doesn't make any difference what the product is. We're going to make a million dollars.' They are the ones who cause the most harm to our industry. What is unique about the industry is that you cannot only make a good living, but truly believe that you are benefiting other people while you're doing it."

The Origin of Multi-Level Marketing

The door-to-door salesman of the 1920s and 1930s is the parent of today's multi-level marketing industry. The Fuller Brush Man would knock on your door with a smile on his face, ask you to select a sample brush as a gift, give you a catalog and announce that he would return in a few days for your order. How could you not order something when you returned his catalog to him! And then there was the Hoover Vacuum Man who cleaned your carpet. For many years, a vacuum cleaner was known simply as a "Hoover."

The First Multi-Level Marketers

The first multi-level marketing company is thought to have been organized by psychologist William Casselberry and Lee Mytinger, who sold Nutrilite vitamins through what they called the C & M Marketing Plan.

They had been selling the products of the California Vitamin Company directly since 1934. However, in 1941 they established a new program by which distributors could earn a bonus of 3 percent of the sales by people they personally sponsored into the organization. When sponsors and their recruits had sold $15,000 worth of products, the sponsors could set up their own profitable wholesaler relationship with the people *below* or *downline* from them in the recruiting chain. New wholesalers were called "breakaways" because they had broken from the sponsor's organization to create their own wholesaler relationship to the company. To encourage sponsors to develop successful breakaways—though they would lose profitable wholesaling business—C & M Marketing gave the former sponsor override royalties on the sales of a breakaway's organization of distributors. These distributors were connected financially to the people who sponsored them and to the people they in turn sponsored.

> What is unique about the industry is that you cannot only make a good living, but truly believe that you are benefiting other people while you're doing it.

The Party Plan

During the early years of the industry, 1940s to 1960s, widespread experimentation occurred. The "party plan" of the 1950s is attributed to Frank S. Beveridge, the former Fuller Brush executive who founded Stanley Home Products. Beveridge noted that one distributor in Maine had become exceptionally successful by demonstrating the product to groups of women in private homes. Whether or not he originated this innovation, Beveridge certainly perfected what became known as the "party plan," soon widely copied by other direct-selling organizations.

The party was a more efficient use of the salesperson's time, demonstrating to a roomful of people rather than to one prospective customer. And the hostess did much of the work: issued invitations, served refreshments, provided the location, and probably screened her guests for interest in buying. Although the party plan was an effective way to take advantage of social ties, it was also a limiting one. A distributor could only rarely go back to a hostess as a party sponsor, and a hostess could invite her friends for only an occasional party. Multi-level marketing is infinitely more practical, making deeper and more sustained use of social networks.

Spin-off Groups

C & M Marketing prospered using the network form of organization until the late 1950s, when management problems threatened. What happened next bore remarkable resemblance to the Protestant Reformation. One group of Nutrilite distributors in Michigan, headed by sponsors Rich DeVos and Jay Van Andel, formed the American Way Association and sent representatives to California to company headquarters. DeVos and Van Andel decided that, though they would continue to sell Nutrilite, the supply of the product was too precarious. They began to manufacture goods for their downline recruits to sell. In 1959, they incorporated Amway, a contraction of American Way, now the world's oldest and largest multi-leveled direct-selling company.

Even before the formation of Amway, others began to copy C & M Marketing's organizational innovation. Stanley Home Products became a multi-level marketer, and subsequently several successful Stanley distributors went off to found their own network companies. In the 1950s and early 1960s former Stanley distributors Mary Kay Ash, Mary Crowley and Brownie Wise founded, respectively, Mary Kay Cosmetics, Home Interiors and Gifts, and the Tupperware sales force. A few years *after* the formation of Amway, Dr. Shaklee formed his company in the mid-50s.

The Early MLM Distributors

The direct-sales marketers for this new organizational structure were mostly women who had completed high school, but with little or no college. The profile of the early MLM distributor was a politically conservative female, more overtly religious than the average American. Their household income was slightly above the national average. Some of the same issues that are driving women into our industry today opened the way for the MLM sales approach of the 50s, 60s, and 70s: jobs with low status and low pay; the increasing insecurity of employment; the degrading atmosphere of much of the professional and managerial work; and the increasing costs of sustaining the employment relationship. Yearning for a little extra pocket money, these women discovered that in the labor force the pay was low, the work unfulfilling and stressful.

Direct selling, a modest industry during these three decades, promised something that the labor force couldn't offer: status, freedom, and friendship.

Integration of Work and Family Life

As far back as the very earliest days of Amway, the separation of people's work lives and their family lives posed a serious challenge to their values. Appealing to women who were already disrespected in the workplace, MLM offered them an alternative. By choosing Amway, for example, they could have their dignity back and spend more time with their families. Amway offered continuity between the two aspects of their lives. This philosophy is still prevalent and powerful in our industry today.

From the earliest days, building the "legs" of organizations through the family tree was strongly encouraged. Having husbands and wives work together and bringing in parents, children, brothers and sisters was all a part of the family unity that laid the foundation for the MLM industry. This philosophy is particularly noticeable, then and now, in some of the oldest and most established companies, such as Amway and Shaklee.

The metaphor of family in MLM tradition reaches beyond blood ties to the extended family created in the business. From earliest times, the loving, nurturing relationships between distributors have long been fostered.

"I love you, brother," can be heard on closing phone calls around the world, not between siblings, but between male distributors working to help each other achieve dreams and goals.

Early MLMs Were Cause-Driven

It becomes easier for those of us in network marketing today to understand the common threads running throughout our industry as we look back and study its history.

These early companies shared a common mission as it related to their particular line of products. Nicole Woolsey Biggart succinctly describes this in her treatise on the direct-selling industry, *Charismatic Capitalism.* The first theme was tied to an ideology of wellness and environmentalism, and included such companies as Shaklee, Nutri-Metics International, Herbalife International, United Sciences of America (USA Vitamins), Avacare, and National Safety Associates (NSA). The second theme was products that were self-enhancers, and usually included cosmetics, clothing, and accessories. Mary Kay Ash built her company on the belief in the value of entrepreneurism and in the confidence one gains by looking one's best.

A third common set of ideologies involves products that were supportive of the family and home. Tupperware stresses that their products preserve nutrients and protect the family's health. Art Williams, one of the most dynamic speakers and writers in the industry, created an army of distributors fighting against the most unlikely cause, the whole-life insurance industry. A. L. Williams' distributors argued that converting from

> Direct selling...promised something that the labor force couldn't offer: status, freedom, and friendship.

whole-life insurance to its term insurance helped provide a family with financial security.

But there was always the linkage of product, opportunity, and belief, a very effective union because of the highly personalized nature of an MLM presentation. It was always critical for a multi-level company to have a cause—a belief in something beyond just making money. Almost all of the early companies laid a foundation of their business as being a means of touching people's lives by giving them opportunities for better health, a safer environment, enhanced income, or self-esteem. And, in that sense at least, the opportunity was an important force for good in the world.

Along with that, a personal story was encouraged. First, relating to your product line, what happened to you as a result of using these vitamins or cosmetics? Later, that personal story was extended to the opportunity. What happened to you (in the corporate world) that led you to find solace in this business? Without a doubt, MLM distributors believed in the transforming power of their product line and business opportunity.

Exaggerated Product or Income Claims

The industry was built on trust. Having a revered founder coupled with the testimonial of a respected acquaintance was an effective combination in selling products. However, this trust made the industry susceptible to false claims.

As distributors became larger in numbers and began sharing their exuberance about the healing power of their product or the income possible in this industry, the battle between the regulatory agencies and MLM companies began. Often, an FTC agent sitting in someone's home would ask poignant questions, baiting the presenter to say something in violation of the code. When that distributor succumbed, the company and distributor were both slapped with a fine and the situation publicized in the media.

As this marketing approach developed over time, the public began to equate MLM with pyramid schemes. It was during the 1970s (what has come to be known as "The Legitimacy Era") that the industry struggled to earn its credibility as a legitimate channel of distribution. The pandemonium of this pioneering stage of development, what Richard Poe has termed "Wave One," came to an end only in 1979. Following an acrimonious investigation, the Federal Trade Commission determined in its own courts that Amway, and, by implication, network marketing in general, was a legitimate business, not a pyramid scheme. This Amway decision became famous and played a significant role in carrying our industry into the next phase.

Historical Legal Challenges to the Industry

In 1975, the Federal Trade Commission sued Amway, alleging that it was an illegal pyramid scheme. Four years later, the court ruled in favor of Amway. As a result, a legal interpretation was established that still determines today the criteria for a legal network marketing company:

- A generous buy-back policy (usually 90 percent of the wholesale price paid from all re-sellable products returned);
- The ten-customer rule, which means that distributors must retail products to at least ten non-distributors per month; and
- The 70-percent rule, verifying that at least 70 percent of all previous wholesale orders have been sold or consumed before any subsequent orders can be placed with the company.

The 1979 Commission decision did find that Amway's claims about the amount of money distributors could earn were indeed deceptive. The order accompanying that decision prohibited misrepresentation of the amount of profits, earnings, or sales that distributors were likely to achieve. The order also requires that assertions of above-average earnings must be accompanied by clear and conspicuous details of either the average earnings of all distributors or the percentage of distributors who actually earned the amount claimed. In 1983, Amway ran an ad that allegedly did not include the proper disclaimer. In May 1986, they settled the dispute out of court by paying a $100,000 fine.

For the past two decades since this 1979 landmark Amway decision, these criteria have governed the industry. The earnings-claim rule is still an accepted practice in the industry and reporting average earnings at each level is gradually being adopted by most legitimate network marketing companies today. Besides proffering the truth, it also provides distributors with legitimate means of setting realistic financial goals.

Questioning the 70-Percent Rule

Only recently has the 70-percent rule come under scrutiny. The true spirit of this ruling was to eliminate front-loading and stockpiling. In years past, it was common to find people buying into a certain position in the compensation plan with an up-front purchase of several thousand dollars. This is where the term "garage-qualified" was derived. Not because they had customers to whom they could sell the products, but merely to hold their position, they would order hundreds or thousands of products each month and store the excess product in their garages. The 70-percent rule was designed to eliminate this practice. By counting personal consumption as part of the 70 percent, it still effectively accomplishes this.

Perhaps not completely grasping its original intent, certain courts have thrown out the "or consumed" clause, ruling that all wholesale purchases must be retailed to non-distributors only. Furthermore, they have ruled that no commission, bonuses, or overrides be paid on product personally consumed by the distributor.

Leonard Clements, host of "Inside Network Marketing," and author of the controversial book of the same name, has spoken with numerous individuals in the offices of state attorneys general over the years. Ironically, he found that only one, Michigan, the home state of Amway, offered the explicit opinion that personal consumption does not satisfy the 70-percent rule.

Very likely, there is no network marketing company that truly retails 70 percent of their sales volume to non-distributors. The argument is still being put forth by the proponents of the industry that it should make no difference whether products are sold to customers or consumed by distributors. What matters is that the products are being consumed by an end user and not piling up in the garage. While the FTC is treating even newer companies that place adequate emphasis on product movement more respectfully, regulators seem to be selective about whom they target for this "violation." They pursue fledgling companies that appear to be pyramid scams rather than legitimate networking companies and, quite reasonably, leave the Amways, Shaklees, and Herbalifes unchallenged to conduct business as usual.

Changing Perceptions about MLM

For years, network marketing has been equated with pyramid schemes. The misconceptions and confusions about the difference pervaded the industry. Often inappropriate and misleading earnings claims were made. Some methods of introduction used in the early days left people less than enthusiastic. The industry was known for inviting people over for dinner and, during dessert, whipping out a white board and beginning to draw circles.

It is not my intention to defend these early days, but, admittedly, doing business then was much harder than it is today. You ended up stockpiling products in your garage, distributing small amounts in the backs of station wagons (hence the name "distributor"), receiving your larger check and cutting smaller ones back to your organization. It took great determination to survive those days. And yes, undoubtedly, mistakes were made.

Attrition has always been high in our industry. Out of the 200,000 Americans joining a network marketing company every month, more than 85 percent of them quit within the first 90 days. That is because network marketing is a business that demands effort. In the early stages, it is some of the hardest work most of us have ever done, and the return for our effort is very small. Most people don't have the patience to persist long enough for success to take hold. So most people do quit...the business, but continue placing product orders for years to come. It is those continuous orders, month after month, and year after year, which provide serious network marketers with the promised long-term residual income.

"The attrition or turnover ratio is recorded as very high in direct sales. But, actually, turnover is not a bad thing," suggests Neil Offen. "It is based on the motivation of people. When you have a large number of women, for example, coming into Avon for Christmas money and they work only one month and quit, technically that represents a 1,200 percent turnover because it takes twelve of them to equate to one full year. But this is meaningless if those people earned extra money and achieved their objective."

These negative perceptions are beginning to dissipate as more and more professionalism is introduced to the industry. The scars of the past are still visible, for example, in such TV shows as *Chicago Hope*, where we find the pesky doctor who harasses everyone to sign up under him. But little by little, we are moving into a new era of network marketing tolerance by the regulators, acceptance by the media, and respect by those leaving the corporate ranks. The industry is stepping up to be counted among the serious economic contributors. A major university teaches network marketing. A sitting United States President acknowledged the industry by a video presentation at a recent DSA gathering. Network marketing has come of age and is leading the way into a new entrepreneurial era.

Training Period Necessary

Education is the key to rising above this negative public perception. That is one of my objectives in writing this book. An apprenticeship is a part of every business and ours is no different. Network marketing is sufficiently different from conventional business that everyone should find a mentor and learn the unique aspects of this industry. Wealth does not come easily to those who feel they must do everything themselves. Rather, it comes to those who understand the value of training others. Training and duplication are the essence of building a large, dynamic network organization.

Kay Smith, a longtime veteran of the industry, owes much of her success to having put this principle into practice. While building a consulting firm, Accents on Health, in the 70s, Kay also wrote a monthly nutrition column called *Kay's Corner* and hosted a radio program, *Health and You*.

It was during this phase of her life, more than 25 years ago, that Kay first heard of multi-level marketing. A product was brought to her by an enthusiastic MLM distributor who indicated that this was better than the product she was using with her clients. After testing the product with doctors, it became apparent to Kay that the distributor was right. Instinctively, Kay shared her excitement about the products with her clients. At the end of the month, she was amazed to receive a sizable bonus check and realized that she had just "leveraged" her income through network marketing. Using her immense credibility, as she told her readers and listeners, they used the product and, in turn, told their friends. For Kay, it was an entirely new kind of income, and she quickly became convinced of the power and effectiveness of this new burgeoning industry.

"In the beginning I didn't have any resistance to the concept. I just didn't understand why I was getting a check. Back then there wasn't anyone to guide or teach us. If you think about it, professionals in all fields must go through a set form of training in order to learn their career. Network marketing is no different. Newcomers to the business must learn the basic steps in order to duplicate themselves."

Because it appears deceivingly simple, some professionals make the mistake of thinking they don't need to go through their apprenticeship in our business. But familiarizing yourself with the simple but critical differences in our industry can determine your success.

Success Is Infectious

This business is less about looking good and sounding eloquent than it is about making large numbers of ordinary people look good and sound eloquent about their chosen product and company. If you understand this, you understand one of the core principles of the networking industry. Kay Smith grasped this early on. During her early days in MLM, Kay was drawn into the political arena, fighting for women and children's issues. Her expanding sphere of influence led to her appointment to Presidents Reagan and Bush's Roundtables, and the Senatorial Inner Circle, to advise on business issues.

It was soon after that, in the mid-80s, that Kay joined her present company as one of the early pioneers. Thanks to her and a handful of other committed and visionary leaders, this company went on to become one of the largest and most respected network marketing companies today. Kay's organization alone is responsible for sales in excess of $70 million a year. As the President of Career Development, Inc., with nearly 70,000 people in her organization in 25 countries, she travels the world training others to build their own businesses.

Her success has given her the freedom to pursue other outside interests. She served as President of the National Association of Women in Business organization (1985-86). She has been nominated to the International Who's Who of Professional and Business Women (1989). Appointed to the Women's Inner Circle of Achievement (1993), she loved to work with kids in distress. She helped educate teens about business through the Entrepreneurs Roundtable (1994-97). Kay Smith was awarded the distinction of being appointed to Nova Southeastern University's Entrepreneur Hall of Fame (1996) and chosen to serve on the University's board, one of the largest and most prestigious in the country. Most recently, she was distinguished in the Network Marketing Hall of Fame (1998), for her accomplishments in this field.

Today, from her home in Hillsboro Beach, Florida, she spends her professional time as a business consultant working with corporate executives, entrepreneurs, and others seeking to maximize their business and personal potential.

"Network marketing has given me the financial freedom, as well as the time-freedom that I have always wanted. I learned that if you work hard on your job, you can make a living, but if you work hard on yourself you can make a fortune."

Blending the Old with the New

The evolution of one of the oldest companies tells the story of the transition of the industry from the first days to contemporary times. Dr. Forrest Shaklee was one of the earliest pioneers in network marketing when he founded his company in 1956. Like so many of the first MLM companies, the Shaklee products were cause-driven.

Dr. Shaklee believed in an ecologically-harmonious world where people respect the natural balance, avoiding, when possible, the use of environmentally-harmful products and choosing instead to use biodegradable ones. The company motto, "In Harmony with Nature," was a vision far ahead of its time. In keeping with the approach of these early days, Dr. Shaklee's intention was not to have his distributors sell products. Rather, he wanted them to personally use the products, experience the benefits, and through the emotional appeal of testimonials, share those products with others. Perhaps you remember, as I do, the "Shaklee lady" from the 70s who would stop by once a month to take our order. This philosophy is still commonly used in networking companies today. What has changed is the door-to-door approach.

"One of the greatest challenges facing our company," says Don Karn, Senior Vice-president for Sales and Marketing, "is finding a balance between keeping our founder's vision alive, which grounded us so well in the past, while going forward with innovative plans and strategies with

> This business is…about making large numbers of ordinary people look good and sound eloquent about their chosen product and company.

> We see more young professionals looking for an avenue that will enable them to own their lives and have time with their families and friends.

the new management team. As we work with the field, we see more and more people who are in transition, looking for a way out of the routines and demands that arise from their jobs. We see more young professionals looking for an avenue that will enable them to own their lives and have time with their families and friends. For these reasons, it is evident why there is a definite increase of professionals coming into our industry."

Shaklee's sale force today consists of more than three-quarters of a million distributors worldwide, a half a million in the United States alone. One of the great things about Shaklee is that they are the epitome of stability, having distributors who are still with them since 1956.

"We cherish those early pioneers who built this company," says Jim Whittam, Ph.D., President and CEO of the Shaklee Companies. "At our annual conventions, the loudest applause goes to these still active veterans as they come to the stage to receive their much-deserved honors. After all, we are a health and wellness company...with integrity...combining the old and the new to make a difference in our world." Shaklee is symbolic of the industry's transition from the early days of the industry to contemporary times.

CHAPTER 12

From Single-Level to Multi-Level Marketing:
1980-1999

The Technology Era—that time in the 1980s and 1990s when rapid freight delivery, computerization, global expansion, innovations in telephony, the Internet—dramatically impacted the growth of products and services moving through the network distribution channel. Many of us witnessed this first-hand and were in fact on the playing field during this incredible, explosive period in network marketing history.

During the 80s, more people were becoming aware of the fact that large incomes could be generated through this industry. That fact attracted more serious players to the field. In the last half of the decade, leaders in network marketing worked closely together to determine more effective ways to network and move greater volume of product. There was little concern about working only within one's organizational line. Leaders crossed lines because the only thing that mattered was a system that worked.

One group targeted salons as a means of moving products; another tried massive video pass-outs to promote the business; yet another left provocative notes that looked like $20 bills lying everywhere. If one distributor created a newspaper ad that drew responses, everyone copied it. It was a time of excitement, fervor, and searching for systems.

The old-time network marketers have their own version of "walking miles to school through rain, sleet, and snow." In comparison to the ease of doing business today, they will tell you how lucky you are. You no longer have to stock inventory in your garages, personally fulfill orders, keep track of all the paperwork, or stay up all night taking phone calls for product orders from people in your downline. By relying more on systems, procedure, media, and today's technologies that simplify and standardize much of our work, ordinary people will find our industry a delight. Today, we simply direct customers to a toll-free 800 number and the company fulfills the order, credits us with the sale, and generates a computerized commission check at the end of the month. With each new technological innovation, our distributor role becomes easier and easier.

Nineties Bring Extensive Changes

Serving as president of the Direct Sales Association since the 1970s, Neil Offen has been in the network marketing industry for the past 28 years. Neil indicates that, without a doubt, the most extensive changes in network marketing have occurred over the past ten years. There was a time where 20 percent of the DSA members were multi-level and 80 percent were single-level. Today, all but two of the 45 companies that presently have submitted applications to the DSA are multi-level marketing companies.

Although begun in the 80s, network marketing literally invaded the service industry in the 90s. MCI Communications began to sell long-distance telephone service through Amway, and went on to become the number two long-distance telephone service supplier, right behind AT&T. U.S. Telecom Inc. established an alliance with Network 2000, an independent network marketing program later known as Sprint, attracting more than three million customers. Excel Communications, founded in 1988 in Dallas, accelerated from $30.8 million in revenues in 1993 to more than $500 million in 1995. The following year the company launched an Initial Public Offering (IPO) and literally doubled the stock value on the first day.

This is indicative of what can happen when basic services are released to the network marketing industry. There is no better way to market them than a friends-telling-friends campaign and now that the door has been opened a crack, the flood of possibilities will come rushing through.

Writing about network marketing in June of 1999, a Texas newspaper reported: "You know the industry is attracting many home-business entrepreneurs when a book titled *Your First Year in Network Marketing* makes Barnes & Noble's best seller list."

Legal Challenges Facing the Industry

Our evolution has not been without hardships and battles. As an industry, we've been challenged by regulators, politicians, the media, and those apparently threatened segments of corporate America. Some of the criticisms have been well founded and our response to them has helped take us to the next level of professionalism. Others have been ludicrous. But because they were the big guns and we were the groveling peons, we had to treat the ridiculous and the sublime with equal respect. Either way, the legal challenges tell an important part of the story of the development of the network marketing industry.

In 1986, Mark Hughes, founder of Herbalife, drew regulatory attention to himself when his 700,000-member company reportedly hit $500 million in sales the previous year. The Food and Drug Administration repeatedly investigated the company for making false product claims. Although admitting no wrongdoing, Hughes agreed to pay $850,000 to the California State Department of Health Services.

Similarly, A. L. Williams settled out of court with a Prudential Life Insurance agent who claimed A. L. Williams agents made misleading comparisons between whole-life and term insurance. Never mind the fact that his organization sold more term life insurance in 1986 than Prudential, industry leader until then.

Practically no pioneering or emerging corporate leader in the industry has gone unchallenged by consumer groups and government agencies.

Nu Skin Falls Prey to Legal Inquiry

During his 14 years with his company, Steve Lund, now President of Nu Skin Enterprises, has noted with satisfaction that more and more professionals are coming into the network marketing industry.

"I think that Nu Skin played a significant role in that healthy transition, as we created a compensation plan grounded solidly in real business economics—an attractive force for any professional." Theirs was an innovative compensation plan for its time.

> "You know the industry is attracting many home-business entrepreneurs when a book titled *Your First Year in Network Marketing* makes Barnes & Noble's best-seller list."

As many of you may know, I was one of those professionals who was drawn to Nu Skin. Over more than a decade, I built my organization with this remarkable company. Just at the peak of our growth, in 1991, Nu Skin faced one of the most disastrous moments of its young life. Led by Attorney General Frank Kelly of Michigan, several attorneys general began an investigation of our company. Their questions were pervasive. Were we a pyramid scheme? Were certain distributors making false product claims? Were they exaggerating their incomes? Did the Nu Skin corporate office take strong enough measures to control the field distributors? These and other questions were raised by Frank Kelly and the Federal Trade Commission. Connie Chung, Barbara Walters, *Nightline*, *USA Today*—every major national TV show and newspaper—seemed to revel in our demise.

On July 9th, 1991, the Frank Kelly vs. Nu Skin drama was played out on the front page of *USA Today*. The headlines read: "Marketing Tactics Draw Scrutiny"-"Highflying Firm's Strategy Smacks of 'Pyramid Scheme,' Some Charge."

We read on.

"Michigan Attorney General Frank Kelly has issued a notice of intended action against Nu Skin, charging the company is 'operating an illegal pyramid marketing scheme.' Nu Skin is careful to point out that its official literature forbids many of the trappings of the typical pyramid scheme: distributors don't get bonuses for enlisting new distributors, and they can return unsold products."

Those of us who swallowed that bitter pill sat in front of our televisions ten days later to watch a *Nightline* broadcast with Barbara Walters sitting in for Ted Koppel. Frank Kelly was interviewed along with Mike Smith, one of the lawyers representing Nu Skin. Our company came under a barrage of attacks from the attorney general. Kelly held up a graph of our compensation plan and pointed to it, saying, "See, it even looks like a pyramid!"

I, like every other loyal Nu Skin distributor, found it agonizing to watch. We spent hours on the phone with each other, desperately trying to hold things together. This caused so much needless devastation to the lives of countless innocent Nu Skin distributors, blindsided by the backlash that followed.

The fiasco took ten months to resolve. In the end, Nu Skin was determined to be an honorable and legitimate company. Shortly after Frank Kelly won his re-election, he dropped all charges against Nu Skin. Some minor adjustments were implemented which are still in effect today. The company extended our product-return policy from 90 days to one year and required a review of all independently produced training and recruiting materials to make certain they conformed to industry standards. Thereafter, the company began providing average distributor earnings information at all levels and created a more extensive distributor activity review program to ensure everyone's compliance with company and government guidelines.

But beyond that, there were no changes in our compensation plan, no changes in our marketing approach, and no changes in the essential make-up of network marketing. In fact, from that point forward the Direct Sales Association and the Federal Trade Commission heralded Nu Skin as the benchmark by which other network marketing companies would be measured.

By January 1992, stories ran all over the country: "Five States Finalize Investigations of Nu Skin International: Settlement Reached." For all that hullabaloo, two-thirds of the distributors dropped out that year, checks dropped as much, and good people, caught by surprise, were completely devastated in their personal lives. Some lost their homes and many gave up on the industry, swearing never to return. All this because of the political antics and media hype begun by one Michigan Attorney General.

Once a network marketing company had reached a high level of success, it was in the radarscope of the FTC. In January 1994, Nu Skin was again fined for false representation of income earnings (and this is key) "without proper substantiation that such earnings are typical of Nu Skin distributors." Additionally, the FTC claimed that "it was deceptive for the respondents to fail to disclose that only a very small percentage of Nu

Skin distributors earned more than a small monthly income." The issue was not whether a certain number of Nu Skin distributors in fact earned the $60,000 to $80,000 their first year as claimed by some Nu Skin distributors, but that they didn't put this in perspective against the vast number who did not.

The FTC had a point, but it's a fine line. The distributors saw the glass partially full and excitedly presented this. The FTC saw the glass largely empty and was dismayed that the company permitted its distributors to make such a claim. A compromise was reached by having distributors put their "glass partially full" view in perspective with how much of it is partially empty. In this way, distributors can present what is possible based on what others have done.

This case is very similar to the 1986 Amway case. Unfortunately, the public at large doesn't read the fine print. Their subconscious absorbs only the headlines: "Network Marketing Company Fined."

A Path Littered with Obstacles

Unfortunately, both California and North Carolina have recently declared that personal consumption no longer satisfies the 1979 landmark Amway decision regarding the 70-percent rule and that no commissions or bonuses can be paid to distributors on personally consumed products. This ruling is incongruous with the original intent, implying that the majority of consumers are precluded from becoming a distributor. It makes no rational sense for someone to be paying retail prices for a product they can get at wholesale simply by calling a toll-free number and signing up. To force 70 percent of all consumers of network marketing products to pay retail over wholesale defies logic and basic common sense.

Marvin Higbee, formerly the General Manager of Forever Living and now CEO of Life Force International based in San Diego, California, indicated that his company has introduced a concept called "Referral Marketing" to their field. Instead of setting a wholesale price and a retail price, everyone purchases products at a factory-direct price from the company. This approach is very appealing to professionals and especially attractive as the company expands into foreign markets. It eliminates the entire issue of sold versus consumed.

The State of California has now ruled that any type of sales aid or live training is not "commissionable." At least this ruling is based in common sense. I can easily accept the restriction that we not be compensated for prospecting and training materials that prepare us and our peers to be better at the role of distributor, but may be compensated for the sale of actual products and services.

SEC Battles International Heritage

One current legal case that is definitely giving the industry a huge black eye is the incident filed by the Securities and Exchange Commission (SEC) against International Heritage Inc. (IHI). While the company appears to have had a legitimate product, the issue was that a number of distributors (contrary to company literature) essentially delivered a message that promoted the opportunity this way: "All you have to do is put money into our company and you will earn commissions off of everybody else."

As reported April 2, 1999, in the *News-Observer* in Raleigh, North Carolina: "Larry Smith, co-founder of IHI and one of 20 co-defendants in the case, appears to be on the run. The SEC recently filed a motion for a default judgment against Smith, who had been residing in Greenville, South Carolina, contending that he has relocated without leaving a forwarding address. Smith failed to appear at a deposition for the SEC's civil complaint against him and IHI, which accuses the company and the individual defendants of three counts of fraud, filing false reports, and illegal sale of unregistered securities. IHI co-founder Stan Van Etten, the company's president and CEO, said Smith is rumored to have sold all of his assets and left the country."

The penalties being sought by the SEC include the return of $1.2 million in commission fees that Smith received from IHI in addition to $96,719 in interest and a fine of up to $110,000. The SEC characterizes Smith's commissions as "ill-gotten gains" from an illegal pyramid scheme that generated more than $150 million in revenue. IHI is liquidating its assets under federal bankruptcy laws after going out of business in November 1998. Company officials, who always maintained that they were operating a legitimate business, blamed the publicity surrounding the SEC complaint for the company's downfall.

The SEC has further said that Smith participated in Gold Unlimited, which the agency described in a court filing as "another notorious pyramid scheme...Smith's sudden disappearance," the SEC argues in a brief filed in federal court, "can only be construed as an attempt to avoid being deposed."

Without knowing any more facts, it is difficult to argue with these closing remarks of the SEC. It is cases such as this one that label our industry as a pyramid scheme. When the general populace reads this news about the challenges of one company, and knows nothing more about our industry, they are hard pressed not to form an opinion about the entire industry.

Long-Term Growth Potential of the Industry

Beyond those deserved investigations by the FTC, overall, the probing-for-probing's-sake seems to have died down.

"When franchises first came on the scene, they were viewed very skeptically by the various regulatory agencies. They were heavily regulated for a while, and now they have become very well accepted. Network marketing has gone through much the same thing. It is just now beginning to get to the phase where the regulators are accustomed to the industry and recognizing it for its contributions to society and the economy," attorney Ed Wainscott points out.

"Network marketing is moving into a more professional arena," states Marvin Higbee. "There are a couple of major shifts that are affecting the industry. The shakeup in corporate America that is leading so many to seek financial security elsewhere together with the enhanced hybrid compensation plans emerging in our industry are attractive and growth producing for professionals today. The burgeoning technology with all of the information available on the Internet has eliminated the 'door to door' sales approach and literally 'opened the door' to welcome in these new entrepreneurs."

For well over a decade, many of us have had the privilege of watching and participating in the growth of this industry. On a global scale, we have gone from 8.48 million distributors moving $33.32 billion worth of products in 1988 to 31 million distributors moving nearly $100 billion worth of products at the close of 1998. The facts speak for themselves. The growth of this industry cannot be denied.

> When franchises first came on the scene, they...were heavily regulated...and now...have become very well accepted. Network marketing has gone through much the same thing.

> The burgeoning technology with all of the information available on the Internet has eliminated the 'door to door' sales approach and literally 'opened the door' to welcome in these new entrepreneurs.

Changing Perceptions of the Industry

Last year Citigroup, the world's largest financial services firm, cut its workforce by 6 percent (10,400 workers). However, its network marketing subsidiary, Primerica (formerly A. L. Williams Company), continued to expand. This is indicative of the turnabout going on between corporate America and network marketing companies and divisions.

If you look at strategic alliances that major corporations have formed with direct-selling companies, it is clear that conventional businesses are seeing the direct-selling industry as a viable channel of distribution. Amway is now selling Rubbermaid, Tupperware is selling Disney products and Avon is selling Mattel.

In 1990 the industry was 90 percent female but, by 1997, 35 percent were male and the actual numbers of men participating continue to rise. There may be several reasons for this drastic increase of men joining the industry:

- More men are seeing how successful their wives have been.
- Many have been laid off and downsized from corporate management positions.
- White males between 45 and 60 in particular are looking for alternatives to corporate America because many of them are being replaced at 40-plus.
- Men are seeking the empowerment of controlling their own investment image through direct selling and network marketing.

Universities Introduce Network Marketing

Dr. Charles King recalls network marketing's introduction to the University of Illinois at Chicago. "In 1990 we had a major economic

189

recession in the U.S. As a result, the interviewers stopped coming to campus. We were graduating hundreds of students a semester who weren't getting jobs. Our alumni were coming back to us, victims of downsizing and looking for help. We had nothing to offer them. My background in marketing led me to look at alternative career paths—home-based business, franchising, and direct selling. Through this research, I backed into network marketing."

Mark Yarnell and I were first invited as guest lecturers to Dr. King's class back in 1992. With each subsequent visit, we observed an increasing buildup of excitement and receptivity among the UIC students. They began with a reserved attitude and advanced to a genuine interest, asking penetrating questions.

On one visit, while finishing up our class, Paul Uselding, then Dean of the Business School, sent a note to Dr. King inviting us for lunch. Over multi-course Italian cuisine, we shared stories about network marketing as an entrepreneurial opportunity.

The student body's reaction to our lectures intrigued Dean Uselding. As we talked, the idea of having the first network-marketing certificate course at an accredited university began to surface. The Dean undertook a yearlong process to get the seminar approved provisionally for a special one-time event.

It was critical that the seminar be well attended, cover its own costs, and not discredit the school in any way. In November 1994, the first class was held with approximately 100 students from all over the United States and a handful from abroad in attendance. It was a success, and true to their nature, these students "networked" the class. They went home and told members of their organization who, in turn, told others. Today, there is a waiting list to enroll for the program. (To learn more about the UIC seminar, check the Resources section in the back of this book.)

In fact, the course established the UIC certificate seminar in network marketing as the industry leader in professional education and distributor development. We have now carried the UIC certificate seminar to Seoul, Korea, and are scheduled to carry it into Australia this year. Dr. King is negotiating with university connections to take it to several other countries. Thanks to the University of Illinois at Chicago, the UIC Certificate Seminar in Network Marketing represents a true breakthrough for the credibility of the industry.

And now a virtual university is also a part of the ongoing education of new professionals joining the industry. MLM University, founded by Hilton Johnson, specializes in teleconference classrooms taught by virtual professors offering "sales coaching for network marketers who hate selling." I have enjoyed being a part of this new phenomenon.

Network Marketing on Wall Street

"The Direct Selling Investor," a monthly bulletin that reports on the publicly held Direct Selling companies, is produced by Paul Adams, Vice President of Sales and Marketing for Video Plus.

"There has been public involvement in the network marketing industry for a number of years. But in the last few years we have seen this number grow to as many as 30 companies," he says.

"Unfortunately, I see some trends where companies are going public and looking for survival money instead of growth money. On the positive side, I do see growth. I see the chance for the distributor base to not only enjoy being involved as a small business owner in their own home based business, but also to be part owner and share in the growth of the very company they are helping to build. They actually create their own marketing arena."

Video Plus has two publications. The first and oldest one, the "Direct Selling Stock Watch," is a one-page, at-a-glance look at the industry's market activity for the preceding month. With this publication, Paul has put together a reasonably complete list of the direct-selling publicly traded companies. The "Direct Selling Investor" takes that basic information and expands on it by researching and reporting on public information that had an impact on the industry stocks' rise or fall for that month.

In the mid-90s, we distributors were quick to point to the 20 companies that were then traded publicly on NASDAQ and the New York Stock

> Thanks to the University of Illinois at Chicago, the UIC Certificate Seminar in Network Marketing represents a true breakthrough for the credibility of the industry.

Exchange as a sign of our evolving maturity as an industry. Our reasoning was that, in order to file an Initial Public Offering (IPO), these companies had to establish standardized accounting procedures and be open to SEC scrutiny and control. Therefore, the companies that "go public" establish and maintain high standards of business practices that elevate the character of the entire network marketing community.

We also were pleased (and boasted) that investors' initial response to the publicly traded network marketing companies was outstanding. *Upline* magazine, an industry trade publication, maintained an "Upline Index," which tracked the financial performance of these publicly held network marketing companies. In 1996, this Index showed an increase in stock market value for our industry of over 63 percent. This was phenomenal when compared to the Dow Jones Industrial Average increase of only 33 percent and Standard and Poor's 500 Index increase at 34 percent. This two-fold gain of the network marketing industry over traditional corporations created considerable excitement among savvy investors.

But as Paul points out, the industry couldn't possibly sustain those kinds of margins long-term.

"If you look at the network marketing industry as a whole over the last couple of years, the publicly-traded companies have not performed as well as the industry standard. Some of that has to do with the fact that many of our public companies didn't have as much sizzle as some of the hi-tech industries that have made the stock market go through the roof recently. Also, historically, the direct selling industry doesn't thrive as well in times of prosperity."

Paul is right. Looking back over the history of network marketing, we have always prided ourselves that our businesses continued to thrive during recessions and financially hard times.

"From what I am seeing happen in the direct selling industry," Paul reflects, "at least from a market performance standpoint, the overall economy of the U.S. is overpowering. We don't see a lot of people jumping from their great hi-tech jobs to a home based business. In the most recent 'Direct Selling Stock Watch,' we show the year-end change for 1998 was down 19 percent in market performance. This relates back to the almost unrealistic growth that is happening in the hi-tech sectors and related arenas. However, the stock value of a handful of publicly traded network marketing companies, such as Royal Body Care and Excel, thrived during this time in spite of the odds."

In 1998, Pre-paid Legal became the top performing company on the American Stock Exchange. May 13, 1999, just one year later, they had the privilege of ringing the opening bell of their new home, the New York Stock Exchange.

Speed of Technology Attracts Many Professionals

"The Internet businesses are drawing in many professionals who have never before been involved in network marketing," says Jerry Campisi, a long-time veteran of the industry whom you will meet later in this book.

"If you think about it, how did the Internet or Yahoo grow to what it is today? It developed by one-on-one word of mouth, one person sharing it with another person sharing it with another. And that is why so many Fortune 500 companies are interested in our channel to the customer. They are drawn by the power of networking."

Network Marketing as a Global Force

Network marketing is a worldwide phenomenon. According to the World Federation of the DSA, the top countries for moving at least one billion dollars worth of products through direct sales/network marketing are the following:

Country	Retail Sales	Number of Sales People
Japan	30.2 billion	2,500,000
USA	22.2 billion	9,300,000
Brazil	4.045 billion	1,839,044
Germany	3.6 billion	335,000
Italy	2.1 billion	340,000
Korea	2.1 billion	909,000
Taiwan	1.74 billion	2,360,000
Canada	1.6 billion	1,300,000
Mexico	1.4 billion	1,200,000
UK	1.396 billion	400,000
Australia	1.2 billion	650,000
Argentina	1.074 billion	429,000

> **The Internet businesses are drawing in many professionals who have never before been involved in network marketing.**

Beyond question, the advancement of technology has united the world. It is as common to receive an e-mail from Europe or Australia as it is to receive one from our next-door neighbor. With the advent of Amazon.com, it is as ordinary to have the Yarnell books sold to a customer in South Africa, India, or Australia as it is within the continental United States. The Internet was designed for relationship marketing—personal, one-on-one interactive selling, educating, and informing kind of marketing—on a worldwide scope. The Internet is ideal for our industry. Consequently, global expansion is an inescapable by-product of this phenomenon.

If interplanetary communication becomes a reality, no doubt network marketing will lead the charge.

I may be among the first to volunteer for Mars, now that I'm single again, since most of the bright, witty, and sensitive men from this planet seem to find solace there...according to the eminent Dr. John Gray (*Men are from Mars, Women are from Venus*).

CHAPTER 13

Technology and the Internet

Bill Gates of Microsoft predicts that by the year 2010, there will be two kinds of businesses: those on the Internet and those out of business. Oh, sure we can say Bill Gates is biased. The fact is that the Internet is the single most powerful force to invade our planet in this lifetime. It is right up there with electricity and the telephone in terms of global impact. It has changed the process of communication as we know it faster than any other medium in history. Radio took 38 years to reach 50 million listeners. Television took 13 years to reach 50 million households. The Internet has taken only 5 years to reach 50 million users!

Since 1992, Al Gore has been calling the Net "The Information Superhighway." But, as more and more of us around the world zoom back and forth across this virtual superhighway, we realize it is easier than driving a car on any interstate. And more economical, too. Gasoline prices keep going up, and cars are costing us more every year. But the price of the vehicles that we use to negotiate the Internet—our computers—keeps going down while their power, speed, and memory continue to increase. We can buy good PCs today for less than $1,000, and several manufacturers are producing them for less than $500. So, "superhighway" may even be a bit horse-and-buggyish. We're much more like those characters on *Star Trek* who boldly go where no one has gone before. We're in space...in cyberspace.

To be sure, the personal computer is not as omnipresent as a TV. But consider this: about half of the adults in the U.S. now have access to at least one personal computer, either at home, in the workplace, or in school, and most of those computers are connected to the World Wide Web. With the advent of web TV, even those without a personal computer can enter cyberspace via a hand-held device connected to their TV. In *Business @ The Speed of Thought*, Bill Gates reported in 1998 that more than 60 million Americans were using the web regularly, up from 27 million the year before. He predicts that by the year 2001, more than 60 percent of U.S. households will have PCs and that 85 percent of those homes will have Internet access. In *The State of the Net*, author Peter Clemente reports that the Internet "is exceeding the growth rates of all previous communications technologies including the cellular telephone, VCR, television, radio, and conventional telephone." Internet traffic is doubling every 100 days, and in the not so distant future people without Internet and e-mail access will be compared to those without a telephone.

On-line shopping? Whopping increases here. In a 1998 report, Jupiter Communication estimated that on-line shopping is growing at a compound annual rate of 69 percent, which means that in 2002, we will see Americans spending $41 billion on-line. There is no doubt that network marketing will have its share of these growing on-line sales.

More People in Cyberspace

Thanks to the Internet, most American businesses have their own web sites. Each month, more and more retailers, manufacturers, banks, schools, and government agencies are turning to the Internet to provide on-line information. In 1998, Special Prosecutor Ken Starr used the web to disseminate his 445-page report on Bill Clinton. And more than six million people read the *Starr Report* on the Net in the first weekend after its release. Every major movie, every TV series has its own web site. So do the Los Angeles Lakers and the New York Yankees. As Peter Clemente said in

> By the year 2001, more than 60 percent of U.S. households will have PCs and...85 percent of those homes will have Internet access.

1997, "The Internet has evolved into a state-of-the-art communications matrix through which new ideas and technologies can be shared on a global scale, almost instantaneously."

The Internet itself has more than doubled in size every year, partly because Internet technology has made everything easier. We used to get our Internet data through the equivalent of a straw. Now, with cable feeds and wireless communications becoming available to almost every cybernaut, we are getting our data through the equivalent of a water main. The technical name for this expanded new flow is "bandwidth" and, largely because of competition between telephone companies, cable companies and wireless providers, bandwidth is getting wider. That means that, once we get to a site in cyberspace, we won't have to wait more than a few milliseconds to be running around that site. Click here. Click there. Click, click, click and we're everywhere. (I don't know why we want more speed, but it is definitely the measure of the Web's value. So we have two choices: either stop the world-as-it-is and get off, or hold on tight. Whee!)

The Internet & MLM

What kind of business is best transacted on the Net? The electronic equivalent of door-to-door selling? No. Sending unsolicited mail to the masses—spamming—is outlawed in certain states, and it makes regular e-mail users react with anger. In other words, spamming doesn't work.

According to Clemente and a good many others, the Net is best used in the one-on-one "relationship marketing" I have mentioned before. Some have dubbed this new phenomenon "internetworking," believing that there is no quicker, more effective, more credible way to establish a network than through the Internet today.

The Internet is changing the very essence of how we will do our network marketing. Network marketing companies are setting up web sites so they can provide both distributors and customers with answers to everything they need to know and didn't know how to ask. Exactly what makes the web so fitting for network marketers?

1. We can target specific marketing messages to specific individuals, including those identified through their on-line behavior patterns.
2. We will find that the individuals who are with us are there because they have already chosen to pay attention to us, and because they find our products will be useful to them. If they don't respond, they're not interested. If they do, they're already sold.

> # Network marketing companies are setting up web sites so they can provide both distributors and customers with answers to everything they need to know and didn't know how to ask.

3. We can get instant feedback from our customers.

4. We will find that cybernauts have money to spend.

5. We can offer our customers much more in-depth product information than we can in any print or broadcast ad, and we can be as creative as we want. Advances in software, like Java, to use one example, make it possible for our web sites to sing and dance in color. And we can change our message whenever we wish. (We can't do that after we've printed thousands of brochures. On a web site, ink never dries and full-color publishing is free.)

6. Our customers can order their products on-line, instantly.

7. We can sell from anyplace in the world to anyplace in the world. If what we are selling is information, they can download that digitally through the Internet within seconds.

8. We can resell them, with follow-up services and products.

9. We won't spend a penny on paper or postage.

As Richard Poe said in *Wave Three*, "...the wealthiest moguls in history have always sought to escape the slavery of linear income. They accomplish this by leveraging the time and energy of others leaving themselves free to plan grand strategies, start new businesses, or just enjoy life!" Many of us are receiving, not 1 percent, but 5 percent and sometimes more, on the efforts and sales volumes of thousands.

Web Sites Build Network Organizations

Through cyberspace, we now have more innovative ways for reaching out to prospective business associates, and for keeping in communication with them once they are there. But we can't rush in, thinking that the Net itself is a panacea. It's not, unless we have a plan.

198

The plan works like this: first, you approach people about your business. Then send them to your company's web site or your own replicating site that links to the company. For those with know-how, you can build your own site or convince your smart cousin Becky to do it for you. For a modest investment, you can hire a creative web site builder. They will know how to make a site attractive to visitors. After all, if your site is amateurish, people will quickly move on. For those less savvy in Internet mechanics and lingo, you can purchase an easy-to-use web site builder as a software program already in template form. "Where do I get this?" you ask. Where else but from your nearest network marketer.

Some web sites are becoming more like TV commercials. Check out www.macromedia.com. There you will find a dozen examples of cutting-edge web sites for corporations that have hired site developers to craft some very powerful interactive events giving us sound, music, words, and even animation. Those in network marketing who are using such advanced technology have the most cutting edge direct-sale web sites in the industry. Leaders utilizing such avant-garde tools are also able to provide their team members with their own Internet presence.

Creating your own web site can be adventurous and exciting and, note this: you do not have to start from scratch. On the web you can copy any idea or symbol and adapt it to meet your company's needs. There are no copyright restrictions for anything found on the Web. The other side of the coin, however: know that others will assuredly copy your creative designs as well.

But, even if you have your own Web sites constructed, I have to insert a word of caution here: those personal web sites should be linked very tightly to the web sites of your companies. You don't want to go off on your own, or encourage the distributors in your organization to go off on their own. If you have a strong lead in the offing, believe me, you don't want her surfing the Net and reading someone else's pitch. Nor do you want anyone in your company building a site and then disappearing. A web site can be a miraculous thing, but, like a garden, it needs constant attention.

What if you, or one of your people, put up a web site and then forget it, or, worse, leave the business? That web site will soon become obsolete and misleading, but it will still be up there in cyberspace, providing people with the wrong information about your company. Nothing could be worse for the network marketing business as a whole, because the wrong facts and figures will tell people they can't believe in us. And, as we know, believability is more important, in any kind of sales, than everything else put together. So, although it can be valuable to create personal information on your own web site, it would behoove companies not to let reps put up their own public web sites that attempt to duplicate the information already available on the company's site.

With that understanding, let's say you now have your web site set up and linked to the proper places. Then what? You still want to reach out to people, like you always have, generally beginning with your own circle of friends. That is the genius of network marketing, and it always will be. Make people aware of your site and/or your company's web site where they can find everything spelled out for them. This is one of the most effective, economical, and effective methods for anyone in network marketing to follow through with a prospective associate.

And after your prospects visit? Many web sites allow the prospect to send an e-mail from the site directly to you. If this happens, it's easy to follow up with them in old-fashioned ways, like the telephone. As one successful network marketer relates, "What I have found is that after people have read my information on the web site, it's very easy to converse with them on the phone, because now they know who I am, and trust is already established. It's as if I'm a long-lost buddy. I don't even know them, but they know me. It makes prospecting very easy."

Building Community on the Web by Referral Marketing

The convenience of saving time and money is drawing more and more people to shop and make price comparisons on the Net. Following the example set by Amazon.com, many established companies such as J. C. Penney, Barnes & Noble, Lands End, Eddie Bauer, and OfficeMax are encouraging consumers to purchase through the Web at a discount.

Launching in the first quarter of 2000, DOYOUWOW.com Inc. is offering affiliates the opportunity to form a new Internet community based on developing personal and professional relationships. Participants can save time and money by shopping more efficiently at their own *free* on-line store that will be a portal to access the on-line stores of hundreds of different merchants. In addition to receiving a percentage back on all of their own purchases, DOYOUWOW.com Inc. will be given the opportunity to earn income without any major change in their lives, and be provided a resource of valuable information on how to live a healthier and richer life.

So what is unique? The creation of the cultural aspect of the site. The ability to participate without any out-of-pocket expense coupled with the power of word-of-mouth referral marketing is expected to build a loyalty factor among its affiliates that will keep them wedded to this Internet community.

According to a company spokesperson: "This is a look at the future. While maintaining a focus on success principles and family values, DOYOUWOW.com Inc. is merging the growth of e-commerce with the power of 'relationship' or referral marketing, and presenting it in a package that allows anyone with an e-mail address to participate."

For every dollar spent, affiliates will receive credits that can be cashed in or used for other purchases. As affiliates begin to personally refer other affiliates who in turn refer other affiliates to DOYOUWOW.com Inc., they can earn a percentage of all the purchases in their referral network. Although margins will be small, this can begin to add up and generate a good income. As each participant assists other personally referred affiliates to refer others, and in turn to assist them to refer others, this business model can create a growing community of participants. As more and more affiliates choose to educate themselves on success principles and living healthier, richer lives while also shopping as they normally would through their personally owned Internet-based stores, this professional model can duplicate itself into colossal income for a vast number of community builders.

We've already witnessed massive response on such web sites as MyFamily.com, AllAdvantage.com, MyShopNow.com, ShopNow.com and SixDegrees.com—all of whom offered a free membership and received more than a million sign-ups within the first 60 days, with one receiving that many in the first week. These experiences serve as a role model for Internet-based companies who will begin building a networked community on the Web through referral marketing—a clear sign of the direction our industry will take in the 21st Century. (See Resource section in back for more information.)

Other Technology and the Web

There's a new wrinkle in telephone technology, called virtual offices or unified messaging systems. They are like having your own electronic secretarial assistant. You give out one phone number, and that's the number everyone has for you. When anyone calls that number, no matter where you are, you get a ring. Your phone system tracks you down through the numbers you input, keeping you always "in touch." You can even check your e-mail from the phone. This technology is likely to be a major element in the future of network marketing.

And then, after you've elicited some genuine interest? Your prospects or team members won't have to wait for material to arrive in the mail or wait until the next local business meeting is held. You simply send them back to the web site, where they can receive instant answers to their questions, and explore the areas that are most important to them. Certain prospects will want to review profile information on the company. Others will be more interested in product testimonials of actual representatives.

Flexibility is the key. Some will now be intrigued enough to listen in on the regularly scheduled teleconference calls offered by many companies and top-level field representatives. If the Web isn't convenient for your prospects, they can make use of voice-on-demand messages available 24 hours a day. If they like what they hear, they can retrieve a fax-on-demand executive summary or a product catalog. Using these tools with the Internet can be a powerful combination.

I have found, for example, that answering an e-mailed question is much more time-efficient than answering the same question on the phone. We can do it whenever we want, on our timetable, not our customer's or associate's timetable, generally with an answer that we have saved in our computer for easy reference.

Now, as cybernauts, you will be able to respond right away. There's nothing worse than promising you will stay in touch with your customers or team members, and then failing to deliver. That destroys your credibility and wilts their blossoming enthusiasm.

> Internet-based companies...will begin building a networked community on the Web through referral marketing—a clear sign of the direction our industry will take in the 21st Century.

Many network marketing companies are now providing "downline" information on-line. With this system in place, you need no longer wait for monthly printouts from the company headquarters to learn about the growth of your organization. You need only look into the company's web site, enter a password, and check on your personal information and that of your entire organization. This data can tell you such details as who just signed on, the personal volume of each member, and your organization's entire volume broken down by team builders.

Strategies in Action

One representative who has maximized his use of the Net to build a successful network organization is Brett Dabe. From his home in Hamilton, Ohio, he built a national business selling communication products and services through effective use of his personalized web site.

"Once a prospect has been qualified through some sort of one-on-one interaction," he states, "the Internet can be used to elevate the level of interest immediately. The prospect will not have to wait for something to come in the mail, but will receive information immediately."

In addition to the Net, Brett also uses voice mail, fax-on-demand, and conference calls through a sophisticated unified messaging system. Using the telephony available on the Net, prospects can call Brett directly from the Internet or request information from him 24 hours a day from anywhere in the world, simply by typing in their telephone number, and clicking a button. Then, his messaging system will send them the information they want, let them listen to different recorded messages, or it will allow them to talk to him personally right from the Internet.

"With this system," Brett describes, "we can check our voice mail and we can fax people back all through the Web, which means we have no usage charges."

Brett has been able to do this with the technical support of an organization called TeamSolo™, in Birmingham, Michigan, under the direction of Gregg Corella.

"Our product can be used by small-office and home-office workers, network marketers, and corporate users," Gregg explains. "We are a true one-stop shop when it comes to support and infrastructure on a general scale, as well as on a specific scale for network marketers."

As executive vice-president of GoSolo™ Technologies, Gregg indicates that his company is in the process of completing some innovative developments to further advance unified technology: voice recognition will identify your commands, speaker verification will know who you are without a password, and the text-to-voice feature will read your e-mail to you in a near human-like voice.

Gregg Corella's TeamSolo™ provides Brett with personalized dynamic web pages combined with the state-of-the-art unified message service, which contain a photo of Brett, a thumbnail biography, and facts about his company and its service.

"All members of our team are given their own personal user name and password which is provided to prospects. As a result, everyone benefits...and has fun doing it," says Brett. "By taking web sites to this next level, the screen takes on the character of a live production, which can bring warmth and feeling to a web site."

In some ways, this approach of a unified technology emulates the methods and success of the franchising industry. Potential holders of franchises with McDonald's, for instance, go to Hamburger U. in Illinois, run by McDonald's, to learn tried-and-true methods that have worked for decades. If they follow the system, franchisees succeed, often beyond their wildest dreams. But improved efficiency and consistency is always the key.

For Brett and his wife, Rachel, this tightly duplicated system protects the integrity of his company and service. It restrains new people from making outlandish claims.

"I want to take the 'hype' out of network marketing," Brett says, "giving it a professional touch. The web site we are using appeals to the people who would be interested in both our products as well as our business opportunity."

In order for network marketing companies and proven field leaders to improve their utilization of the Internet with more professionalism, check out the Team Solo™ Unified Technology in the Resource section at the back of this book. If you are new to the industry or have not yet reached a solid leadership status in your company, invite your corporate and field leaders to visit the site and check out this technology.

The objective is to help bring more professionalism to the industry by creating dynamic ports of quality-controlled information that can be duplicated over and over again, thereby reaching a great diversity of people— different ages, sexes, races, educational levels, and religions and cultures.

The advancement of technology and the popularity of the Internet will have a profound effect on the rise of the network marketing industry as a profession.

"We know the network marketing profession stands alone as one of the greatest opportunities for wealth that can be acquired on the road to personal freedom," Brett says. "Through the Internet we've found a way to show prospective representatives how they can take the networking industry to the next level and do the same thing we've done."

The advancement of technology and the popularity of the Internet will have a profound effect on the rise of the network marketing industry as a profession.

CHAPTER 14

The Next Era of Referral Marketing:
The 21ˢᵗ Century

The next phase of network marketing is clearly going to be a new work culture and a new economic paradigm. In that burgeoning environment, network marketing is fast transitioning into referral marketing, and, as such, is becoming the next major profession. Neil Offen predicts that over the next decade, 200 million new representatives will join the direct selling industry on a global basis. That represents nearly a 700-percent growth ratio over the 31 million distributors estimated in the industry today. And much of that growth will be on the basis of people building Internet networks through personal referrals.

Already more than 50 percent of the American public has purchased goods or services through direct selling. Why? They say because of product quality, uniqueness, and money-back guarantees. I would add: because it is there in front of them, being recommended by their best friend, their sister, or their boss. Our industry hasn't reinvented the wheel. We have taken the oldest, most effective form of advertising, word-of-mouth, and found a lucrative and legitimate way to make money. What is new, relatively so, is our method of compensation and our means of communication.

We observed what happened with the deregulation of tele-communications. The network marketing industry is ready to step in and assume a similar Herculean role with the deregulation of electricity. Companies are lining up to deliver all home services—power and gas; pagers, local, long-distance, and cell phone services; virtual offices and follow-me phone systems; Web TV, web sites, and Internet service providers, just for starters. The goal is to deliver this with one easy credit-card payment. Add to that the ability to shop from home, make price comparisons, and ultimately make a selection, all through the Internet, in a shopping mall owned by you or a friend. And who will be making many of these sales and being compensated for them? Network marketers, of course!

Tech Trends Boost MLMs

Jerry Campisi joined network marketing long before it was fashionable for professionals to enter the industry. For 20 years he had been a business and financial consultant, helping companies grow from national to international status. He was at the top of his career, earning a great income, but as he put it, "my business was running me instead of me running my business."

His wife, Debbie, with a degree in neuro-diagnostics, headed up the second-largest seizure unit for children in the United States. Much of this work involved a type of brain surgery that would stop the seizures. Although she loved her work with the children, the responsibilities of her job as a department supervisor were constantly stressful. As she dressed to leave for work at 6 a.m. every day, her life went one way and Jerry's another.

It was in 1985 that they first learned about the network marketing industry.

> Over the next decade, 200 million new representatives will join the direct selling industry on a global basis.
> That represents nearly a 700-percent growth ratio over the 31 million distributors estimated in the industry today.

"What intrigued me about this industry is that I could help the average person become successful," Jerry says. "In my previous work, I felt limited to helping rich people get richer."

He came to realize that network marketing is just another way to distribute products to the end user. Instead of going through middle management, advertising, and retail stores, the dispersal of profits is apportioned throughout the network organization.

The more he delved into it, the more Jerry was unable to find fault with the company, the compensation plan, or the products. The company was just getting underway and was marketing youth-oriented skin care products to aging Baby Boomers. While many professional men might have had difficulty identifying with the product line, this didn't bother Jerry.

"Although I couldn't relate to this niche, it didn't mean I couldn't capitalize on it. In business, you often have to separate yourself from your emotions in order to get objective answers to these questions: Is the company growing? Are you at the right place in the market penetration so that you can really benefit from it?"

Jerry's background led him to think in terms of return on investment rather than what others might think about him being in the personal care business.

"When you're in business, the only thing that really matters is return on investment," he says. "If you make decisions based on what other people think of you, you will never be successful in any business. The advantage that I had coming from my background was realizing that if a business that distributed cow manure and packaged it for fertilizer could have a high return, it could be a multi-million-dollar business. Who cares what the business is as long as it is a legitimate product with a real end consumer, and a good R.O.I.? Business decisions must be based on awareness of what is happening in the world around us."

Jerry cites the three phases of market penetration: (1) innovation, when only two percent of the leaders enlist and begin driving the business; (2) infrastructure, when about 15 percent of the leaders begin entering the market; and (3) diversification, when 70 percent of the market actually moves the product. "When Reebok first came on the scene," he says, "the majority resisted the chance to get involved because the sneaker was considered too expensive. A few risk-takers caused that company to receive product recognition, and the demand outstripped the supply. They couldn't set up the stores fast enough to handle the inventory."

> **Instead of going through middle management, advertising, and retail stores, the dispersal of profits is apportioned throughout the network organization.**

Jerry and Debbie made a good evaluation 14 years ago, but success didn't come overnight. They struggled in their first two-and-a-half years. Jerry credits Debbie with the two realizations that changed their fate: (1) the importance of building new groups rather than just managing existing groups, and (2) the willingness to change direction if something wasn't working.

"At first, we were selling anyone and everyone into the business," he says. "We weren't looking for someone who was a self-starter, who was entrepreneurial. And if you sell a non-self-starter into the business, as soon as you leave them alone, they will fall apart. They have to have discipline and perseverance in any profession they choose. I couldn't give them the inner strength. They had to have it within themselves. I realized that most people are procrastinators. But if I could find the person who was serious, we could at least give them the tools to change their lives."

Jerry defines the two questions to ask: (1) Are you serious about owning a home business of your own? (2) Is the timing right for you to take advantage of it? Unless the answer is yes to both, the prospect is not ready to take the plunge.

The most common recruiting mistake is to suggest that the new distributor is going to make $10,000 a month almost immediately. It could happen, but it's rare! The prospect will see through this.

The Campisis saw their networking company grow from gross annual sales of a few hundred-thousand dollars to a billion-dollar company today. They have tens of thousands of people in their organization and are members of the $10-million-dollar circle, indicating that they have earned at least this much in commissions through their business over the years.

Though they are most certainly set for life, the Campisis have come out of retirement to participate in the opening of their company's newest technology division. Why? Because they see the great potential of the

Internet and they see it as yet another way of helping their people. Jerry maintains that "Technology and the Internet are going to have a profound effect on our lives—whether we like it or not. In the early 1900s, farming made up 35 percent of our economy and the service sector was 30 percent. Today farming is 2 percent and the service sector is 75 percent. The Internet, the ideal service medium, will have an overwhelming global impact."

E-Commerce Takes MLM to Next Level

The role of the Internet in direct sales is being taken quite seriously by the DSA, with a full standing committee to deal with all aspects of recruiting on the Net. Many companies have executives serving on that committee.

According to Neil Offen, "One concern is having recruiting going global and getting people into countries where the company hasn't registered and it isn't officially allowed to do business. While this could represent a challenge, it is also driving international expansion. The biggest and most innovative aspect of the multi-level marketing form of direct sales is the cross-border sponsoring."

Leading MLMers are looking at ways to let people order everything from lipstick to salad bowls through their web sites, but they are being careful not to alienate their established network of sales representatives. Avon, the largest company of its kind in the world, took the first step toward on-line selling nearly two years ago. Companies such as Nu Skin are throwing themselves into the virtual market, selling nutritional vitamins and nutritional supplements on the Internet. Amway has affiliated with Microsoft to form Quixtar, an e-commerce site purported to be the largest e-commerce web site ever. Some of the newest networking kids on the block, such as Smart-Mart and Horizons International, are jumping into e-commerce with both feet.

Although electronic commerce is difficult to monitor, Jupiter Communication expects total on-line sales to grow from $12 billion in 1999 to $41 billion in the year 2002, while Forrester Research sees it reaching $108 billion by 2003. What is selling?

Product Category	Percentage
Home/Family Care Products (cleaning products, cookware, cutlery, etc.)	32.2 %
Personal Care Products (cosmetics, jewelry, skin care, etc.)	25.9%
Services/Miscellaneous/Other	18.2 %
Wellness Products (weight-loss products, vitamins, etc.)	17.9 %
Leisure/Educational Products (books, encyclopedias, toys/games, etc.)	5.8 %

One company, AllAdvantage, has created a way for Internet users to make money while they are using the Net without threatening or competing with their primary business. By displaying the view-bar which advertises certain companies, products, or services while surfing the Net or e-mailing friends, they will be paid for this advertising. And, not so surprising, the company is using an MLM compensation as each person introduces someone else to the concept. Because it is non-intrusive and costs nothing to Internet users, this is another sign of the times.

A Veteran Sees E-Commerce as the Future of the Industry

Many industry pioneers, who could easily retire, are once again excited about these new trends. After 20 years of MLM involvement, experiencing all of the ups and downs that inevitably go with active participation in our industry, Bill Hyman is more enthused than ever about network marketing. The reason: e-commerce possibilities leave him sleepless in Milwaukee. His story portrays, as well as any, the history and evolution of this industry through the 80s and 90s, leading us into the 21st Century.

When his dad used to ask him what he wanted to be when he grew up, Bill Hyman's answer was "a professional bum." As Bill reflects back, he acknowledges that this might have been a 12-year-old's definition of MLM success: leisure time and the money to enjoy it.

A high-school drop-out, Bill spent what would have been the last half of his high school years unloading ships in the port of Elat, Israel, or selling potatoes door to door in England. Returning home after two-and-a-half years, one thing Bill knew was that he could sell. With a strong desire to start his own business, and without knowing the first thing about automobiles, he enrolled in the Milwaukee Area Technical College to learn how to work on cars. His plan was to gain enough knowledge to open his own shop and be his own boss. But after six years of being an auto mechanic, Bill learned something important: he hated working on cars.

With long hair and a straggly beard, Bill walked into an upscale suburban home in Milwaukee one Sunday afternoon in July 1979, to attend his first MLM meeting. It was a day he will never forget. Bill remembers the man doing the meeting as a curious sort. Pudgy with very curly hair, he paced a lot and contradicted himself even more. But he was his own boss, making $3,000 a month, more money than a car mechanic could imagine then.

As Bill describes it, in his first 18 months, he fell flat on his face. At his first meeting, he sponsored one person who bought his kit, and never even picked it up. But he was driven by the realization that in this business he could be self-employed, help people, and make money without working on cars. Finally, persistence paid off. In the next 18 months, he turned one fifth-level customer (a customer five levels below his personally sponsored distributor) into a business builder (a company representative seriously putting together an organization of distributors), and together they created 35 leaders in Bill's organization.

"Two years later I was making more money in a month than I ever made in a year as a mechanic and was the number three distributor in the company. By July 1983, I was able to trade in my old beat-up Volkswagen for a brand new Mercedes and to move from my one-bedroom alley apartment to a four-bedroom home on two acres of land. I was in heaven."

It was just one month later that Bill called the home office and found no one there. They had gone out of business, and he had lost 2,500 distributors and all of his income.

"This was the greatest moment of panic I'd ever faced in my life. I didn't have any other source of income. My former wife had a small income from her job, but we owed more on the monthly house mortgage than I used to earn in total. I didn't know where to turn."

Making a New Plan

Still hooked on network marketing despite the bad experience, Bill joined two other companies before discovering the one with which he was to achieve his greatest accomplishments. Once again he started from scratch. His company at that time was not attractive to business people or to professionals. So the only way Bill felt he could make his distributors successful was through a detailed, step-by-step training program. He developed a training system that anyone could follow, implement, and duplicate. This course in the practical aspects of network marketing became his trademark, propelling him into overwhelming success in his next venture. He started a once-a-week class called "Success Seekers," which included daily homework assignments to teach effective work habits to less-experienced distributors.

Bill found that it was far easier to build an organization with those who had already developed their leadership skills in other careers. Those who have contacts, credibility, a good work ethic, and bring those qualities to their network marketing business, are the people who go right to the top. But the majority of those joining at that time were inexperienced. Bill believed that those who were willing to work and pay their dues through serious personal development would find success in network marketing.

After only 18 months part-time with his new company, Bill had 4,000 distributors in his organization and was making over $20,000 a month. As this company gained momentum, and Bill's checks continued to climb, he focused on bringing in professionals. He found one of his leaders by cold-calling various businesses in Florida, and another through a classified ad that he ran in *Business Opportunity Journal*. It was these experienced business people who were primarily responsible for Bill's monthly check increasing to $30,000, even $40,000, in a single month. Three years later, he had made millions by recruiting good leaders and replicating his simple training system for non-leaders. After more than a decade, his organization spans the globe with over 60,000 distributors. Bill's training system is used by dozens of network marketing companies in numerous countries around the world.

> **Those who have contacts, credibility, a good work ethic, and bring those qualities to their network marketing business, are the people who go right to the top.**

E-Commerce Expands Horizons

With his organization stabilized, and the excitement of building it gradually diminishing, Bill began looking for ways that he could make his next mark in the industry. While searching for new and better means of making his training materials available generically, Bill stumbled on something completely by accident that he feels may alter consumerism as we know it today. He discovered e-commerce, and when he let his mind wander to the possibilities of this medium for the networking industry—to describe him as excited is an understatement.

Shopping trends over the past 50 years have advanced from individual stores, to department stores to shopping malls to catalog telephone orders to QVC television shopping and now to shopping on the Internet. For the first time in network marketing history, individuals have the chance to own their own Internet commerce mall, with dozens of name-brand stores and services. Regardless of how many purchases are made from however many different stores, the buyer need only check out once. Every store from which a purchase is made immediately receives the demographic information on that shopper, and can track the commissions back to the distributor. This is possible because of a patent-pending, copy-written technology that referral-stamps this shopper to the distributor whose mall site they've utilized.

After 20 years in the business, Bill has found his passion all over again. He envisions countless distributors becoming wealthy by drawing a small commission from those customers who visit an electronic mall. He feels this is just the tip of the iceberg that network marketing, coupled with technology, offers for development in the coming millennium.

As Bill looks back over his years in this industry, he offers this reflection: "If you get with the right company at the right time, you don't have to worry about singles and doubles. You can hit a home run.

"But all of that comes only after a lot of trial and error. I believe that network marketing is the greatest self-development course on the face of the planet, leaving you open to learn more about yourself and others than almost anything else you can do. Network marketing is one of the few professions where you can watch wallflowers turn into rose gardens."

The Second Generation Takes Over

As we move into the new millennium, we will see more children taking over their parents' networking businesses. And that fact alone will

> **For the first time in network marketing history, individuals have the chance to own their own Internet commerce mall, with dozens of name-brand stores and services.**

account for some of the transition from the old way of doing things to fresh, innovative approaches.

Amway

Amway has come a long way from its 1959 days of selling vitamins and soap out of the basement of the DeVos home in the western Michigan town of Ada. Theirs is an important story to tell, because this company is the grandparent of network marketing. The original Amway founders, Rich DeVos and Jay Van Andel, have now passed the baton onto their sons, Dick DeVos, Jr. and Steve Van Andel, both men in their mid-40s who walk in their fathers' footsteps.

Amway fields an army of three million distributors in 45 countries. The company reports that sales have tripled since 1991, reaching $7 billion in retail sales, thanks to rapid growth overseas. Estimating roughly a wholesale volume of half of that amount, which is how standard industry calculations are made, Amway clearly is in the number one position of network marketing companies. Amway doesn't generally report earnings, but its publicly traded affiliates in Japan and Hong Kong are on record having earned a combined $295 million on revenues of $2.5 billion, as reported at the end of their third quarter report in 1997. The DeVos and Van Andel families own 80 percent of the two companies, a stake worth $3.4 billion.

On the way to achieving that size, Amway has acquired a reputation for controversy. For the past year, they have been involved in legal battles with Procter & Gamble Company. P & G filed suit alleging that some distributors from Amway were involved in rumor-mongering and slander saying that P & G had ties to Satanism. A U.S. District Court in Houston dismissed this case in May 1999. Apparently so outraged by this insinuation, P & G had earlier retaliated by also filing a restraint of trade suit against Amway alleging that their distributors were prohibited from buying any other products than those sold by Amway. In March 1999, this case was also dismissed in a Utah Federal District Court.

Why would a behemoth like P & G bother with a little gnat like Amway? I can only conclude that network marketing has taken enough of a bite out of the P & G market to become annoying.

That controversy has extended to the political arena as well. The founding families are ardently conservative, fervently Christian, and enormously influential in the Republican Party. Over the past decade, Amway has been a major GOP contributor. In 1996 it tried to donate $1.3 million to televise the GOP convention on Pat Robertson's cable channel but backed off when Democrats criticized the donation as a ploy to avoid campaign-finance restrictions.

Now, it's up to the eldest sons of the founders to carry on a small-town entrepreneurial legacy for one of the nation's largest privately held companies. Steve Van Andel and Dick DeVos, who serve as chairman and president respectively, face challenges their fathers never knew, including intense family pressures. And unlike their fathers, the new leaders harbor ambitions outside Amway. Both have indicated that they won't spend the rest of their careers in the business. While Steve Van Andel is vague about his plans, Dick DeVos has made no secret of his hope to run for political office, possibly a U.S. Senate seat.

The company still operates on the system the founders created in the 1950s. Rich was the seller and Jay kept his eyes on the books. The lives of the Amway sons have been intertwined since childhood and it shows. The co-CEOs are given to finishing one another's sentences and yield to one another in public. "In essence, Dick and I speak as one person," says Van Andel. "When we make a decision, the decision is the two of us making it." Their early years with the company were also shaped with controversy, much of it stemming from their distributor system.

"We are far more vulnerable than any company because of our (open-door) policy and the low cost of entry," Dick DeVos declares. The average monthly gross income before expenses for U.S. distributors is just $88, according to the company, which reports that most work for Amway part-time. Amway distributors earn profits on sales and bonuses, but they make more money from their recruits. To make $25,000 a year, a distributor needs to have 70 distributors, each generating $200 in sales a month.

Amway depends on super-distributors to fill the ranks as distributors drop out. To do that, the top-earning distributors have developed lucrative parallel businesses selling motivational tapes, books, and seminars. This element of Amway continues to be a controversial aspect of how it does business among network marketers in other companies. But there is no question that regardless of profits or loss, the Amway loyalty is resolute and, for many, has become a way of life.

The new leaders have also perpetuated the Amway tradition of political involvement, which dates from the 1979 FTC case.

"Government," Rich DeVos asserts, "has the power to sink you, destroy you—and you better pay attention."

Dick DeVos, who is very much at home in the political arena, reveals that Amway will remain committed to its political involvement. "We are not going to run away and hide on the issues." Associate network marketing companies should feel extremely indebted to the longtime political savvy of this direct-sales pioneer. Without Amway's 1979 courtroom victory over the FTC and their continued guarding against this fox's attack on their hen house, our industry would not be where it is today.[1]

Because of Amway's prowess in the industry, the Van Andel and DeVos charisma is significant to the network marketing industry. Quite frankly, I hope Dick DeVos does seek a major public office. It would be intriguing to see what might happen if a known network marketing personality sought a major public office, backed by ten million industry supporters.

The Birth of New Vision

It isn't just the old-guard companies that are passing the reins of power onto their children. This is happening even with the newer breed of companies. Benson Keith "BK" Boreyko has been involved in the industry for nearly 30 years. Lest you think he is an old man, he got his start at the age of nine.

"My parents were in Amway and I wanted to do something to help. So my father sent me out with a little tote tray to drop off at a neighbor's house. A week later, I'd pick it up and find out what products they wanted to buy. When I got out of high school, I became a distributor and went profit-sharing direct with Amway. After about three years, when I turned 21, I felt that it was time to get a real job, so I went to work with a Fortune 500 company in advertising.

"At this time my family made a move and joined another networking company, Matol Botanical. Working at my job 50 to 60 hours per week, I didn't have time to work with the family in this company. But after a year, I saw my brother, Jason, who was previously a bellman at a local hotel, making $8,000 per month. Since I felt I'd taught him everything he knew, I decided to start working the business again part-time. After about three months, I was able to go full-time. At least I had tried working on both sides of the fence and knew, beyond a doubt, where my heart was. For the next ten years of my life as a distributor, I was earning about $40,000 a month and had life by the tail."

In 1994, the Boreyko family fell into some hard times. Their mother developed a brain tumor. The company they represented went into bankruptcy. They faced their first Christmas without their mom and without a royalty check. Many of the distributors, both within and outside of their organization, were distraught, looking to the Boreykos for solutions. The entire family spent most of the holidays discussing the situation. With thousands of distributors waiting for them to come out, the Boreyko family emerged from their time in solace. They made the momentous decision to launch their own company, "New Vision International."

"I believe that the reason our company made it," says BK, "was because of our parents' reputation. We had 1,900 of our distributors signed on with our company the day we launched on March 20, 1995. Everyone in our company believed in what my parents had done and what they stood for. They knew that they could trust us. Integrity is a huge selling feature for any company."

As part of its mission, the company chose to target those professionals who can no longer find a home in corporate America.

"We will begin to see more and more people working twice as hard for half the money," BK says.

"In network marketing, we are a business that allows people to capitalize on the natural network that they have established over the years. People in their 40s and up are perfect for this type of an industry because they know people and are respected in the workplace. After all, their credibility is their strongest asset. From a company standpoint, we recognize that these displaced executives and business owners are professionals, and we need to look and act professional ourselves in order to be able to attract them."

With Ben Boreyko's recent death, his children are left to carry on the business. The family philosophy lives on—if you look after the newest person, everything else will fall in place.

"My dad always said 'you can't have a lot of big shots without a lot of little shots,'" BK recalled.

As I walked around the New Vision facility with BK, it was evident from the warmth between himself and every employee and distributor I met that this basic belief had passed on from father to son.

What Does This Mean for You?

You have now been presented with a brief history of the evolution of our industry. You have been informed about the good along with the bad. Perhaps you have even had some of those nagging rumors about our industry explained. I have taken you from the days of single-level direct selling to the first days of multi-level direct selling, and from the early phase of MLM to its evolution into a more sophisticated world of network and referral marketing. In the remaining chapters, I will share the challenges and the vision of the future through the eyes of the corporate and field leaders from this exciting industry.

"I think that the most powerful sales setting on earth," says Nu Skin's Steve Lund, "is an informed person with a personal relationship to a customer, able to share the merits of the product. I am so confident in the strength of this marketing channel as a means of providing information about products, that I am convinced that, wherever society may take us, direct selling will be in the heart of it."

Whether you decide to participate in this exciting industry or not, you will be hearing a great deal about it. Network marketing is destined to lead the way into the next century and become the leading choice of entrepreneurs. These self-starters, fed up with the norm, are characterized as people who take advantage of opportunities. They are resourceful, creative, independent thinkers, hard-working and optimistic. They perform as innovators, risk-takers and visionaries. These new entrepreneurs are individuals who seek personal fulfillment, want more freedom in their lives, wish to grow in their own self-mastery, perhaps have altruistic goals, and recognize the essential need for ongoing financial security. If this

> Network marketing is destined to lead the way into the next century and become the leading choice of entrepreneurs.

description fits you or the person you'd like to become, you owe it to yourself to seriously examine your own entrepreneurial options.

If it is fear that holds you back, know that this is a normal emotion. Once I was in New Zealand contemplating (not too seriously) going bungie jumping. It was an old man and woman who influenced my decision. While flying in a bi-plane over Milford Sound, the gentleman turned around and asked if I'd been bungie jumping yet.

"No, have you?" I inquired with disbelief.

"Sure, it's free if you're over 65," he replied in a matter-of-fact tone.

"Okay, I have to ask you one thing....Were you afraid?"

"Omigod, yes! As I stood over that raging river with just a little rope tied around my ankles, my heart was in my throat."

About that time, his 75-year-old wife spoke up and said, "Oh, honey, it was a cakewalk."

I went bungie jumping because an older woman shamed me into it. And, truthfully, it was only the anticipation that was so frightening. Once I made the dive (a truer description of a bungie jump), and was floating in air, pulled up and down, and up and down again by the tug of the elasticized rope, I thoroughly enjoyed the experience. Most of our fears are merely apprehension of what might come. Rarely do we hear people express fear in the act of rushing into the burning building or fighting waves at sea to save a life.

Unless we have been afraid, we cannot know courage. It is courage that stems from fear. It begins with a belief in ourselves. This belief together with the building of our confidence overrides our being paralyzed by fear. Fear can be a healthy emotion. It can energize and stimulate us. Instead of holding us back, it can drive us to perform even better...if we have the courage to take that next step.

How many have lost their health for the sake of making money...and then have had to sacrifice their hard earnings to restore their health? Loss of health is something to be feared. A possible solution for the future is not. If you have any reservations about network marketing, I hope your fear will lead you to have the courage to stay open to the prospect...and get back with the person who introduced you to this book.

CHAPTER 15

Countering Challenges Leads to
New Level of Professionalism

Thanks to the technological revolution, the network distribution era is manifesting itself in every corner of the world.

"It's necessary to stop the operation of pyramid sales," pronounced Wang Zhongfu, director of China's State Administration for Industry and Commerce, "since it has begun to hurt social stability and economic development." This statement made in April 1998 came as a result of unscrupulous pyramid scheme operators who disguised their fraudulent practices as direct-selling firms. Until then, the direct-selling industry had had an excellent record of economic and social contributions to the Chinese economy since 1985 when Avon first entered the market (followed by Amway, Mary Kay, Nu Skin, Sara Lee, Sunrider, and Tupperware).

This announcement didn't make headlines around the world, but in China it caused a mini-revolution. The announcement was the prelude to a government ban on all types of direct selling, including network marketing. For several million Chinese people, the restriction crushed their hopes and destroyed their chance for economic well-being. Mobs reacted in various cities across the continent, toppling cars, smashing windows, seizing hostages, and storming government offices. At the end of the violent outburst, ten people were dead and more than 100 wounded.

A new age is dawning for network distribution, something that China's Marxist rulers had not banked on. Within just a few short weeks after Wang's proclamation, they were compelled to create "conversion regulations" to require that products be sold at a fixed price (as opposed to wholesale and retail markup) directly from a fixed location (storefronts) with distributors acting as agents on behalf of the company. As long as these storefronts were in place, the network marketing distributors could still go door to door to sell their products and benefit from the compensation plan.

With these changes, Chin-ning Chu, president of Asian Marketing Consultants Inc. of Antioch, California, confirmed in June 1998 that network marketing had resumed in China, with the government's tacit endorsement.

Says DSA President Neil Offen, "With no DSA in China, we have no idea how many distributors were lost through this ordeal. With about four million on the books prior to the announcement, I am estimating there are at least two million remaining."

Prior to this event, sales for U.S. direct sales companies in China approached $1 billion in 1997. The period leading up to the ban resulted in the approximate losses of more than $200 million in revenues.

Exactly one year later, on April 8, 1999, thanks to the efforts of the Clinton administration and U.S. Trade Representative Charlene Barshefsky, an agreement regarding the future of the direct-selling industry in China was reached between China and the U.S. in World Trade Organization (WTO) negotiations. In a news-breaking press release, it was announced:

"The Chinese have agreed to a binding commitment to remove all market access restrictions on direct selling, including an April 1998 ban, no later than January 1, 2003," a media release announced. "In addition, the United States and China have agreed to inserting language into the definition of 'distribution' in the WTO agreement that includes 'wholesale or retail services away from a fixed location.'"

Offen indicated support for the breakthrough agreement and praised both Chinese and U.S. negotiators, indicating that it was in the interests of both nations and removed a major possible impediment to approval of China's accession to the WTO, which the DSA supports.

In addition, during the interim period, in the China-U.S. working party protocol, China has agreed to develop regulations for direct selling based on the World Federation of Direct Selling Association's World Codes of Conduct, in consultation with the U.S. government and the U.S. Direct Selling Association.

The excitement about the industry is unmistakable. If we are to advance as an industry, we must move forward with respectability and integrity. For this to happen there are still some vexing issues that must be addressed.

Let's look closely at the likely challenges network marketing will face as it evolves into the future. The more we anticipate possible roadblocks, the more likely we will counter them and move toward greater professionalism.

Pyramids Disguised as MLMs

Peter Hirsch, author of *Living with Passion*, has been involved with network marketing for about ten years. Most of Peter's experience has been as a top distributor with two previous companies.

"Had I been asked three years ago what changes I would predict for this industry, my answer would have been: we are entering a time of complete professionalism. Scams are being driven out and we are afforded our due respectability. And now, three years later? Compared to the early 90s, this is the slowest period I have seen in ten years in network marketing's advancement. Professionalism, once on the surge, now appears to have diminished and more pyramid scams are infiltrating our legitimate field, disguising themselves as network marketing."

A good example of the kind of pyramid scam to which Peter is referring recently got "spammed" into my e-mail box. It announced: "Earn $100,000 Per Year Sending E-Mail!!!" Then it gave a lengthy explanation instructing me to send $5 to the name at the top of each of the following reports, placing my name at the bottom of the fourth report.

REPORT #1
"The Insider's Guide to Advertising for Free on the Internet"
REPORT #2
"The Insider's Guide to Sending Bulk E-mail on the Internet"
REPORT #3
"The Secrets to Multilevel Marketing on the Internet"
REPORT #4
"How to become a Millionaire Utilizing the Power of Multilevel Marketing and the Internet"

The following explanation shows how the money will be made:

1st level - your 10 members with	$5	....	$50
2nd level – 10 members from those 10	$10	($5 x 100)	$500
3rd level – 10 members from those 100	$100	($5 x 1,000)	$5,000
4th level—10 members from those 1,000	$1,000	($5 x 10,000)	$50,000

Total $55,550

This is a pyramid scheme because it compensates people primarily for bringing other people into the sales plan rather than from the sale of legitimate goods or services. This is nothing more than a glorified chain letter. The reports are not stand-alone products, but are training materials. The State of California has ruled that such materials cannot be counted as commissionable volume. Do not be taken in by one of these scams. More importantly, do not mistake a pyramid scheme for network marketing. You wouldn't want to hurt your credibility by recommending this kind of program to people who look up to you. Remember, it takes years to build up trust and only a few seconds to destroy it.

"So," continues Peter, "I see integrity as the challenge of our times. Integrity springs from a commitment to a set of philosophical principles to which we adhere in all situations and use as a standard for our decision-making. If the scams are not curtailed, then we can expect to see much more regulatory involvement. Normally I wouldn't want the federal government in my life or in my industry, but I believe network marketing is at a critical juncture: either our industry must be made to conform to some significant ethical standards or be prepared to lose some of our best people.

"The painful reality is that network marketing companies must come to appreciate, far more than is being exemplified, the deep significance of integrity as a moral guide for all our actions. Short of that, the companies that circumvent this imperative will eventually lose or be acquired by those who have made integrity the hallmark of their functioning."

Do not mistake a pyramid scheme for network marketing. You wouldn't want to hurt your credibility by recommending this kind of program to people who look up to you.

Need for Government Regulation

Peter isn't alone in seeing a need for government regulation.

"As we move into the future," suggests Steve Lund of Nu Skin, "we need to keep working to overcome the integrity issues that continue to plague our industry until they are resolved. People want to do business with people they can trust."

Although he admittedly has mixed emotions, Steve believes a uniform regulatory program is necessary for the direct-selling companies.

"That has to be better than the current gridlock of several complex federal regulations combined with 50 conflicting state regulations. However, my skepticism is that the federal government would be able to understand the complexity of our industry sufficiently to create such a framework without doing damage to the fundamentals of the business."

"I would also like to see federal legislation that actually legitimized the industry," adds Jerry Campisi. "Right now, with 50 different regulations in 50 different states that govern the networking industry, it's absurd. Just like franchising in the 60s, it was difficult to get through Congress because the representatives thought it was just another way of getting an up-front fee. Little did they realize it was an entirely new way of doing business. Today hundreds of millions of dollars are generated through the franchising industry with it representing nearly one fourth of the Gross National Profit. It has gained worldwide acceptance, but this came as a result of Congress legitimizing the industry by putting laws into place that regulated everyone equally. I see that coming very soon for network marketing."

I too am hoping for federal regulation. With the financial backing of the established MLM companies, together with ten million distributors writing their state legislators, we deserve and should get a fair hearing. We can only hope that they will use the 1979 Amway decision as a precedent and starting point for 21st Century legislation.

"The best place to begin is for owners to found companies for the right reasons, and not simply to 'get rich quick...and then leave,'" says Ray Faltinsky, co-founder of FreeLife International, a nutritional company based in Milford, Connecticut. "I feel that company founders should have a higher vision than simply 'making money.' When this 'higher vision' becomes the driving force of the corporate leaders, encompassing their mission, then we will begin to see companies endure long-term. They must see the bigger picture and not feel compelled to change their comp plans for the latest hype; they don't come out with products with little or no research to back up their claims.

"What we're really talking about," he concludes, "is the integrity of the people coming into the industry, both founders and distributors alike. Neglecting this higher vision will turn people off on the industry. I'm hearing this from the leaders in our field. Marketing execs who continually jump from one company to another lose credibility with their friends and family. Everyone, corporate executives and field leaders alike, must have stability and consistency to succeed. I foresee many more mergers between network marketing companies in the future, which, hopefully, will rid the industry of those 'come and go' companies who are devoid of that higher vision of building on integrity and fostering stability."

Companies and Regulators Must Agree

Richard Brooke has been the president and owner of Oxyfresh, a small network marketing company, for the past 12 years. He has been directly involved in the industry for over 23 years. He proposes that our industry needs its methodology more suitably delineated.

"One thing clearly needed in our industry is to redefine network marketing," he says. "We all know that the process is threefold: using the products, selling the products, and enrolling others to do the same. Using the products takes no time and is a basic expectation of every distributor. Selling the products takes more time but has little financial reward. Even if you had a thousand customers who are direct to one distributor, depending on the price and profit structure, that effort might represent $4,000 or $5,000 monthly income. The payback just isn't there to retail a lot of product. And it becomes even more cumbersome if the company has no retail direct program. If a customer calls up their distributor and says 'I need a bottle of this or a tube of that,' the time and energy it would take to provide that service is not a cost-effective action. So the place to spend your time is in the third arena—to build an organization by recruiting other business builders."

But as Richard is quick to point out: "Therein lies the catch. From a regulator's perspective, if you put more emphasis on engaging other distributors rather than selling products, by their definition of network distribution, that is a pyramid scheme. To their way of thinking, there is something wrong with spending all of your time recruiting, when, in fact, that is what all truly successful networkers do. So we are living a lie and it needs to be validated. We need to accept the fact that the definition of network marketing is different than direct sales."

Direct-selling companies are represented by a few full-time, skillful salespeople selling large quantities of their products within a geographical territory. Network marketing is a different paradigm. It is not a few superstars doing large quantities of sales, but rather a lot of people doing a little bit each.

You can hire 100 superstar sales people and motivate each of them to sell $10,000 worth of product each month. Or you can have 10,000 network distributors sell $100 each month. They both equal a million dollars in sales.

The network marketing industry today still suffers from a lack of respect because we are caught in this Catch-22. As long as regulators demand that networkers conform to the perception of a business as having retail emphasis alone, when MLMers are primarily dedicated to building an organization, the incongruity will persist. The time has come for regulators to categorically address this issue: unlike single-level direct sales, multi-level marketing is a lot of people doing a little bit.

Need for Relevant Uniform MLM Laws

Early on, you may remember our discussion about the famous Amway decision made some 20 years ago that played a significant role in carrying our industry into the next phase. As you may recall, the key element differentiating Amway from a pyramid was its "70-percent rule" which required a distributor to verify that 70 percent of his previous order had been consumed before he could reorder. The networking industry has governed itself by that rule ever since.

In the summer of 1992, two former distributors who had ostensibly lost some money in their business filed suit against their company, a health and skin-care company called Omnitrition International. In July 1994, the trial court dismissed the case, known as *Webster v. Omnitrition*, which had alleged that the company was, among other things, an illegal pyramid scheme. The trial court granted a motion for summary judgment concluding that, based on the facts submitted, as a matter of law, the plaintiffs were unlikely to prevail at trial.

The plaintiffs' attorneys appealed the case and a three-judge Ninth Circuit panel remanded the matter for trial. The panel issued an opinion that contradicted, in part, the 1979 Amway decision. The Ninth Circuit said an MLM company is a pyramid scheme unless 70 percent of its products are being sold to customers outside the company as opposed to being ordered and consumed by distributors who are part of the company.

Network marketing attorney Ed Wainscott says, "These judges said a lot of things that I consider to be 'dicta,' that is, a statement that the Court makes, offering its opinion, but it is not central to the Court's ruling."

In other words, the judges' *opinion* was to deny the validity of any network marketing company to be able to serve as a wholesale buyers club. By suggesting that, unless 70 percent of all orders in a network marketing company go toward retail sales, it is a pyramid scheme, this opinion invalidates the rights of distributors to count personal use as commissionable volume. While seemingly ridiculous, it was only a dicta opinion; the actual decision was to remand the case to trial court.

On March 20, 1998, this case was settled out of court. For a period of five years, the Federal District Court retained jurisdiction on the reasonableness of changes to Omnitrition Rules and Regulations. For a period of 12 months, Omnitrition was required to "provide...reasonable evidence of its compliance with its refund policy, 70-percent rule and ten-customer rule."

Leaders from the DSA are dealing assertively with the question by lobbying state legislatures to clarify their "anti-pyramid" statutes.

"We now have an anti-pyramid substitute for the language we've been using in the industry that has been enacted by the 1999 Montana State Legislature and signed by the state's governor," Neil Offen proudly reports. The DSA is prepared to go, state by state, to develop a uniform code of anti-pyramid law, and once and for all determine a uniform policy for the rules governing multi-level direct sales in the United States. This standardization of a code of industry practice will fulfill one of the missing elements needed to make our industry a verifiable profession.

I encourage state legislators, lobbyists, and concerned citizens to check my web site or the Resource section at the back of this book for "Uniform MLM Laws" to get a copy of this bill. You may want to work with the DSA to introduce a similar bill into the next legislative session in your state.

It would take a grass-roots effort, person by person, state by state, and country by country, to effect this much-needed uniformity for our industry. Jane Fergason, an attorney with Gardere & Wynne, a Dallas-based law firm who represented Omnitrition in the case, commented, "Hopefully, through legislation encouraged by the industry and the DSA, education of governmental officials, and self-regulation by direct-sales companies, the misleading and controversial language of the Ninth Circuit Court will become meaningless in time."

Bonding Product and Technological Companies

There seems to be a connection between technological and product-oriented networking companies. Each is coming from opposite ends of the spectrum, but the ultimate purpose of each is to retail products to an end consumer. Kenny Davis, one of the principals with Smart-Mart, a two-year-old company out of Dallas, as well as director of its network marketing division, sees the convergence.

"It is good to see a company like Avon that was previously built on direct sales now coming into the network marketing world," he says. "Our technology company, like Avon, is stressing retailing, but on-line retailing. We are a department store on the Internet. We are delivering, at cost, tens of thousands of name-brand products like Tommy Hilfiger, RCA, Donna Karan, Armani, and we are still paying commission on them. Our approach is to build a large customer base like a Sam's Club, utilizing network marketing as the driving engine to that. The distributor force is marketing all of those products while also building an organization of distributors who will in turn bring in their own retail customers."

The regulatory agencies should find relief in the approach used by Internet retailing companies. While the reality is that they are building a network like any other multi-level company, the perception is that they are returning to a retailing emphasis.

231

Controlling Product and Income Claims

"I think the greatest damage to the professionalism of our industry is the marketing and promotion of programs and products that are either blatantly inappropriate or in a gray area," says Richard Brooke. "Most companies are willing to promote their programs and products in these marginal areas in an effort to generate fast sales. Some companies get away with it and some don't. Unfortunately, this bleeds over into advertising. No one makes more false-income claims than network marketers. Often presidents of companies, presidents with high standards of integrity, are forced to cross over the line in order to survive and keep up."

Historically, in order for a start-up company to come out of the chute and experience success before it runs out of money, owners and managers will tolerate outlandish product claims. The president and management know full well that the distributors are going overboard in their hype of certain products, but they make no attempt to stop it. Why? Fear of sinking before they can stabilize their little boat in the rough financial waters.

It is generally more difficult for a network marketing company to get underway because most are undercapitalized. Many of the companies recognized today as giants in the industry began with only a few thousand dollars. Most of them had to substitute hype for capital in the early days.

When those very rare companies do develop a semblance of financial stability, then they can also afford to develop integrity and enforce their policies. Or as is more often the case, once they are doing well enough to be noticed, they get a visit from the FTC and are reminded, by virtue of a fine, that they should straighten up their act.

The quest for international expansion seems to be another factor in a company's marketing practices. Companies naturally want to be in the black as soon as possible, but there are countless rules imposed by the governments of countries into which the company is entering. The company must impose those rules; otherwise they risk being fined or completely shut out of that country. But the stricter they are about imposing those rules, the longer they remain in the red. So when a few aggressive distributors make it possible for the company to open in the black by conducting activities prematurely in the new country, there is a strong inclination for the company to look the other way, or, at worst, give them a token slap on the wrist.

These types of marginal activities by company owners and managers seriously damage the reputation of our industry. Good people are hurt.

Distributors become angry. The "us" and "them" nature between the field and corporate management becomes a wide chasm. If we want to avoid this, we must begin by elevating the level of integrity by which we play the game. This virtue should begin at the top and trickle throughout the distributor force. The simple truth should begin in company literature, in advertising, in the equality and fairness of policy enforcement.

Lorene Crom, a successful distributor with a four-year-old nutritional company, agrees and suggests that the respectability of our industry relies heavily on the veracity of the field force.

"In order to elevate the bar of professionalism in the industry, we must raise the standards of how we present the opportunity," she says. "No more 'get rich quick' presentations that convey a pyramid scheme. This is hard work. Just ask anyone who is in this business today and has persevered through months and even years of struggles, challenges, loss of key leaders, media misinformation, etc."

Part-time Catch-22

The part-time capability of Network Marketing is a Catch 22 for the industry. "On the one hand, it sets the industry apart allowing professionals to maintain their careers while also 'lifestyling' this business," Connie Dugan points out. "On the other, the very part-time nature of our industry sends a message to the traditional professional world that we aren't to be taken seriously."

Rick Jordan and I share one aspect of network marketing in common: we both began as part-time professionals. Rick still is part-time. He owns two insurance agencies, a hand car wash, and is a partner in several fast-food restaurants. He has done well in business, and didn't want to relinquish his years of building up client relationships or revenue in his insurance business, but he wanted to protect himself from the shrinking insurance commissions.

Giving up a few hobbies, and with careful time management, Rick began his networking business part-time with the goal of diversifying his income. He used the same work ethic in this business that he had in insurance. He set aside one hour a day to prospect. He never deviated from that hour, not even to make a sale or close a client. For both Rick and me, consistent activity was especially critical to our part-time business venture. But it didn't all go smoothly for Rick, as he relates.

"After a year and a half, I hit a wall. My business wasn't growing fast enough and I was frustrated and ready to quit. I talked to my upline mentor who restored my confidence and my belief. In the next six months, my income grew over 300 percent." Living with his family in Laguna Niguel, California, now in his sixth year of working consistently at a part-time business, Rick's income is nearly a half-million dollars annually.

An attitude change about professionalism is needed—not just in our industry but across the board. Part-time does not and cannot signify "not serious." As we enter the 21st Century, there will be innumerable part-time, earnest, effective new entrepreneurs emerging. Their part-time or transitional status in our business must not diminish their stature or their respect as professionals.

New Professionals Demanding More

Looking back on his years in network marketing, Richard Brooke reflects: "I've seen a dramatic change in this industry. The first major transition came at the distributor level maybe about ten years ago. It became evident that the quality of the distributors showing up to pursue the opportunity was vastly different than the last ten or 20 years. Before, the majority of people getting involved tended to be less sophisticated. If they found a product that they really liked and could talk decently about it, they could make some money.

"But what showed up about ten years ago was a new class of society, with more education, a history of higher incomes, higher expectations for themselves, and were able to figure out the mathematical advantages of network marketing. This new group of entrepreneurs joining the industry discovered that if they could leverage themselves on an unlimited basis, they could do this business with no employees, or at best, maybe one

---

As we enter the 21st Century, there will be innumerable part-time, earnest, effective new entrepreneurs emerging. Their part-time or transitional status in our business must not diminish their stature or their respect as professionals.

---

assistant to keep track of their business. This wave of a new breed of network marketers came in concert with the opening of free markets and the development of communication infrastructure around the world."

Dave Schofield, President of Rexall Showcase, is also seeing this changing environment with more well-educated professionals joining the industry.

"In our own company, approximately 30 percent of our distributors are healthcare professionals and 70 percent come from management or executive ranks," he says. "Most of our people would not have been likely candidates for network marketing 15 or 20 years ago. But so many individuals are not content with their typical corporate jobs. They are looking for other opportunities to develop their own businesses, to be free of time constraints and politics, to take control of their lives! Network marketing is a perfect alternative for them."

Richard Howard, president and co-founder of Eventus International, credits the professionals coming into the industry as a significant reason for the maturity and expansive growth of the industry. Or is it the other way around? For many networkers, money is not the primary motive. Unlike traditional business where so many workers are held back, professionals in our industry are driven by the high expectations their team members have for them.

Education Essential for Networking Professionals

Avon is an icon in the direct-sales industry with more than 2.5 million members in 130 different countries. After more than 100 years of direct-selling, Avon moved from single-level to multi-level marketing in 1991 to give their representatives a better earning opportunity. After seven years of a learning curve, they have seen enough to make a further commitment to the network marketing approach as a viable way of moving their products.

This decision, from such a respected direct-sales company, speaks volumes for the industry. Out of the nearly half a million independent Avon contractors in the United States, 6,300 of them have shown an interest in moving into the new network marketing division of their company. Avon now is in the process of retraining this group to be network marketers, and it is not the only company discovering the power of network marketing and incorporating this as a division within the corporate umbrella of their present company.

> So many individuals are not content with their typical corporate jobs. They are looking for other opportunities to develop their own businesses, to be free of time constraints and politics, to take control of their lives! Network marketing is a perfect alternative for them.

After 18 years, the Dallas-based direct-sales company, Beauty Control, began to see the potential for upside growth in network marketing and formed an MLM division, Eventus International. Mike Moseley, director of sales development, indicates the new division was launched with nutritionals and will expand into skin care products.

Referring to the challenges still ahead for the industry, Mike observes, "We have a ways to go to get past the credibility gap. In the past, the industry had a lot of get-rich-quick scams happening. Continuing education and creating alliances with major universities, such as the University of Illinois at Chicago (UIC), will definitely help move us to the next level of professionalism.

"I believe network marketing is going to continue to become stronger. If you look at all the new companies that are entering the industry every day, and then look at the total revenue that is being produced every year, it is evident that the industry is growing exponentially. In ten years, network marketing will undoubtedly be a major force as more and more people will be searching for an alternative means of generating an income."

Evertrue Bell, one of four regional trainers for Avon, feels strongly that "network marketing is a salvation for companies that are mature like Avon. For us to bring incremental advancement to our business and our independent contractors, we have to embrace multi-level marketing. However, it is almost the opposite of what we have been trained to do in the corporate arena. Traditionally, corporate teams are accustomed to being in control of their own business. Network marketing is all about empowering the distributors to take the business to the next level through education and duplication.

"What I'm seeing in our industry is that the administration is having difficulty letting go of some of that control. We are seeing people in management responsibilities but with no training to prepare them for working in the networking field."

Peter Hirsch shares this same concern. "People are used to being trained in their professions and jobs—it is a necessity in both conventional and networking businesses. If you bring someone into this business and they quit within the first 90 days, I believe a large part of the responsibility rests with you. Did you slip up on the requirement for 'sponsoring' someone? What about their training? Was the focus on training 'quality of life' or on 'how much money can I get?'"

As we develop on-going training programs, we will meet one more criterion needed to be recognized as a profession.

Technology Doesn't Replace Relationships

We're already seeing network distribution companies using conventional advertising as a way to search for new distributors and build brand-name awareness for their company. More and more, companies are promoting their web sites and allowing customers to order through them.

"The old model of retailing—driving across town to make product deliveries—is outmoded with the advancement of technology," notes Richard Brooke. "Very soon, all retail business will be ordered directly from the company off its web site, fax, or toll-free number."

Despite all these technological advances, we must not lose sight of the human aspect of MLM. For technology to be effective in this industry, people need to hear other people tell them about the products, services, or business opportunity. Once the human contact is made, then the prospective business partner or customer can be directed to the technical central site.

Need for Improved Compensation Plans

John Kavanagh has been in the network marketing industry since 1988. Residing in the Chiswick district of London, after working in two companies there, he took a sabbatical from the industry until some of the major missing ingredients were in place. After using his year for study and research, he arrived at some conclusions about compensation plans that he feels the industry must address.

"The manner in which people have traditionally been compensated for their efforts has been a challenge for companies throughout the history of the industry. This has left a trail of disenchanted individuals who have put in a lot of hard work, energy and time, as well as sacrificing their family togetherness to pursue a dream. Despite this, those same people who have left the business are continually pulled back in because of the vision and the concept.

"There are changes going on since I was disillusioned with the industry. A handful of companies have reinvented the compensation concept and have had the boldness and the vision to recognize the Jurassic Park nature of the old plans. The logic should be this simple: 'If you spend so much money with us and you have made the commitment to order that product directly from our company, and if you recommend it to others, we will pay you so much of a percent on all the people you introduce. And if you or your family spend a little more each month, we will even pay you on those people whom your people refer to us.'

"This is the underlying theory upon which network distribution is based. It drives the distributors' monthly commitment to order from the company and use their products; it determines the distributor's ability to access bonuses and commissions within that compensation structure. Beyond that, there should be leadership bonuses for the people who intend to take this further and duplicate themselves. What I am describing is a uni-level plan with a breakaway element. Some will argue that this type of plan limits distributors in terms of having the big volumes of a breakaway, but what is good is that it allows a greater number of people to work within the system, doing a little or a lot, as they so choose.

"In the early 1990s, we saw network marketing as a challenge here in Europe. The learning curve here is a much shorter one than in the States. People in Europe expect a higher standard from day one. Many U.S. companies have come to Europe ill-prepared, but they only work in disarray for so long before they fail. People expect more professionalism here; otherwise they are not interested. Clearly, the networking atmosphere is

> The old model of retailing—driving across town to make product deliveries—is outmoded with the advancement of technology...Very soon, all retail business will be ordered directly from the company off its web site, fax, or toll-free number.

changing worldwide, but I especially see it here in Europe. The energy of the people in the industry is more vibrant and those looking at network marketing as a career choice are finding well-grounded logic in doing this business.

"I see the future of this industry as very exciting, moving rapidly towards far greater credibility. As a business, there is no concept anywhere in the world today that is this powerful. No other enterprise is set up to be as influential globally. No other industry comes as close to changing people's lives and empowering individuals from all walks of life. And no other profession brings so much vision, inspiration, and recognition into people's lives."

Women's Income Level in Network Marketing Not Up to Par

While women still outnumber men as distributors in this industry, as a whole, we are not yet generating the same income. The inspiring women exemplified in this book are still the exceptions. As we face the dawning of the Entrepreneurial Age, a strong female side in both men and women will particularly reveal itself in those professionals seeking balance, nurturing, and integrity as necessary aspects of their work life. And with the fostering of these qualities in our industry, I believe, inevitably the money will follow.

It is this female factor that enhances what I love to call "relationship marketing." Ours is a business built on relationships. Both men and women who possess a strong feminine side often find that their innate sense of values embraces a remarkable capability for kindness and concern for the well-being of others.

You may recall the 1992 Olympic trials in the women's marathon event. The runners were off. The leaders had been pacing themselves perfectly. Then there was a jam-up at the water table at the fifteen-mile mark. One minute Janis Klecker was leading the pack; the next she went crashing to the concrete, flipping over on her back, forcing Cathy O'Brien to leap over her. The amazing part is what happened next: Cathy came back to help Janis up—and Janis went on to win the race.

Cathy O'Brien lost the race—but she won the hearts of everyone looking on. That kind of behavior is the stuff of which network marketing is made—people winning by helping others win. Women are naturals at this. We have done wonders to help raise the level of integrity and deepen human values in our industry. Now it is time that we step forward with

> As a business, there is no concept anywhere in the world today that is this powerful. No other enterprise is set up to be as influential globally. No other industry comes as close to changing people's lives and empowering individuals from all walks of life.

confidence and belief in our gifts, and command the respect and income that we deserve.

Past Challenges Become Prologue

We will one day look back and remember the 90s as the decade when outsiders began to look seriously at our industry. According to a June 23, 1995, article in *The Wall Street Journal*, the total number of network marketers in the U.S. increased 34 percent between 1990 and 1994. It's obvious that the industry is expanding exponentially. With the strength of this surge in interest, we must become more dedicated to enhance the education of new MLMers as well as the general public.

It is also incumbent upon us to guide these new professionals joining our ranks to live within their means until their income revenue stabilizes. Far too many networkers live beyond their means, buying into the dream and living it before it is sensible. Some will create a good life within our industry by reaching for the stars and earning an income to match. Others will find a sense of freedom by keeping their feet planted solidly on the ground and cutting back on their lifestyle for the sake of personal happiness. Both avenues are signs of success.

Given a better understanding of network marketing and a new breed of professionals joining our ranks, perhaps start-up companies will be less inclined to use dubious methods of selling products and recruiting new distributors. This would result intrinsically in a higher standard of integrity, which, in the final analysis, is the answer to the core of MLM challenges in the next century.

CHAPTER 16

Vision of the Future as a Global Community

I am convinced that we are entering the Entrepreneurial Age. I believe that the entrepreneurs who will transport us across the threshold of this new era will be legions of network marketers, carrying the banner that signals our inalienable rights to lifestyle freedom, personal fulfillment, and financial security.

After nearly three decades in the administration of the direct-selling industry, having watched the World Federation of Direct Selling Associations spread into 140 countries, Neil Offen is bullish about our industry.

"I think direct selling, of which network marketing constitutes the largest part, will recruit over 200 million people in the next ten years.

> The entrepreneurs who will transport us across the threshold of this new era will be legions of network marketers, carrying the banner that signals our inalienable rights to lifestyle freedom, personal fulfillment, and financial security.

> **"You strengthen our country and our economy, not just by striving for your own success, but by offering opportunity to others...Your industry gives people a chance...to make the most of their own lives and, to me, that's the heart of the American dream." —William Jefferson Clinton.**

Using the Internet and the world of technology, together with traditional approaches, positions the industry to be in the right place at the right time."

Support for our industry is coming from high places today. "You strengthen our country and our economy, not just by striving for your own success, but by offering opportunity to others...I've followed your industry's growth for years now...Your industry gives people a chance, after all, to make the most of their own lives and, to me, that's the heart of the American dream." This was a videotaped statement prepared for sales representatives of the DSA, which is made up almost entirely of network distribution companies. Released at their September 1996 convention, these words were spoken by the President of our United States, William Jefferson Clinton. This alone is a measure of how far the industry has advanced from its humble beginnings of just a few decades ago.

Internet Bringing Families Together

"Network marketing is nothing more than getting a product from the manufacturer to the end user by eliminating some of the middlemen and the advertising," states Jerry Campisi. "With this as the objective, clearly the Internet will carry our industry into the next phase of dynamic growth. I believe the future will look more like Amazon.com, where it is incumbent on companies to give real value to the customer by marking products at the same price or better than what can be purchased through conventional means. Through the Internet, customers can be serviced at any time and as often as needed. That will create customer retention and a far more service-oriented and cost-effective way of doing business through networking."

There are several web sites currently being developed that use the Internet to draw together families who are separated by geographical distancing. They offer an Internet Family web site; families who once were too separated to share in the joy of the latest birth, anniversary party, new home, or grandchild's birthday party, simply click on the family web site. Like Bill Gates, they are selling software. It can be offered to anyone in the world, in any country, at any time of the day or night. If you want to have your own family web page, you just download it to your computer. From a network marketing perspective, this type of site builds community, an essential quality for any successful Internet service provider.

Jim Brown, President and founder of SkyBiz 2000, offers one such site. "We wanted to include three facets in our business plan: (1) a tutorial program that would educate the masses who have never tried going on the Internet before; (2) a marketing arm that could instantly reach out to the global community; and (3) finances and a back-end support system that would be there to personally help those buying into our program," Jim says.

Uniting families on the Net is a growing phenomenon. There are several sites reaching out to families today and more coming on-line. *My Family Builder* is one such site through which, in addition to the family album concept, families and friends are drawn together to share family treasures, newsletters, and hand-me-downs with each other. They are invited to have regularly scheduled reunions in the chat room; introduce family businesses to each other; utilize a common address book and family calendar to recall each others' special days by sending cards or gifts; and, of course, research the family tree. Even relationship skills and crisis lines are being developed and made available. (See Resource section at back of book for more detail.)

FlashNet, an Internet service provider based in Ft. Worth, Texas, since 1995, has taken a stand on family values for their customers. Says Lee Thurburn, founder and chairman of the board, "In keeping with our family mission, we have introduced CleanNet, removing from our server certain newsgroups containing child pornography and other illegal and inappropriate activities."

Terri Frey, president of FlashNet's network marketing division begun in 1997, feels that the positive message this sends more than offsets the loss of a small customer base who might object to this restriction. "We have set the stage for FlashNet Marketing Int. to be the leading edge for

243

an Internet-based, e-commerce, network marketing company of the 21st Century. We have been building to this day for the past two years."

Let your mind wander for a moment to the business possibilities. These companies aren't just in the direct downloading business. They are in the network marketing business. Because there is no manufacturing cost, no warehousing, and no shipping, they can afford to share more of the wealth with their distributors, who, in turn, have no barriers to building their business. The distributors are not only sanctioned to do business in all 50 states, but will easily be at liberty to do business in every country in the world.

Consider what it would be like to first put your international team in place with a simple product such as a software program, then over the years, sell new and more tangible products through the existing organization. Consider the fund-raising potential for churches, universities, and community organizations looking to raise money for a cause in keeping with their personal missions. This entire concept opens up staggering possibilities!

International Expansion Possible by Merging with Internet

Much of what we've discussed is targeted toward the impact of network marketing in the U.S., but, as Richard Brooke sees, there is explosive potential outside the country.

"Recently, my wife, Rashon, and I were in Asia for our company," Richard recalls. "What is amazing is to watch how those people's eyes and hearts light up about the opportunity to earn a respectable income, knowing that they can transcend their own country's borders, economy, and culture. They can earn money based on the American, Australian or European economy and not be restricted to their own, somewhat tenuous, monetary system."

International expansion of your network marketing organization is one of the most exciting and potentially lucrative phases of your business. But it can also be one of the most frustrating, unless you know what you're doing or have good leadership from an upline team member. Having access to the Internet and the myriad technological advances can be a key component in keeping lines of communication open.

Erik Rasmussen, a longtime MLMer, recently purchased a new computer and searched the web for a business opportunity for his fiancee, Patricia. He discovered a network marketing company utilizing e-commerce through technology and networking. He believes e-commerce will explode through the marriage of the Internet and network marketing.

The upside and, from a legal perspective, the downside of Internet e-commerce is that there are no restrictions in place to control cross-border sales.

Erik had stumbled onto an opportunity that is global from day one. "In two and a half days, we already have over 100 people we've sponsored by using this technology," Eric says. "I will go on record telling you that by using the e-commerce principle, I believe that this organization will grow within the next 18 months to within a quarter of a million people. In my mind, unless we as networkers successfully tap into this technology phenomenon that is occurring, we are missing the boat. I think that it is incumbent on corporate leaders to make a massive effort to integrate the two, technology and networking, if we are going to grow major network marketing organizations internationally." E-commerce will have a dramatic impact on our industry, our lives, and our economy.

Technological Advancement Enhances Growth

All of these dramatic changes in how both conventional and network businesses are conducted are possible because of the ongoing advancements in technology. We are just seeing the tip of the iceberg of the real impact of the Internet on our communications, international expansion, product pricing, customer service, e-commerce, and shopping on the Net.

"With the Internet as an added boon, the industry is going to continue to grow and grow," comments Rudy Revak, CEO and founder of Symmetry, a San Jose, California, based nutrition company in business since 1995. "It's an incredible tool for putting our business into the hands of millions of people who want a home-based, seamless, global business."

There are many vendors who, understanding this phenomenon, have created profitable businesses by supplying the MLM industry with the

> International expansion of your network marketing organization is one of the most exciting and potentially lucrative phases of your business.

245

necessary tools to conduct business. Among them is Mac Oswald of Sound Concepts in Vineyard, Utah. (See Resource section at back of book.)

Mac recalls the days when being at the head of a network organization meant loading the products into the cars of your distributors from your garage.

"Today, the operation has gone professional," he comments. "Instead of being just a sales and delivery specialist, each network marketer these days is the CEO of a personal corporation."[1]

Stuart Johnson is no newcomer to network marketing. A distributor at the age of 15, he has always been drawn to the industry. In August of 1987, he founded Video Plus, a supplier of audio and video cassettes in Lake Dallas, Texas, to the network marketing industry. (See Resource section in back of book.)

What is evident to him is that the companies strictly in it for the money come and go, and in the process, give the industry a black eye. In contrast, the companies that are product-focused are the ones that last over time.

Blake Roney, the founder and now Chairman of the Board of Nu Skin Enterprises, attributes the quality of the company's products to their long-term success. "Lots of companies that we've seen come and go placed their emphasis on the money. We tried to keep our focus on having 'all of the good and none of the bad' ingredients in our products. Nu Skin was the first company that said you could return your products...whenever. As I look ahead, I like what I see coming. As an industry, we've moved from looking like a fair—get your vitamins here, over here, get your lotions— to truly becoming part of a marketing system that rewards higher-quality products. With more emphasis on consumer protection coupled with marrying ourselves with modern technology that combines direct selling and the Internet, the opportunity can only get better."

Another example that illustrates this point is Ken Rolfsness, an American living in Brisbane, Australia, who maintains that you must first believe deeply in the value of your product before you can ask others to invest in it. It was the healing power of his product that first drew Ken, and now he is so enthusiastic about it that when my secretary finished transcribing my recorded interview with him, she asked, "How can I get some of that juice?" He humbly credits his product's value more than himself for his early success.

"In all honesty, with no prior experience in network marketing, I didn't expect my business to take off this fast. I really liked the product, but from the beginning, I was negative about the business opportunity," he says now. His recruiting method is straightforward.

"I give the tape about the product to friends and associates asking for their opinion," he says. "After listening, if they respond positively, I follow up with some literature on the product. If they are still excited, I invite them to a meeting being held in the area. There, a top distributor in our company introduces them to more information about the product and the business opportunity that accompanies it. About 90 percent are signing up. Once they join, I teach them to duplicate this system and to target, as their first goal, bringing three new distributors into the business under them." Ken's company has just introduced a web site as well.

"There are many more people in the business today," Stuart Johnson notes, "who look at the industry as a profession and a long-term investment instead of a hobby. These are the people (like Ken) who are succeeding.

"I am somewhat skeptical of using the Internet as a recruiting tool. But long-term, the Internet will be a significant communications tool. Everything that we have done over the past five years on satellite and through current media forms, we will be able to do even more effectively on the Web, because you can find and download in a matter of seconds just exactly what you need. It's about access versus broadcast: getting whatever you want, whenever you want it, from wherever you are."

Speaking of 24-hour-a-day access, network marketing now has its own radio show, exclusively on the Internet. That's right! It's called Freedom Radio and presently is a two-hour program that can be pulled off the Net 24 hours a day.

"Despite its futuristic source," says Paul Saunders, managing partner for Your Radio Mall, "it looks and sounds like a regular talk radio show. Complete with disc jockey, newscasts, and laid out in an effective magazine format, it is designed to be accessible and informational to a distributor anywhere in the world."

As a regular program contributor to Freedom Radio, it brings me full circle back to my talk-radio days. I used to host a talk show in the 70s and early 80s in San Francisco, Denver, and Reno. I am virtually doing the same thing, except that now I pre-record from my home. Only with Internet broadcasting can we be heard from anyplace in the world. Those of us making an "appearance" on the show will share some perspective of the business, and make our books, tapes, and materials available through the radio mall. The station owners plan to promote the program via the Internet as well as through various industry trade magazines.

The process to tune in is simple. If you want to listen to the show, go to www.yarnell.com and click on the Freedom Radio icon. A radio station delivered by the Internet is one more step to bring professionalism to this industry. It's as close as your dial—well, okay, as close as your Internet browser.

Says Kenny Davis, "The last 20 years of how this industry has been run will not dictate the next 20 years. Technology is inherently changing the way we do business. It will reinforce the already catapulting trend of home-based businesses with checks being issued and printed right off the Internet."

Also enhancing the way we research network marketing companies, the Internet will see a new MLM on-line resource site called mLmSuccess.com which features an extensive database of network marketing companies worldwide and a search function to identify companies by product or service. Users can also locate distributors for each company by region anywhere in the world. This will include articles by some of the industry's most respected authors and trainers. (See Resource section at back of book.)

Media Is Drawing Professionals

We have made some great inroads in the educational arena because of certificate courses like that offered at the University of Illinois at Chicago. There have been notable strides with the media since the 80s, with positive articles appearing in *The Wall Street Journal*, and such magazines as *Success*, *Forbes*, *Home Business*, and now our very own *Network Marketing Lifestyles* publication. The very existence of an industry magazine that can be purchased by subscription or off the newsstand is in itself a step forward for the industry.

"The power behind *Network Marketing Lifestyles* stems entirely from the power of network marketing and its professionals," says its publisher, Ridgley Goldsborough. "Our mission at the magazine is to be so enormously successful that we give all of the credit to the industry and distributors where it is rightfully due. My belief is that if our success is big enough and loud enough, there is a reason for them to talk about us and by a logical extension, about network marketing as an industry."

"MLM is changing for the better as the press has turned quite positive," notes Greg Martin, Chairman of the Board of ShapeRite Concepts.

"Instead of being highlighted as some big item, network marketing is now being mentioned and accepted by the media. We have a favorable regulatory climate. It doesn't seem that the industry as a whole is under siege or attack from any agency."

Economics Enhance Growth

It's a two-way street: the impetus of the economy intensifies the continued growth of network distribution and our industry, reciprocally, strengthens the economy.

"As big corporate players continue to invest in the industry, and as more sophisticated and professional distributors join the industry, leading the way with very powerful sales management and communication skills," predicts Richard Brooke, "this industry is going to continue into explosive growth. But what's even more dynamic is the stock investment potential. If you have a network marketing company with tens of thousands of distributors, you have a built-in and extremely enthusiastic group of prospective buyers."

With approximately ten million network marketers reported in the United States today, better than one out of every 20 adults is involved in our industry. Looking ahead, Richard sees that becoming one out of every ten adults, and into the next millennium, five out of every ten. Why? The basic desire for a balance of lifestyle freedom, personal fulfillment, and financial security is prevalent among society at large today and is no longer reserved for the elite. As lives get busier and more frenetic, the idea of having freedom in all its manifestations is going to be more and more valuable to people.

Stephen M. Pollan, author of *Die Broke*, promotes a systematic, educated, leveraged system for living which allows you to maximize your assets to their fullest while you're alive. If you adhere to these principles, you will live well, spending your money wisely, sharing the fruits of your labors with your children while you're still alive, and have the final check to the undertaker...bounce. Those finding solace in this solution are a perfect fit for network marketing. Such people realize that a wealthy person is not necessarily one who has the most, but is one who needs the least.

Richard points out, "Not everyone demands such extravagant incomes with the fastest cars and the fanciest houses. Many are adjusting their values and deciding that they would rather raise their family on $4,000 a month and have 90 percent time-freedom than $14,000 a month with no freedom. And because of these changing values, I think network marketing will continue to be huge."

If this theory is correct, many of the predictions that have been made over the past decade make sense. Alan Greenspan, chairman of the Federal Reserve Bank, is credited with having predicted that network marketing will have an even stronger impact on the economy than the franchising industry had. Franchising now represents about one fifth of the GNP. Some believe that network marketing will represent 50 percent of the Gross National Profits in coming years.

Before Dave Schofield came into the network marketing industry two-and-a-half years ago as the President of Rexall Showcase International, he worked in franchising for 11 years.

"Today, the franchising industry represents approximately 20 percent of the U.S. Gross National Product contributing in excess of $1 trillion in goods or services provided through franchising opportunities. If you look at the networking industry's size globally, we are already close to being a $100 billion market. Within the next one to two decades, I see the network marketing global market being a trillion-dollar industry with the U.S. being between a $100 to $200 billion market. That represents a significant contribution to our national and international economy.

"Of course, the franchising business requires thousands of start-up dollars and the networking industry perhaps a few hundred. The risks within a franchising opportunity are high, with significant investment in real estate, equipment, and payroll. With network marketing, those risks are eliminated." Dave Scholfield left franchising to join the networking industry as a corporate head. That says it all.

Mergers, Acquisitions, and the Industry

A significant number of industry experts predict that we will see more mergers emanating from our industry, with fewer small companies standing on their own. Corporate founders can no longer "fool around" with network marketing companies, starting them on a shoestring budget. They will be compelled to create solid companies to respond to the myriad of serious professionals who are seeking more long-term stability in the industry.

Just in the past year, we have seen The People's Network (TPN), which broadcasts self-help and motivational programming by satellite, acquired by the Oklahoma-based Pre-Paid Legal Services, which offers access to standard legal help through network marketing distributors. Natural World, a small Connecticut-based network company specializing in all-natural products, merged into the Tempe-based New Vision International. A Dallas-based nutritional company, Eventus International, which is a division of Beauty Control, acquired Quantum Leap, another Dallas-based year-old nutritional company.

Acquisitions are even occuring between traditional corporations and network marketing companies. HumaScan Inc. has acquired Cell Tech International and Nutrition for Life International has acquired Advanced Nutraceuticals.

Our own company, 21st Century Global Network, specializing in environmentally safe products, was the first acquisition of Legacy USA, a Melbourne, Florida, company. This network distribution company is the outgrowth of two corporate giants. Legacy USA is a subsidiary of DCV, a $200 million world leader in food and nutrition ingredients.

Says Ted Elias, President of Legacy, "Consolidation of the industry is inevitable because the strong companies will prevail and the weak ones will fall by the wayside. These types of consolidations can only bring greater credibility to the industry, and credibility is the key to bringing network marketing to the next level of professionalism."

Ridgely Goldsborough has witnessed the industry's coming of age. "The scattered energy of a few years ago has been replaced by more education among the distributor force," he says. "And this is largely a result of two things: existing network marketers maturing in their business practices and the influx of more top caliber professionals coming into the industry who are using their corporate experiences to build their network marketing businesses."

Currently, there are many small, start-up networking companies in the playing field which will eventually fail. They can't all survive. The competition is fierce.

"We are in an era that is as hyper-competitive for distributors as I have ever seen," states ShapeRite's Board Chair, Greg Martin. "I have always considered that in network marketing, our 'shelf space' is distributors, but now we are competing for distributors with many other good MLM companies. We are basically in a full-employment economy, which leads to more intense competition for distributors, since it is so easy for them to find a job. But competition is healthy. I feel that it keeps companies focused and honest in offering the best of all aspects of our business.

"This is one industry that, up until now, has resisted consolidation,"

Greg says. "In my opinion, the reason for this is the cultures in network marketing seem to be so different from one company to another that melding them together is very challenging. However, the industry may have an opportunity to consolidate now because the culture among some of the better-quality companies, those that have been around for several years, is not so dissimilar. Size definitely has an advantage in network marketing. Over the next five years, I think we will see a lot of consolidation. It just makes sense."

The days of a company, such as Nu Skin International, starting out with $5,000 and making it to the top of the industry are history. Already there are merger companies forming to enable these alliances. If your company is interested in any form of consolidation, whether it is merging, acquiring, or being acquired, check my web site or the Resource guide at the back of this book to contact "Network Brokers."

Network Marketing as Potential Political Force

As an unofficial and yet-to-be-organized group of people, the power of this body of distributors known as network marketers is growing as exponentially as the income we generate. The DSA is the closest we come to being united, but this is a membership for companies, not individual distributors. We may hold the record for being the largest group of people who share a common purpose but who have not formed an association around our commonality anywhere in the world. Even doll makers and model airplane designers have an alliance.

Domestically, we are three times the size of the National Rifle Association (NRA) that touts three million members. On a worldwide scale, we stand toe to toe with the American Association of Retired People (AARP) who estimates their membership at just over 33 million. We have a burgeoning powerful body of focused, high-spirited members who are goal-oriented and desirous of making the world just a little better. If we ever do formally organize, there is no stopping us!

Several years ago, Richard Brooke, Ken Pontius, Dr. Charles King, Mark Yarnell and I all met at our home to discuss the possibility of leading the way toward the creation of such an organization. We chose against it then. The proposition was larger, more expensive, and more difficult to maintain than we were ready to undertake. Perhaps through the Internet, this linkage will finally occur as a necessary and missing element to our becoming a true profession.

Network distribution will emerge as the most powerful way to reach consumers in the coming millennium.

Frank Keefer, President and CEO of *Network Marketing Lifestyles* magazine, emphasizes that our survival depends on cooperation. We will self-destruct if we continue to pick each other's company apart and celebrate when another company goes under. One company's loss is a detriment for us all. "The day will come in this country," Frank predicts, "when national and local elections will be won or lost by the unified voice of network marketers. Let that era begin today!"

Dick DeVos, the second generation co-owner of Amway, has not hidden his interest in running for the U.S. Senate. Whether it is Dick or some other network marketing icon, such a run would undoubtedly put to the test our political efficacy as a unified body. A similar situation helped get Jimmy Carter elected President when his sister, Ruth Carter, now deceased, led a grass-roots campaign for her brother through her ministry. If a U.S. President could be elected through the efforts of a group of loosely organized evangelical followers, it can certainly happen through an assemblage of loosely organized, impassioned network marketers.

Shared Vision for the Network Marketing Industry

In February 1999, more than 100 students at a network marketing seminar participated in an exercise to develop a vision statement for their business. Here's what they came up with:

Network marketing is a profession that empowers people globally to maximize their potential to create a business by providing high-quality products and services through personal relationships. Through our entrepreneurial and cooperative spirit, which embodies our core values of credibility, honesty, integrity, compassion, accountability, respect, and trust, we will perpetually strive for a higher level of self-mastery, shared knowledge, and enhanced quality of life, while realizing our personal and financial freedom.

253

Richard Poe, noted author of *Wave Three* and *Wave Four*, is not alone in predicting that network distribution will emerge as the most powerful way to reach consumers in the coming millennium.

In his newest work he writes: "Only 20 years ago, our government questioned the very right of this industry to exist. Now, the world's greatest superpower champions MLM across the globe. Major corporations flock to it. Dictatorships quiver before it. This is the roar of Wave Four, thundering like a fast, distant tsunami. Soon, the tidal wave will strike. When it does, business will never be the same."

As the corporate executive was the hero of the 20th Century, so I believe that the entrepreneur will be honored in the 21st Century. But it will be a new entrepreneur, not one climbing corporate ladders, nor satisfied merely with amassing financial accomplishments. The 21st Century entrepreneur will seek the balance of lifestyle freedom, personal growth, and self-fulfillment, having a solid financial base with enough left over to share the wealth.

In a world that is otherwise competitive and greedy, cutthroat and selfish, there is a growing number of us who are searching for a more spirit-filled life. We realize that what is most valuable is not *what* we have in our lives, but *who* we have. We know that it only takes a few seconds to open profound wounds in persons we love, and that it takes years to heal them. We hope to live in the presence of human love and, even if not fully understanding it, become more worthy of its gift. We seek an environment where we can express our concern for the human plight. We need only find a "how" and our thirst will be quenched.

> As the corporate executive was the hero of the 20th Century, so I believe that the entrepreneur will be honored in the 21st Century.
> But it will be a new entrepreneur, not...satisfied merely with amassing financial accomplishments. The 21st Century entrepreneur will seek the balance of lifestyle freedom, personal growth, and self-fulfillment.

> Because of the impassioned, determined drive of so many professionals to find a vehicle for making a living while also having a life, the first century of this new millennium may well become known as "The Entrepreneurial Age."

With each passing interval of time, with each technological advancement, with each progression of the human spirit, the vision is gradually unfolding. Referral marketing is rapidly developing into a well-balanced and convivial profession that makes it possible for people from all walks of life and from all parts of the world to utilize their talents to the fullest. Establishing a business, preferably one based in their home and entirely within their control, they design a mission reflective of their goals. Carefully selecting products and services that are sought-after but rudimentary, they proudly refer the concept to family and friends. The team to which they belong fosters a synergetic spirit cooperating to create a working environment that encompasses certain basic human values: credibility, honesty, integrity, compassion, accountability, respect, and trust. Members endeavor to advance each other's personal development and continued education, while building a healthier lifestyle that includes both personal and financial freedom.

Because of the impassioned, determined drive of so many professionals to find a vehicle for making a living while also having a life, the first century of this new millennium may well become known as "The Entrepreneurial Age." It is here, in the environment that they have created, that these gentle souls, these new professionals, will be empowered to, at last, live joyfully in the presence of human love...with time to celebrate its mystery.

INDEX

Pontius, Ken 252
Ponzi scheme xii
Popat, Narenda 38, 48
portfolio, financial 11
Pre-paid Legal Services 193, 250
preeminent purpose 152
presentations 115–116, 127
pricing yourself 65
Primerica (formerly A.L. Williams
    Company) 189
priorities 156–157
problem solving 151
Procter & Gamble Company (P&G) 216
product and income claims 232–233
productivity 12
products
    belief in 109–111
    best-selling 212
    checklist for researching 93
    cost 125
    distribution 12–13
    e-commerce 211–212
    exaggeration 173
    nutritional 15
    volume 125–126
professional emigrants 32
professionals
    attitude change 234
    and home businesses xiv–xv
professional slavery xvi
professions, principles for choosing 129
promotional volume 125
prospective business associates 73, 94,
    198–200
prospective business partners 90, 140,
    147, 237
prosperity 15, 19, 36, 149, 192
purpose 151, 163
pyramid schemes 225–226, 229–230
pyramids
    illegal 119–121
    legitimate 121–122
    misperceptions 130
    symbolization xii–xiii
    vs. multi-level marketing 168

Q

qualities of a network professional
    courage 107–108
    open-mindedness 104–105
Quantum Leap 251
quitting 122–123
Quixtar 211
quiz on attitude 41–44

R

Rasmussen, Erik/Patricia 244
Reebok 209
Reeves, Richard 39
referral marketing 126, 186, 200–201
regulation 223–225, 227–228
regulatory agencies 173
relationship marketing 73, 125, 197
relationships
    long-term 9, 74
    personal 73, 77, 127, 167, 253
relationships and technology 237
Republican Party 217
researching successful companies 95–96
restraint of trade 216
retail direct program 228
retailing products 127, 174, 231
retirement
    baby boomers 26
    savings for 25–27
Retirement Confidence Survey 21, 26
return on investment 209
Revak, Rudy 245
Rexall Showcase 235, 250
risk-taking 61
Rohn, Jim 135
Rolfsness, Ken 246–247
Roney, Blake 246
Rousseau, Jean Jacques xv
Royal Body Care 192

S

Saito, Fugi 49
salary 5, 20, 22, 111
Sansone, Joseph 37–38
Sara Lee 223

ENDNOTES

CHAPTER 1
1. Belton, Beth, "Women Jumping Off Corporate Ladder To Start Own Business," *USA Today,* May 31, 1996.

CHAPTER 2
1. Armour, Stephanie, "Job Seekers Still Struggle: Unemployed Hit Brick Walls Even In Good Times," *USA Today*, Jan. 28, 1998.
2. Armour, Stephanie, "Age Discrimination Concerns Differ For Women," *USA Today*, Aug. 24, 1998 and "Women In Workplace Encounter Obstacles: Females Face Age, Sex Bias On Career Path," *Business Week*, Sept. 16, 1998.
3. "Retirement: Time To Kick Back and Get A Job?," *Business Week,* 1994.
4. Parker, Laura, "Too Old? Yeah, Right!", *USA Today*, Oct. 23, 1998.
5. Armour, Stephanie, "Tight Labor Market Squeezes Pay Raises," *USA Today*, Nov. 23, 1998.
6. Hannon, Kerry, "Stocking Up For Retirement Bull Run Rewards Savers," *USA Today*, May 19, 1998.
7. Hannon, Kerry, "Retirement Plans Aren't Just For The Big Players," *USA Today*, June 5, 1998.
8. Yarnell, Mark B., "The Greatest Motivator," *Success,* Dec. 1993.
9. Miller, Rich, "Americans Raid Savings To Spend," *USA Today*, Nov. 3, 1998.
10. Armour, Stephanie, "Lower-Rung Workers Come Up Short On Job Perks," *USA Today*, Aug. 10, 1998.
11. Smart, Tim, and Gleckman, Howard, "O.K., Back To Work," *Business Week*, Dec. 20, 1993.
12. Armour, Stephanie, "EEOC Sets Guidelines To Fend Off Retaliation," *USA Today*, May 27, 1998.
13. Armour, Stephanie, "Employers Hope Spirituality Lifts Workers' Morale" *USA Today*, May 14, 1998.

CHAPTER 3
1. *US News & World Report*, May 26, 1997.
2. *US News & World Report*, March 18, 1996.

CHAPTER 14
1. Vlasic, Bill and Regan, Mary Beth, "Amway: The Kids Take Over," *Business Week*, February 16, 1998.

CHAPTER 16
1. Chu, Paul, "An Upline's Wisdom On A Disk," *Network Marketing Lifestyles*, April 1999.

RESOURCES

AllAdvantage
An Internet-based company that pays those using the Net for advertising, and encouraging others to advertise, via a view-bar on their screen while sending e-mail and surfing for information; www.yarnell.com: click "Network Marketing Tips and Info" icon and go to the bottom of the screen to link to AllAdvantage.

Brilliant Compensation Video
A video that answers standard questions and objections by Tim Sales; www.yarnell.com: click the "Network Marketing Training Materials" icon, then click "Brilliant Compensation Video" to order or call 800-460-8604 (U.S.) or 775-826-5947 (outside U.S.).

DOYOUWOW.com Inc.
An Internet community of people (which costs nothing to participate) seeking information about self-improvement, building family relationships, more efficient ways to shop, and an income opportunity through personal referrals; www.yarnell.com: click "Internet and Technology" and click www.DOYOUWOW.com Inc.

Earnware Corporation
A phone messaging system for business development by John Valenty; www.yarnell.com: click the "Unified Messaging" icon, and then click "Earnware" or call 760-634-4282.

Millionaires in Motion
A generic training and support center for the Network Marketing industry created by John Kalench; go to www.miminc.com: or call 800-388-1748, fax 619-467-9504.

Freedom Radio
An Internet-based radio network dedicated to network marketing; to listen or download to your web site, go to www.yarnell.com: click the "Freedom Radio" icon and then click play to listen while you continue to surf the net or explore the Yarnell web site.

mLmSuccess.com
An on-line resource site featuring an extensive database of network marketing companies worldwide and a search function to identify companies by product or service or locate distributors for each company by region: www.yarnell.com and click on "Internet and Technology," linking to mLmSuccess.com.

MLM University
A virtual campus with virtual professors teaching via scheduled teleconference classes founded by Hilton Johnson; www.mlmu.com or call 954-491-8996.

My Family Builder
A *free* Internet-based tutorial program building family unity on the Net. This will be linked to an e-commerce site where, once the community base is created, a referral business can be built based on sales from shopping on the Net; see www.myfamilybuilder.com.

Network Brokers
A brokering company owned by Rene Reid Yarnell designed to assist in acquisitions and mergers between network marketing companies; www.yarnell.com: click "Network Brokers" or call 800-300-1489.

PM Marketing Lead Generation Program
A pre-screened lead generation program offered by Peter Mingils; www.yarnell.com: click the "Network Marketing Tips & Info" icon, followed by "Lead Generation" button or call 904-445-3585.

Sound Concepts

Produces customized audios, videos, compact discs, and business cards for the network marketing industry. *Direct Source,* their call center and fulfillment services for sales and training aids, can be reached by calling 800-544-7044. *MLM Tools* is their on-line supplier of network marketing books and tapes and can be accessed on the Web at www.buyMLMtools.com.

TeamSolo™ Unified Technology

A professional web site design linked to a unified phone messaging system by Gregg Corella; service intended for companies and leaders with large organizations; www.yarnell.com: click "Unified Messaging System" followed by "TeamSolo" button or call 888-219-9341.

Uniform MLM Laws

A DSA-approved uniform anti-pyramid law hoped to be implemented in all 50 States; to assist in getting this to your state, go to www.yarnell.com: click "Uniform MLM Laws," download the bill, and send a copy to your Congressman from this site.

University of Illinois (UIC) Network Marketing Certificate Seminar

Certificate course taught by Dr. Charles King and Rene Reid Yarnell; www.yarnell.com: click the "UIC Certificate Seminar" icon or call 630-790-6050.

Video Plus

A supplier of video, audio, and printed communication tools to the direct selling/network marketing industry throughout the world; www.videoplus.com or call 800-752-2030.

Your First Year in Network Marketing

A training book for new distributors by Mark Yarnell and Rene Reid Yarnell; www.yarnell.com: to order click the "Yarnell Books" icon or call 888-285-6316 (U.S.) or 801-225-9520 (outside U.S.).

Yarnell Books and Training Materials
All audio, video, and book materials produced by Mark Yarnell and Rene Reid Yarnell; www.yarnell.com: to order click the "Yarnell Books" icon, "Network Marketing Training Materials" icon, or call 888-285-6316 (U.S.) or 801-225-9520 (outside U.S.).

To reach Rene Reid Yarnell
rene@yarnell.com
800-300-1489 message

CONTRIBUTORS

Paul Adams	Video Plus	vendor	800-752-2030
Tom & Bethany Alkazin	NewVision	distributor	800-500-0456
Marc Barrett	Nu Skin/BigPlanet	distributor	303-526-2288
Evertrue Bell	Avon	corporate	www.Avon.com
Tom and Lynn Bissmeyer	Rexall	distributor	303-973-5396
BK Boreyka	NewVision	founder	www.nviworld.com
Richard Brooke	Oxyfresh	founder	www.oxyfresh.com
Jim Brown	SkyBiz 2000	founder	www.skynary.com
Kerry Brown/Richard Larkin	Dynamic Essentials Inc.	distributors	250-658-1258
Wayne and Fran Brown	Life Plus	distributor	714-968-7375
John and Sherrie Busswood	Enrich Int.	distributor	604-929-4897
Steve Campbell	I-Link	distributor	801-818-4000
Jerry and Debbie Campisi	Nu Skin/Big Planet	distributor	561-795-8198
Jonell Clark	Golden Neo-Life Diamite	distributor	770-270-1554
Gregg Corella	TeamSolo	vendor	www.teamsolo.com
Lorene Crom	NewVision	distributor	
Brett Dabe	Excel Communications	distributor	888-683-4949
Daria Davidson	Rexall	distributor	800-647-4421
Kenny Davis	SmartMart	corporate	www.smartmart.com
Janice DeLong	NewVision	distributor	480-860-4519
Kathleen B. Deoul	Nikken	distributor	410-602-1665
Connie Dugan	Oxyfresh	distributor	843-842-6577
Ted Elias	Legacy USA	corporate	www.legacyusa.com
Tom Entwistle	Rexall	distributor	800-987-7341
Ray Faltinsky	FreeLife Int.	founder	www.freelife.com
Jane Fergason	Gardere & Wynne	attorney	214-999-3000
Roland and Virginia Fox	Oxyfresh	distributor	509-926-1720
Terri Frey	FlashNet Marketing Int.	corporate	www.flash.net
Ridgely Goldsborough	Network Marketing mag.	publisher	ridgely@upline.com
Jonathan Goldsmith	NewVision	distributor	888-309-8613
Marvin Higbee	Life Force Int.	corporate	800-531-4877
Wayne Hillman	Life Force Int.	founder	www.lifeforce-intl.com

Peter Hirsch	FlashNet Marketing Int.	distributor	800-310-3117
Joe and Sandra Hornsey	Neways	distributor	800-554-8825
Richard Howard	Eventus International	founder	www.eventus.com
Robert B. Hydeman	Mannatech	distributor	972-233-6243
Bill Hyman	Horizons Interactive	distributor	414-569-7599
George and Julie Iddon	TriVita Way	distributor	604-943-4181
Dani and Hans Johnson	Symmetry Int.	distributor	800-875-6858
Rick Jordan	Rexall	distributor	949-496-5158
Laura Kall	Big Planet	distributor	203-454-9928
Richard Kall	Nu Skin	distributor	561-241-3976
John Kalench	Nikken	distributor	619-467-9667
Russ & Linda Karlen	Nu Skin	distributor	702-363-5343
Don Karn	Shaklee Corp.	corporate	www.shaklee.com
Duff & Suzie Kaster	Oxyfresh	distributor	800-457-0684
John Kavanagh	LifeForce	distributor	onelife@compuserve.com
Frank Keefer	Market America	distributor	410-827-5791
Charles King	UIC Certificate Course	professor	630-790-6050
Richard Larkin/Kerry Brown	Dynamic Essentials Inc.	distributors	250-658-1258
Ken and Karen Long	Legacy USA	distributor	541-258-5533
Peggy Long	Legacy USA	distributor	623-825-1994
Steve Lund	Nu Skin Ent.	corporate	www.nuskin.com
Greg Martin	ShapeRite Concepts	board chair	www.shaperite.com
Rick Mathaney	Karemor Vitamist Int.	distributor	704-559-5900
Ladd McNamara	Usana	distributor	800-346-2183
Peter Mingils	PM Marketing	vendor	904-445-3585
Mike Moseley	Eventus Int.	corporate	www.eventus.com
Mary and Warren Nelson	FreeLife Int.	distributor	877-689-3261
Tony Neumeyer	Enrich	distributor	604-929-6613
Neil Offen	Direct Selling Assoc.	president	www.dsa.org
Wayne Paulson	BodyWise	distributor	877-924-7000
Ken Pontius	Enrich	distributor	602-661-0977
Erik Rasmussen	SkyBiz 2000	distributor	775-825-7892
Rudy Revak	Symmetry Int.	founder	www.symmetry.3000.com
Ken Rolfsness	Melinda	distributor	011-617-3273-7990
Tim Sales	Nu Skin	distributor	818-348-3029
Paul Saunders	Your Radio Mall	partner	paul@yourradiomall.com
Dave Schofield	Rexall Showcase	corporate	www.rexallshowcase.com
Neal and Kim Secrist	Rexall	distributor	800-SECRIST (732-7478)
Kay Smith	Nu Skin	distributor	954-783-8171
Betty Sung	Nu Skin	distributor	011-886-22378-8888
Vivian Thompson	Rexall	distributor	800-883-6705
Lee Thurburn	FlashNet	founder	www.flash.net
John and Shelleen Valenty	NewVision	distributor	800-266-6221
Ed Wainscott	Streich Lang	attorney	ewainsco@sllaw.com
Liz Walcher	Mary Kay	distributor	505-437-4271
Carol Waugh	Arbonne	distributor	800-373-2591
Jim & Candy Webb	NewVision	distributor	800-418-9577
Doug Wead	Amway	distributor	dougwead@dougwead.com
Jim Whittam	Shaklee Companies	corporate	www.shaklee.com
Mary Lou and Bob Wilson	Enrich	distributor	817-279-6624

Rene Reid Yarnell, at her very core, is an educator. Her career began in the classroom in the sixties and expanded to talk radio and television shows in the '70s and '80s. Her life has taken her from the cloister of religious life in the '60s to the exposure of public life in the '90s. Rene received her B.A. and M.A. in Theology, after spending four years as a Roman Catholic nun. Since 1988, as a businesswoman, she has been heavily involved in the network marketing industry while also serving in the elected position as County Commissioner in Reno, Nevada. In 1991, she entered into a 'marriage and merger' with Mark Yarnell and worked with him as an advocate for the network marketing industry. Now on her own, residing in Reno, Nevada, she is seriously pursuing her writing.

Having built a successful organization of more than 200,000 marketing representatives worldwide crossing 27 countries, Mark and Rene became known in the network marketing industry for their numerous books, tapes, articles, and training series. They were instrumental, with Dr. Charles King, in creating the first Certificate Course in network marketing which Rene continues to teach at the University of Illinois at Chicago and abroad. They are the recipients of numerous industry awards including the Leadership Award (1992) and Distributors of the Year Award (1995) from the Multi-Level Marketing International Association; the Leadership Award from Financial Upline Press (1995); the distinction of "Greatest Networker in the World" by *Upline* Magazine (1997); and they have been inducted into the Network Marketing Hall of Fame by the International Directory of Network Marketing (1998).

To Order Books

Please send:

_____Copies of *The New Entrepreneurs*

at $15.95 each _____   Total   _____

Nebraska residents add 5% sales tax   _____

Shipping/Handling
$3.20 for first book
$1.10 for each additional book   _____

TOTAL ENCLOSED   _____

Name_____

Address _____

City _____State_____Zip_____

❑ Visa   ❑ Mastercard   ❑ American Express

Credit card number_____

Expiration date_____

Order by credit card, personal check, or money order. Send to:

The New Entrepreneurs
500 S. Geneva Rd.
Vineyard, UT 84058

Or order TOLL FREE: 888-285-6316
outside the U.S. at 801-225-9520

or online at
www.yarnell.com